T0188492

Also by Larry Brooks

*Story Fix: Transform Your Novel
From Broken to Brilliant*

*Story Physics: Harnessing the
Underlying Forces of Storytelling*

*Story Engineering: Mastering the 6 Core Competencies
of Successful Writing*

GREAT STORIES DON'T WRITE THEMSELVES

Criteria-Driven Strategies for More Effective Fiction

LARRY BROOKS

WD
WRITER'S DIGEST
BOOKS

www.penguinrandomhouse.com

1 3 5 7 9 10 8 6 4 2

ISBN-13: 978-1-4403-0085-1

Edited by Amy Jones
Designed by Danielle Lowery and Jason D. Williams

TABLE OF CONTENTS

PART IV: THE SUM OF THE PARTS

Foreword

by Robert Dugoni

Many years ago, when I was a boy, my mother handed me what had been her brother's trumpet. She thought it important that a child learn to play an instrument, something about learning the scales being a good way to expand the mind. I don't disagree. I picked up that trumpet and I did my very best to blast air through the mouthpiece with the hope that the bell would emit a beautiful song. I suspect you know what came next. The sound emitted was so horrific, it summoned my father like a foghorn does a ship. He wasn't as interested as my mother in any of his children playing an instrument. With ten children, I guess he figured there was already enough noise in the house. "Take some lessons before you blow into that thing again," he told me. "And never again in the house."

I took lessons. I learned to read music and I learned how to summon notes with my fingers pressed down on the pistons, and my lips pinched and squirting air into the mouthpiece. I never did become very good. I didn't like practicing the scales and the runs essential to learning how to truly play a song well. I wanted to just be able to put my lips to the mouthpiece and magically blast out a tune.

Too often, I find, new novelists feel the same.

There is a misconception circumnavigating the writing world that anyone can write because everyone (or nearly everyone) can string words together. String enough words together in the proper order and you have a sentence. String enough sentences together and you have a paragraph. String paragraphs together and you have a scene. String scenes together and voilà! You have a story.

So, really, how hard can it be to write a novel?

"Just write from the heart!" is one rallying cry far too often given to new writers. "Pour your heart into it!" This advice is akin to my picking up the trumpet, blasting air through the mouthpiece, and believing that a song would magically come out of the bell. I can assure you that was not the case. Oh, you might get lucky and pinch your lips in just the right way, press down the pistons in just the right order, and produce a note. But think of that musical note as a letter. Now carry the analogy one step further. You'd have to get lucky approximately 500,000 additional times, in a row, to produce a novel.

How do you like those odds?

And yet, so many writers do just that. How do I know? Because I was one them, and I soon learned the fallacy of my endeavors. Mind you, I was not a person who had never written when I sat down to type out my Great American Novel. I had been the editor-in-chief of my high school and college newspapers. I wrote for the *Los Angeles Times*. I wrote news articles and feature stories of significant length. I also practiced law for fourteen years and wrote extensive legal briefs.

I had done just enough to think, *How hard can it be to write a novel?*

As Larry Brooks might say, "I didn't know what I didn't know."

Insert the trumpet analogy from above, here. And that is not even commenting on the *quality* of the novel written.

It wasn't until I had received close to fifty rejection letters that I fully grasped that writing a novel is a craft. It is something to be studied and learned. For some, this realization is disheartening—as it was disheartening for me when I realized I couldn't blast tunes on my trumpet without first learning the craft. But for others, myself included, the realization is encouraging. If there is a craft, then the craft can be taught, and if it can be taught, then it can be learned, and if it can be learned, then those odds of stringing the right words together to actually produce a coherent novel significantly improve.

Find the right teacher, and the odds improve exponentially. Find the right teacher with the right material and the odds improve even more.

Enter Larry Brooks.

I first met Larry at a writers conference in Surrey, British Columbia, in October 2013, though I had known of him for many years. Larry's work on the craft of writing had become a fixture on my writing shelf alongside the works of Christopher Vogler, Donald Maass, Sol Stein, Michael Hauge, James Frey, and Steven James. I had his books *Story*

Engineering and *Story Physics* and I soon thereafter bought his brilliant *Story Fix*. We look for those teachers who can take a complicated mess and, somehow, miraculously unravel it. Larry, unbeknownst to him, had unraveled several of my messes before they ever became published novels, some of them ending up as bestsellers.

After our meeting, I called Larry during one of my hair-pulling moments and asked him for advice on how to fix a tangled mess I had created. Larry listened carefully before asking me a series of questions and prodding around the edges of my story premise. It soon became clear that Larry was not going to fix my problem for me. He was doing much more than that. Larry was teaching me the tools I would need to fix not just one problem but the many others I would face down the writing road. Going back to the trumpet analogy, he wasn't going to teach me to memorize one song. He was going to teach me how to play the instrument so that I could recognize and fix my mistakes on my own. I hung up the phone that day buoyed with a sense I had never had before: I might just make it in this writing gig after all.

Larry's books on the craft of writing have always spoken to me because he offers the author no excuses. He isn't there to hold your hand and console you. Larry pushes the writer to flex her writing muscles and to move forward toward that elusive goal of becoming the best author that writer can be. *Great Stories Don't Write Themselves* is the next book in Larry's writing toolkit, and one I eagerly devoured. In it, Larry eviscerates the concept of the untrained author sitting down at her keyboard and typing out a Pulitzer Prize–winning novel. To write a novel, he says, is to have a mission. To understand that mission is to have a clue to the secret of great writing, a sense of the criteria that apply. Larry teaches writers not only the concept of the setup and the hook, but the difference between the First Plot Point and the First Pinch Point, and where in a writer's story the reader should expect to find each.

I know there are many writers out there who don't want to be bogged down by rules and outlines. In the business, we call these writers either "organic writers" or the less-flattering term—"pantsers"—as in, someone who writes from the seat of his pants.

Guess what? I consider myself one of them.

What I've learned over my twenty-plus years in this business is that there are very few truly organic writers, and by that I mean a writer who has never had any training on the craft of any kind but who has managed to achieve success (insert your own definition of success here). At this point, you might be wondering about that theory you've read or heard about. You know, the theory that anyone who puts 10,000 hours into something becomes an expert—like Michelangelo or Leonardo da Vinci.

Sadly, it is more fallacy than theory. As my grammar school baseball coach liked to say, "only perfect practice makes perfect." Read the biographies of the two greatest artists the world has ever known, and you soon realize that Michelangelo and da Vinci didn't just rack up hours like meters in New York City cabs. They spent thousands of hours in perfect practice to perfect their crafts.

You might just be the person who can beat the 500,000-to-one odds. You might just win the next mega-millions lottery too. But the better odds are, you're not. Besides, doesn't it make sense to learn from those individuals who have already put in thousands of hours of perfect practice and who are willing to teach you the skills and tools needed to perfect your own writing?

You can bang your head against the wall intending to break down the wall, but it's far more likely you'll just give yourself a headache. Wouldn't it be so much wiser to open the pages of this book with a pen or a highlighter in hand and absorb what Larry Brooks has to teach? It's a step toward learning the craft, which is a step in the right direction. It's a step toward becoming your own best editor, which is a step toward publication. It's a step toward stringing words together that produce a story so rich and intoxicating that readers experience the story as life itself. The characters feel real. The story rings true. To an extent that their own lives have been transformed by reading it.

It happens. Trust me. It happens every day.

The alternative is that beautiful trumpet, locked in its case, tucked neatly in the recesses of the attic, never to be played, never to be heard.

And right beside it, in a neat stack, are your manuscripts, possibly never finished to the degree required. And because of that, never read.

No writing teacher will ever render the task of writing a novel that works *easy*. If they tell you they can … run. But they can make the work clearer, and the path more accessible, while elevating your creation. That's what Larry and the element-specific criteria he discusses here can do for you. It's the stuff most of us wish we had known much earlier in our journey. You now hold it in your hands. What you do with it is your choice. But what this book can do for you as a writer is something you just might find to be a game changer. As I did.

Robert Dugoni
April 2019

ABOUT ROBERT DUGONI

Robert Dugoni is the critically acclaimed *New York Times*, no. 1 *Wall Street Journal*, and no. 1 Amazon bestselling author of the multi-million-selling Tracy Crosswhite series. The first entry, *My Sister's Grave*, has sold more than 2 million copies, has been optioned for TV series development, and has won multiple awards and nominations. He is also the author of the bestselling David Sloane series, nominated for the Harper Less Award for legal fiction, and the stand-alone novels *The 7th Canon*, a 2017 finalist for the Mystery Writers of America Edgar Award for best novel, and *The Cyanide Canary*, a *Washington Post* Best Book of the Year. His latest novels include the award-winning *The Extraordinary Life of Sam Hell* and *The Eighth Sister*, which debuted on several bestseller lists and elevated him to the #1 ranked author on Amazon. He is the recipient of the Nancy Pearl Award for Fiction and the Friends of Mystery Spotted Owl Award for the best novel in the Pacific Northwest. He is a two-time finalist for the International Thriller Writers award and the Mystery Writers of America Award for best novel, among many other awards and best-of inclusions. His books are sold worldwide in more than twenty-five countries. Learn more at his website, www.robertdugonibooks.com.

Introduction

Writing a great story is all in your head.

Or is it? The better question may be, *should* it be all in your head?

That's the real issue at hand, in this or any other book about the craft of fiction. The destination of the serious author, in any genre, is to gain an understanding of the craft specific to it, and then apply that understanding to the development of a story within your process of choice.

Which tees up one of the most mission-critical memes in all of writing:

Too often we don't know what we don't know.

This is a paradoxical truism by virtue of its very nature. It is also a sticking point.

Because it's that last part—what we *don't* know—where both risk and opportunity await. Of course, none of us know everything about writing a story that works, and few of us know every nuance of the story we are about to write before we begin, sometimes even once we're well into it. This *not fully knowing* applies, as it does for us, to the famous authors we read and the gurus whose workshops we devour. And we certainly can never claim to know what the market will respond to, or why. Nonetheless we soldier on, into the dark woods of the unexplored, defaulting to an acceptance of *not knowing*.

And thus we find ourselves in yet another sort of paradox. Because it is the *acceptance* of what is actually, for lack of a better word, *ignorance*, when piled on top of the sheer volume of what we don't know, that can take us down.

For all of us, storytelling is a navigation of what we know and what we do not. But we can move the needle on that trade-off to our benefit. The more we lean into *knowing* what makes stories work and the more we know about the story we are writing—the earlier we know both of those, the better—the more efficient the process becomes. And ultimately, the more effective the product that results from it.

Sometimes knowledge is misinterpreted as *formula*.

Consider the best dish you've ever eaten. Somewhere there's a recipe for it, even when you or your favorite chef can whip it up straight out of your head. When that recipe varies, the dish nonetheless turns out wonderfully because you know where it needs to end up. But if it varies too much, will it still be *that* dish? Maybe not; it may be inedible. If not for you, then for some. So is that a *formula*? And if you believe that it is, or even if you don't, does that word even matter? The dish works because there is an accepted identification of requisite ingredients, proportions, and preparation that lead to a successful outcome. All of it somewhat flexible, because "season to taste" remains an open invitation. But there are also standards and expectations that tell us not to pour a pound of cayenne pepper into a wedding cake.

Formula is a word for cynics and the uninitiated, often applied to an uninformed perspective on story structure. It is an overly simplistic view in an avocation that is anything but simple. *Craft* is the better word to apply. Craft is the practice of putting *knowledge* to work within an artful nuance of creativity and within a framework of expectation, standards, and best practices. At the professional level, when your intention is to publish, craft becomes essential.

It is important to differentiate between *process* and *product*.

Many, if not most, of the conversations and mentoring about writing stories tend to blend both process and product into a stirred pot of *how-to-write* belief systems. But those are very different core competencies, with very different contexts. The *only* viable standards for process—however you go about it—is that it leads you to a place where you can meet all the inherent criteria of product, which have a universal baseline as well as genre-specific requisites, while still giving you room to innovate.

So while process has but one criterion, product has dozens of specific standards to shoot for.

The goal, or long-game you should strive to play, is to become a very good writer in possession of a great story to tell. The key differentiating word is *great*, because *not* all story ideas are great, nor do they become great because the sentences are eloquently rendered. If they are not inherently great, they must be upgraded in a way that changes the essence of the original. Great stories do not always require brilliant prose, because clean and clear prose that doesn't try too hard is the bread and butter of genre fiction, while literary fiction has a wider interpretation in this regard. That said, all genres are driven by the same story forces—character, dramatic tension, and vicarious experience—and thus the core principles become universal.

Here's the thing, though. Almost every writer at any level, almost every time, *believes* the draft they are submitting *is* great. That conclusion is reached as the consensus of whatever collective knowledge and instinct preside within them. It is based entirely on what they think they know. And—this being the realization that can take you forward toward your writing dream—too often, it is taken down by what they don't.

The goal of this book is to shrink the gap between the two.

Principles and criteria are what feed and nourish our instincts.

They inform all points along the story development process continuum, because they can be applied at the moment of creation, just as they can be retrofitted at the revision and polish stage. That's two points of entry where criteria are concerned. Either way you get there, when the story works, it will be because of how the story reads and unfolds rather than how it was assembled. Because the criteria don't favor any given process. Many roads can take you there, even though many forms of the end product are not as available. And when you arrive, the reader will neither know nor care what your process was.

So if this is true—and I can assure you that it is—process boils down to nothing other than a choice. A comfort level leading to a preference. This is critical context for understanding the bigger picture, where process and product merge into one outcome.

We need to know when we've arrived at a final draft and when we haven't.

This is one of the highest-risk benchmarks new writers, and too many resistant writers, face. How do we know when the story is done and if it's good enough? They stop too soon, before all the requisite bases have been touched—because they aren't aware of, or don't believe in, the term *requisite*—or the scenes remain less than optimized. Or, they don't stop soon enough, which leads to overwriting. Either way, the story is compromised ... unless and until they *know*.

Here's the paradox that results: They *think* they know, but outcomes show that they don't.

The criteria-driven author understands what standards to apply to any given moment of decision along the story arc, including the singular idea that is the embryo for the story (an essential benchmark decision that leaves too many stories dead at the starting gate). Too many writers learn the hard way that not all ideas are a viable platform for a compelling story.

You will soon encounter criteria to apply to your story ideas to ensure that they have the inherent raw grist you seek.

While the purpose of this book is to help you increase your odds of success, know that even with criteria checklists to help us vet our work, writing a good novel or screenplay remains a significant task with a high bar. In an avocation burdened with no shortage of opinions and confused by this-is-how-I-do-it hubris, wisdom and truth are often found in the nuances that reside between the lines. We get to choose for ourselves among those opinions, and we are always alone with the consequences of those choices. There is some facet of truth in almost everything you will hear and read about storytelling, and you can count on some level of variance, imprecision, and assessment that will determine how well you apply any of it.

It is rare, even unheard of, when someone in the writing community tells you that your story idea isn't strong enough. It's as if the default position—to an extent that it is commonly considered to be part of the conventional wisdom—is that a writer can and should write anything they want. Even that they can define what a story *is*, when in fact the idea may not qualify as a criteria-meeting *story* at all. This is no different than believing we can and should eat and drink anything—and as much as—we want, when there are principles that clearly show us we cannot do so and simultaneously seek a high level of health. Ice cream for dinner every day. When a friend or a writing teacher allows you to settle for a thin or weak idea, simply by refraining to tell you that they don't see great potential in your story idea, they haven't served you. Or possibly, they aren't able to differentiate a strong idea from a vanilla one at this early stage. They nod and smile and say, "Wow, that sounds terrific!" When in fact, it actually isn't, at least to someone who understands the criteria for a good story idea at its core. Rejection may be the closest you'll get to an assessment in that regard.

Rarer still is feedback on the core idea when the draft itself is complete. And it may indeed be too late if the idea has collapsed under the weight of what the criteria are asking of it. This is like suggesting to a recent college grad who can't find a job that maybe they should have chosen a different major. That's a decision best vetted before the fact, not after.

Nobody—not agents, not editors, not readers—is waiting for someone to reinvent the genres they love. Rather, they are rooting for someone to excel *within* them. Truth is, for genres other than literary fiction where the principles are more vague and more flexibly applied, agents aren't shopping for the next great *writer* at all. They cling to hope, but that's not the road before them. Rather, they are on pins and needles hoping to find the next great *story*.

Which brings us to another common rationalization that doesn't serve the writer

I've heard many writers say, when confronted with this observation about agents, that they aren't interested in landing an agent at all. Instead, they are going direct to market as a self-published author. As if self-publishing licenses a less demanding standard of storytelling and perhaps a stronger promise of commercial success. Both suspicions are highly flawed. This is like skipping the visit to a doctor and going straight to the radiation clinic to get rid of that lump in your throat. The truth is, any self-published novel that is doing well online would have appealed to an agent, at least somewhere along the line, had they had the chance to see it first.

Not all writers actually understand that.

The truth is, within any genre there are certain expectations in play: genre-specific tropes that you omit or violate at your peril. When a writer isn't aware of those tropes, or worse, when they aren't aware of the criteria that drive toward the universal principles of effective storytelling, the only approach that's left is to *guess*. They apply their instincts to conjure and vet their choices. This is fine if their instinct is up to the task, which is rare among newer writers. They seek to imitate the genre novels they enjoy reading, but without the learning curve that guides the authors of those books. Or—this being the subtext of those who deny structure or diminish the value of story planning—newer writers are seduced by advice that applies more aptly to literary novels, and thus may prove toxic to their genre-centric premise and vision for the story.

They *just write*. Because that's what they've read and heard. That's what a successful writer advised from behind a microphone. Just write. You'll be just fine.

Maybe.

When an experienced professional *just writes*, that, too, is instinct being put into play. But their instinct is almost always at a higher level than that of the new or untrained writer. Novice writers will find an abundance of advice out there suggesting they should go with their gut and just write—it won't be called *guessing* in that moment, but that's exactly what it is when writers go at it without the omnipresent context of knowledge—but you are about to learn how and why this is advice you should carefully parse and vet. It is a process you should understand completely before diving in to that end of the pool. Because when it works, it is because of an informed instinct, not an untested one.

The same principles and criteria apply to any process. Because the bar resides at the same height—it's *way* up there—for either preference.

It is *always* better to *know*.

Know the fundamental tenants *and* principles of the craft, and the criteria that provide target choices for them, including the tropes and traps of your genre. Write from an awareness of what your readers are expecting and the inherent potential of your premise to deliver it. Know where your story is headed—the famous-author rumor that you can succeed by beginning a draft with absolutely no notion of destination is greatly exaggerated and misunderstood; it's a half-truth, valid for half the people half of the time—so you can recognize a better path when it opens up before you, at which point you'll need to know how to retool prior pages that had started out as something else altogether.

Blindly changing lanes mid-journey, without the lights on, can get you killed. *Knowing* is your means of avoiding the temptation to veer too far over the abyss looming at the edge of your lane. You could argue that nobody truly knows what will work best, but the bestseller lists are full of authors who absolutely know what they should shoot for.

Welcome to criteria-driven storytelling.

If this sounds like advanced stuff, it is. You are about to encounter a deep dive into the fundamental knowledge you'll wish you had more fully integrated earlier in your writing journey, perhaps before prolonged exposure to the foggy nature of the writing conversation obscured the view.

This exploration into unlocking your highest potential as a storyteller will unfold in three parts. Each builds a foundation for the next, while in sum reinforcing a core understanding of what makes stories work at a publishable level as well as what may reduce them to mediocrity.

- The first (Part 1) will clarify the power and upside of applying criteria-based knowledge to what has otherwise remained an avocation mired in hope, instinct, and guesswork. And doing so as early as possible, beginning with the very first spark of a story idea. This is antithetical to how many writers approach writing novels, which—in a profession with less than a 5 percent success rate—is precisely the point.
- In Part 2, we will focus on the cultivation and culling of story ideas that lead to premises that have the right stuff, with specific clarity on how to separate the wheat from the chaff in context to the perhaps jarring, but nonetheless provable, realization that not every idea has the raw grist to become a commercially viable story.
- And, in Part 3, armed with a higher level of awareness of how and why your premise will bear the weight of what you should ask of it, we will clear a path through the unfolding parts and essences of story, applying specific criteria to enrich each scene and chapter, every layer and pivot, leading to story endings that will be felt and remembered.

If you're not a new writer and you still pursue the secret sauce that will finally get you in the game, maybe this will be the flashlight in the darkness that takes you there. Even after decades of effort, you may just find an epiphany or two—perhaps much more—in these pages.

PART I

It's All in Your Head

1 The Mission of the Novel, and the Novelist

Decoding the abundant noise within
the writing conversation

A good novel or any other type of fictional story isn't just about *something*. It is about something *happening*.

This is true whether the author realizes it or not. And among new writers, too often they don't.

Virtually everything about the revision and rejection phases of a story's life is, in fact, a push toward alignment with this truth. In commercial fiction, what *happens* is the means by which every other story goal is realized and injected into the head and heart of your reader: dramatic arc (plot), character arc, story world, backstory, suspense, pace, romance, emotion, reflection, dialogue ... even theme. All of it is the consequence of *something happening* in your story.

In literary fiction, *what happens* is often shown within the inner landscape of a protagonist experiencing multiple facets and challenges of life. In genre fiction, while inner demons and emotional backstory matter, *what happens* in the story is almost always external and forward-looking. It happens *to* the hero, summoning the hero down a path that grows darker and more complex as it unfolds, and then it shifts into a context in which the hero happens—takes action, becoming a catalyst—*to* the story.

But even then, showing *what happens* may not be enough to fuel the story. Because the real goal, the bigger goal, the thing professionals do by instinct and new writers seek to master, is to make the reader feel and care about what happens. To make them root for something, and someone.

This is why episodic, slice-of-life stories are risky, especially in genre fiction. Because while they may show what happens, there is too often the lack of a strong macro-thread that gives the reader something specific, something big to engage with and to root for, in context to an external antagonist threatening the hero's goals and needs.

More than a few writers harbor the hope that their novel will change lives.

They hope that it might convey the meaning of life or sell a particular point of view. This is a fine intention when held in the right perspective—it can become the key focus of a literary novel—but until you figure out *what happens* in the story that leads readers to that glorious illumination, it remains just as it sounds: an outsized, albeit noble, literary goal. When the pursuit of that goal trumps the reward of the reading experience itself, as expressed through a vicarious and empathetic dramatic arc and nuanced character development, then you've crossed a line within genre fiction that can take you down.

Our highest and best purpose is to deliver a gift to our readers. But chances are the meaning of life is beyond our reach. Rather, ours is a gift of entertainment and escape and emotion and enlightenment through the presentation of *something happening*. A vicarious journey, perhaps in the form of an emotional roller coaster, a three-hanky ending, or something that touches hearts and enriches minds at the same time. A shock to the system. A story they will *feel*. An experience readers will remember and be thankful for that becomes a return on their investment of time.

Where the meaning of life is concerned, it is best to allow the reader to connect the story to their interpretation of real life, as *they* please. When you imbue your story with the variables and challenges of the world, that will most likely be all the thematic spice the story needs to reach hearts and minds in any genre, including literary novels.

For the gift to emerge, certain principles and criteria apply.

The fundamental truths about what causes a story to work aren't optional or random any more than sutures and staples are optional in a surgical procedure, or wings are less than compulsory in the design of an airplane. Successful genre-centric writers never write from an intention to marginalize the principles of dramatic tension and vicarious experience and emotional resonance to offer up a manifesto about the meaning of life or a biographical slice of life from a fictional character. Rather, they write to tell a *story* that resonates on both a dramatic and thematic level.

Certainly, with the right instincts, a story might eventually emerge simply by confronting the blank page, and it might hit the reader right where they live. But in essence, this approach is the search for a story idea rather than telling a story that meets the criteria for a story that works. Truth is, even when organic story development is your preference, there's a better approach available that allows you to create in context to specific criteria at both the idea stage and within the story execution process.

An under-recognized truth is that the road to efficacy begins at the *idea* stage. From there, guided by criteria and fueled by the inherent allure of the idea that meets them, it extends into the premise, which then fuels an unspooling sequence of expositional scenes and transitions, some of them essential structural milestones. All of these elements of the story are embedded with expectations and standards, which are germane not only at the submission level (agents, acquisition editors, and online readers as they shop for new reads) but also at the story execution level that precedes submission, as well.

These become a checklist for the inherent potential of your story idea.

Readers of genre fiction are expecting a certain flavor of vicarious experience. A lover to be met. A far-off land to discover. An alien dimension to explore. A culture to navigate. A wrong to avenge. Your readers will expect to meet a hero that they can relate to, even if that character is nothing like them. More than anything, they will relate to what the story asks or demands of the hero (which is why anti-hero stories can work). They are drawn to the hero being summoned down a story path with an immediate goal—to run, to survive, to seek clarity, to fight back, to save someone, to conquer darkness and save the day for all.

The common context here is that *there is a goal to pursue*. There *must* be obstacles along the path of that quest, including but not limited to, an antagonistic force, usually in the form of a villain. There will be twists and turns. There will be inner issues the hero must deal with. There will be a second level in play within the narrative (known as a B-story, often a romantic arc for the hero) that eventually connects the hero to the primary story arc. There will be drama, conflict, confrontation, small successes, and major setbacks. Nothing will be easy or obvious. There will be surprises and twists, as new information enters the story in the right places, with the right touch. There will be confrontation that leads to resolution, after which the hero goes forward with the consequences of what has been done. If, that is, he survives, which is not a criterion at all.

Of course, this is Story 101.

What is in unfortunate short supply is an understanding of how to apply this to the *earliest* and most raw form of the story *idea* itself. In the same way that an architect can look at an empty lot and envision a beautiful and functional structure there, the criteria-driven author looks at their idea and, applying criteria, gets a feeling for the foundational potential to bear the weight of all these story facets, parts, and essences. From that understanding, the work of adding layers and specifics and nuance is no longer random, but informed by a level of knowledge about how stories work. As opposed to, say, being struck with an idea and simply starting a draft to see what happens.

To let the story come to you, rather than seeking it out in all the right places, this being a nuance that separates the pro from the rookie (more on this when we discuss how to give wings to a story idea). Writing a draft that hasn't yet discovered its core dramatic thread can work if your instinct is earned and is applied to evaluating the idea itself before you invest a year of your life trying to cull a compelling story from it. The alternative is to apply criteria to come up with a core dramatic arc, even if it only serves as a placeholder within which stronger ideas can emerge.

Here's a scary fact of life for fiction writers: Not all ideas are good ideas. Not all of them, even when they glow in the dark at the first spark of inspiration, can be made to work on all the levels necessary within a novel or a screenplay or simply work at a level that is high enough.

It is asking a lot of a story that's written randomly to not read as if it were written randomly. Great stories don't write themselves.

High-potential ideas can be recognized from standards of criteria.

Too many new writers commit to ideas that aren't really *stories* at all. It may be a good short story idea, or even an idea for a scene in a novel or movie. Like, "What if someone stole your mother's ashes from your car on the morning of her memorial service?" That idea was once pitched to me in a workshop, and the feedback was tough to hear and tough to give. If your idea is more suited to an episode of *The Twilight Zone* than it is a multifaceted, criteria-crushing candidate for a novel—it might make for a good *scene*, but it's not yet layered enough for an actual story—you need to learn to recognize that difference. You'd need to nurture that idea upward, searching for a larger tapestry that might build on the limited scope of that idea. From within that context, all ideas are worthy. But until the idea meets the criteria for a powerful story, which is an issue of both knowledge and instinct, it should remain a work-in-progress.

Here's the best writing tip I've ever heard.

The best writing tip I've ever heard, in my opinion, came in a keynote address at a writers conference. The speaker was a senior New York literary agent with a who's-who client list, who said this: **When a story idea strikes you … *run*.**

Not run toward it. Run *from* it.

Make it chase you. If the idea is fundamentally weaker than it seems at first blush—because certainly, sometimes things strike us in ways we can't defend or understand—time itself, seasoned by an understanding of applicable criteria and through the filter of your instincts, will be your ally in ultimately seeing it for what it is, and what it isn't.

Nobody is standing at the gate giving you a user's manual and a life preserver for your story idea. It's all on you. Rather, the better approach is to juxtapose your ideas against known criteria—this being the focus of Part 2 of this book—all of which reside within that short list of expectations we saw a moment ago. Make sure you go out on a few dates with your story idea before you propose marriage, and make sure you have criteria to apply, informing a sense of knowing what needs to happen, before you do.

The odds invite you to *not* follow the crowd.

While no double-blind, peer-reviewed, data-ratified certification have been made to come up with the following statistic, many professionals conclude that 96 percent of the submissions to agents from new writers are ultimately rejected. The agent may have asked for more pages, they may have made a few submissions with some of those stories, but ensuing rejections contribute to the ultimate 96 percent return rate from agents, who are actually looking for stories that not only work but make readers swoon. It's not exactly a failure rate, because the writer may learn from the rejection—hopefully this is the case—and he may revise to the point of elevating the project. (This statistic was reported in the *HuffPost* and refers to agents exclusively, and fiction exclusively, which is only part of the whole picture. The percentage of rejected submissions through agents who have agreed to represent the work is lower, though still far greater than half, while the percentage of rejected submissions made directly by authors to publishers, without an agent's representation—known in the business as the *slush pile*—is frighteningly higher, well above 99 percent. So the aggregate rejection rate of all novels submitted, however submitted, is actually well in excess of 96 percent. You can find this source here: www.huffingtonpost.com/heather-hummel/why-agents-reject-96-of-a_b_4247045.html.)

That 96-to-4 percentage split is as much a motivating statistic as it is a terrifying one. If nothing else than because it reflects the efficacy—actually, the lack thereof—to a great extent, of the conventional wisdom that dominates the writing conversation.

There *has* to be a better way. What are those 4-percenters doing that the rest aren't, or at least aren't doing *well* enough? Or perhaps more germane, what do they *know* that the rest of us do not?

There are answers to those questions, and their layers, which will unfold before you as continue to read.

Self-publishing doesn't change the math.

It only tears down the barriers to seeing your name on a book cover. In truth, the percentage of self-published authors who reach the sales levels of A-list traditionally published authors is microscopic. The average self-published book sells about two hundred copies, and that average includes the successful slim percentage that have much higher novel sales numbers. And while those authors may have done well in marketing their work online (a different acumen than the writing itself), it is the actual *storytelling*, and the degree to which it delivers principle-driven reading experiences, that will bring readers back, again and again. It is the storytelling that dictates the attainment of a word-of-mouth tipping point required to propel a novel onto a best-seller list. This is true whether you are aiming for a contract with one of the so-called Big 5 publishers or your own series of self-published novels on Amazon.

In terms of the quality of the end product, it really doesn't matter *how* you write (your process), nor does it does matter how anybody else writes (their process). And marketing your novel is what it is, whether you are self-published or traditionally published (the main difference being a traditionally published novel will end up in major bookstores, the self-published novel likely will not). From idea generation to story visualization to drafting and revision, all of it is *writing*. At least in the context of the discussion we are having here. Which means, what others say about *process* may or may not be of value to you, even if it comes from a famous author. Which it often does, because famous authors love to wax lofty about how they do the work.

That common oversimplification—it's all *just writing*—is the pervasive toxic problem within the conventional wisdom itself. It really isn't a simple proposition at all. Ask a published professional how long it took them to reach the A-list and this truth will become self-evident.

But here's a fact, in an avocation in which there aren't many facts.

Behold a liberating truth that can change the trajectory of your writing career: There is no right or wrong way to write a story. Within this hypothesis, I contend that the more an author knows about the principles of storytelling and the criteria that frame them, the more those principles and criteria influence and eventually define that writer's process, as well as their product. It is the degree to which their instincts become sufficiently empowered. And yet, writing without a context of knowing is the default process of new writers by definition, and among frustrated writers who continue to avoid the truth about the presence of principles and criteria.

Once we grow into a state in which our process no longer hinders but actually empowers because it is infused with and defined by the application of core principles and measured against part-specific criteria, the glass ceiling shatters and a suddenly accessible upside is ours to realistically shoot for.

When even the most cynical, mystical, and old school of authors finish writing a scene, they always read it over several times to make sure it works. That's not a pass-fail proposition as much as it is a broader search for ways to make it *better*. In doing that, by definition they are applying *criteria*. Criteria that are, for this kind of writer, largely instinctual. They dwell in that writer's head after being earned and learned over time, usually with the blood of rejection all over their psyche. Newer writers, however, tend to write a scene and then move on from it, trusting that first instinct—that first *version*—of execution. The difference is found in what the writer knows, rather than what they default to.

Which brings us full circle … back to you.

If you know what that enlightened writer knows, then you may succeed in doing an evaluation of your work in the same fashion, with the same instinctual, criteria-driven basis of comparison. But if you don't, if you can't instinctually recognize what needs to be there upon completion, including what isn't there, then you need an external standard to apply. Some hire editors for this purpose, but that doesn't add value at the composition stage, and certainly not the idea stage, where in both cases criteria can empower the scenes as they unfold in real time.

This is how these lists of criteria might change your writing life.

Because, ultimately, they are the things that your fully informed instinct will view as foundational, natural, and expected. They can be applied *as* you write, not just after you write it. It may have taken those old school authors years and a basement full of rejected manuscripts to get there, but you are on the cusp of a better opportunity.

Because the assimilation of element-specific criteria doesn't have to wait until you have a closet full of rejected manuscripts. You don't have to have buckets of blood on your learning curve. An evolved story instinct is available as a body of unassailable knowledge that can be learned before it is earned. They are principles that are easily dissected and validated within stories that work and succeed in the marketplace.

All you have to do to begin your journey of enlightenment as an author of fiction, right now in this moment, is turn the page.

2 Developing a Criteria-Driven Nose for Story

Let's try to understand *why* that ratio—96 percent rejected, 4 percent successful—is what it is. My hypothesis is this: Too many writers aren't doing the work from an instinct, a storytelling muscle, that is strong enough. Which means that not all of the part-specific applicable criteria are being considered. While some claim to be born with the storytelling gene, I believe it's more an outcome of the learning the writer has absorbed, or not, that has led them to where they are.

In athletics, where DNA actually does become a factor, competence is something that is developed over time by applying certain principles with consistency. Over time that application meets a higher standard, which can be defined by criteria. The same is true of writers who *get it*.

In this book, I frequently reference *new writers* and frustrated writers who haven't broken in, who likely haven't yet conquered the learning curve. Those are overlapping yet separate circles of demography. My point of reference isn't a casual assumption, but rather the outcome of many years of working as a writing coach and workshop facilitator, both of which find me reading full and partial submissions and listening to story pitches from new writers.

The difference between a new writer and someone who has been at this a while is quickly discernable. I read and listen to these with great empathy, remembering my own earliest story ideas, which were all ideas in need of more depth. It was only after studying screenwriting that I realized there are given standards available—not just for films, but for any story—and that truth has remained at the core of my work as a writing coach *and* a practicing author of novels.

If this were a keynote, I could regale you for many pages with the story ideas I've heard from the enthusiastic mouths of new writers, including that *lost ashes* concept from the last chapter. Literally thousands of them. Too many were dead on arrival, no matter how well they might have been written. Slice-of-life stories. Theme-pounding pontification.

Thinly veiled *this is based on my life* novels. (Quick note: *Eat, Pray, Love* was a memoir, not a novel, which means different forms and criteria apply.) These are well-intended, smart people who, nonetheless, *do not know what they do not know.*

Knowledge is not only power—it becomes the raw grist of instinct.

Any agent or story coach will tell you that the reason so many of the manuscripts they read aren't strong enough to take forward has to do with the lack of a *nose* for story on the part of the author. Some of those manuscripts are well written, if you are referring exclusively to sentences and paragraphs. Good writing, in that particular context, is a commodity. But—this being a newsflash for many—solid prose is merely an entry-level prerequisite to getting into the audition room. Among that collective whole, it is the outstanding *story* that will be noticed. The industry is looking for the next home run told by a first-round draft choice storytelling prospect.

The great separator and distinguishing attribute of writers who sell their stories, compared to those who don't, is the ability to *conceive and execute stories that glow in the dark.* Too often the *conceive* end of that goal is undervalued. Agents, publishers, and readers want stories that are ambitious, that work at a high level within their genre. Stories that tap into hearts and minds, that are fresh and provocative and lovely and disturbing.

They are less interested in a novelization of the year you spent hiking in Chile after grad school. That's the province of memoir, not fiction.

Notice the duality of that conclusion: *conceive* and *execute*.

Both factors are always in play, and both are essential. You can be talented in one but not the other. In fact, it explains why some authors never fulfill their writing dream: They aren't executing stories from both contexts.

The world is full of karaoke bars that are full of singers who can stand alongside many of the recording artists who have big careers and match them note for glorious note. But truly great *songwriters* are a rarer breed. As authors, we face the exact same paradox, asking us to be the same, yet different, with every story we tell.

At some point, it's all about your brand.

New writers tend to look at known published authors and compare themselves and their work to that level of skill and talent. But doing so can be a seductive illusion. Because success begets success in this business, and it is more difficult to break in than it is to sell your next novel once you've done so at some level of success. Even then, after you've sold a handful of novels, your publisher will expect a home-run novel, and for that you'll need a home-run story *idea*. Two of the best examples of that are the careers of Dennis Lehane and Dan Brown, both of whom published perfectly respectable genre novels that sold fairly well and then rose to a higher level—the top of the mountain, actually—with mega-bestselling breakout novels (*Mystic River* and *The Da Vinci Code*, respectively).

They were already terrific writers. But their breakout novels were built upon the DNA of a story idea that was truly special.

To break *into* the business, or write a *breakout* novel from your less-than-notorious position on the mid-list, a story has to be even *better* than books that fill the shelves at Barnes & Noble, but haven't been seen in the front window yet. The X-factor that makes that happen is the power of the *originating story idea* as it translates to a compelling and complete *premise*. Those authors could write all along. But it was a Big Idea that moved them into a better neighborhood.

And so the question becomes this: How do we nurture and grow our story instincts, beginning at the idea level, so that we might begin to write stories on a level that demands attention and response? What criteria are applied to ideas and premises at that level?

"But wait," the cynic might cry out.

This isn't brain surgery. Which is true, but it's not a valid comparison.

Unless it's a surgeon, or a pilot, or a scientist who is making it. Which is exactly who I've heard from when they undertake the study of story in preparation of dusting off the dream of writing a novel. They are shocked when they learn how complex it is. Too many writers don't acknowledge this as they simply dive into the deep end of the pool without yet knowing how to swim.

It is much more challenging, and rarer, to turn a sow's ear into a silk purse than it is to hone and polish and frame a diamond in the rough.

Our stories are emotional tsunamis and chemical cocktails as much as they are assemblies of thoughts and ideas. The manipulation of a reader's emotions—let's be honest, that's what this is—becomes a multifaceted and subtle undertaking, one that transcends story and embraces principles of human thought, biochemistry, and social engineering, all in the context of history.

If you're thinking there is an advanced degree for this—the venerable Master of Fine Arts, or MFA—you need to understand that an MFA is to an aspiring commercial author of fiction what a law degree is to a politician. Valuable, absolutely worth pursuing. Everything about it will contribute to your success in any genre, especially literary fiction. But the story craft learned in an MFA program is a different contextual breed than what a commercial author working in the genres needs to understand.

The necessary foundation of knowledge comes from *an immersion into the study of the craft* that defines commercial storytelling. Studying it, experiencing it, questioning it, practicing it. There are a multitude of resources that include books and workshops and mentoring programs and blogs and conferences and, most importantly to all of this, the continued analytical reading of commercial fiction for the express purpose of recognizing and internalizing the *principles* of craft that those resources and experiences will show you. You will know it when you see it.

But it is important to understand this: You may not see it until you know it.

It's like looking at an MRI. You and I see contrasting shadows that look like someone spilled coffee onto the film. We really can't tell a thing about the health of the patient. A trained radiologist, however, as well as most doctors, see life and death. They see where problems reside and where danger awaits, and they know what needs to be done about it. They *know*. Just as we need to know our way around a story, good or bad, sometimes with as little as a glance.

The craft informs your instincts about how a story should be conceived, assembled, sequenced, set up, layered, escalated, twisted, imbued with shock and awe, drenched with emotion and a microcosm of the human experience, laced with empathy, and driven forward by tapping into centuries-old theory and practice on how stories are absorbed and remembered. This, if nothing else, enables the ability to take that great idea and actually turn it into a novel that works. While coming up with a decent story idea (for which there are specific criteria) is fairly common, the ability and nuanced touch required to successfully spool it out over 400 blank pages is quite rare. In my experience, I'd say that failure, in the form of rejection, distributes across these two explanations—premise versus execution—at a fifty-fifty rate, some being deficient at both.

Chance and random proximity play a role.

As does persistence and faith substantiated by informed study. But sooner or later a sort of natural selection kicks in, because failure and frustration wear us down. It is the hope of finding a pathway to success, in the form of a keen understanding of principles and craft (versus a blinder faith in an evolving story instinct), that becomes the highest-odds bet we can wager.

Here is where the room divides.

Simply honoring the principles of craft is not the exclusive domain of the criteria-driven author. Because all of us share the mission to write a good story. It's the *driven* part that sets some authors apart. It's how they view and *apply* the craft that empowers their work in an exciting and effective way.

It is the degree to which the criteria for story find their way into your process that defines the opportunity at hand.

If our instincts remain underdeveloped—if our narrative choices have no relationship to what the principles tell us will be the responses they evoke in a reader—we'll remain among the unnamed masses who write their stories in an almost identical fashion, both in terms of process and product. This process is really nothing other than regurgitating our ideas onto the page without being filtered by something other than ourselves. In other words, to just write. Rather, we need to insert something between our brains, where the ideas form, and the page, where they end up. Because, as the data suggests, more than 96 percent of the time in the aggregate our uninformed instinct is wrong, or at least not right enough.

This is about learning to fly.

If you've ever been inside a cockpit of an airliner prior to takeoff, or (more likely) seen this in a movie or YouTube video, you know that the pilot and copilot undertake a very serious and repetitive regimen of going through a robust checklist that covers the entire spectrum of what must be done to ready the aircraft for safe flight. *Safe* being the key word here. Every item on that checklist exists because someone in the past has literally (in most cases) died for it. Every time an airplane goes down, the accident is studied in great detail. Much is learned from those postmortem engineering dissections—just as an informed analysis of a work-in-progress shines a light on the role that principles and criteria play in the storytelling—and it translates to procedures and settings and criteria for the state of the airplane and its instruments that must be checked and checked off (met, without compromise) before anything else can happen.

Stay with me here.

Pilots operate the aircraft, which is no small feat. But even more intricate and complex is the design and building of the flying machine, which is more analogously true to our role as designers and builders of stories. There, too, for each and every one of the hundreds of thousands of parts and programs that come together within the skin of the airplane to become an airworthy vehicle, there are checklists that are applied, checked, and rechecked to make sure the part is worthy and sound, that it has been properly installed, that it is wired properly, and that it interfaces with countless other systems on the airplane, all of which have checklists of their own.

Consider that for each and every critical factor and facet, there is a set of criteria to be applied. Criteria that is reflected in the checklist and for which there can be no compromise. Criteria that are applied over and over by different sets of eyes and in different contexts of operation, maintenance, and repair. It reflects the very best thinking, the very best minds of aviation and design professionals over decades of technological innovation, leading to best practices.

Those folks—pilots, avionics designers, aerospace engineers, quality control auditors, and National Transportation Safey Board accident investigators, who are collectively the authors of the checklists they apply—are all *criteria driven*. As opposed to the old school barnstorming pilot who slides into the open cockpit and *just flies*, without the slightest knowledge of Bernoulli's principle, which explains why 400,000-pound airplanes can lift into the air. They create the designs and the parts in context to something external to themselves, certainly far beyond their gut instinct. And yet, at the point of installation and inspection, the instinct of those professionals still plays a role. It is the combination of knowledge, instinct, and criteria that empowers the entire design, build, and operations processes, resulting in a product that has produced a stellar record of safety, productivity, and benefit. A pilot, as precise as the checklist is, still depends on her "gut," a sense of the moment, especially in the detection of something being slightly off-kilter. All the instruments may report normal readings, but when the plane begins a takeoff roll, the pilot has a window measured in seconds to decide to proceed or abort. That decision, after consulting the data, is pure instinct.

And yet, sitting in coach there is a writer putting the finishing touches to her novel on a laptop, without knowing there are criteria that can be applied to every part and parcel, every nuance and essence, of the story she has just written. She's alone with what she's written, empowered only by her instincts as a writer, by the opinions of what her friends in her writing groups claim to be true, and by her own tastes and opinions. Sometimes even just guessing, too often without anything to compare it to other than her own gut feeling, and soon, that of others, few of which will apply any specific criteria to their own analytical evaluation, either.

That's what being a criteria-driven author means.

Whether at the level of instinct or through an actual checklist of criteria that pertain to specific parts of his novel, the criteria-driven author is always conjuring ideas and developing stories in context to something ... something bigger and more proven than themselves or the personal opinion of someone else. They juxtapose ideas and scenes and drafts against criteria that become a checklist that ensures specific areas of intention and function, that it is all in the ideal and optimal place within the story, that the pacing is right and the emotional experience intended for the reader has the benefit of everything we know about how human beings respond to storytelling at its best.

The mission is to blow your readers away.

Many writers are driven by the lesser mission of simply *finishing*. But when you write toward a target that exists in the context of criteria, you can't help but experience a qualitative upgrade, because that's the entire function of criteria in the first place. You'll more quickly and easily be able to discern whether a given creative choice you've made relative to a specific story point is fair, good, or amazing, because you'll know the context of that moment both before and after it appears. If a better choice is available, you won't have to blow up the story to put it into play, because other criteria have ensured that the surrounding contexts are solid.

This is how being criteria driven helps writers who adopt that context for their work, no matter what their process. It allows them to see the big picture as a target, rather than an outcome over which they aren't sure or don't feel they have full control.

The criteria the writer sitting in coach could apply if she were more aware await you in the forthcoming chapters: first with a focus on story idea and premise (Part 2), and then across the entire arc of the story that expands them (Part 3).

3 What Happens When You Know

Your writing process is infused with and defined by what you believe and what you know to be true, just as it is limited by what you don't know. Both calculations contribute to the outcome of your efforts.

I get it. We have to start *somewhere*. When you open a file for a new story, you probably don't know a fraction of what you need to know *about the story* in order for it to work, even if you do understand the criteria that will render a specific story beat effective. In fact, it is that understanding that will lead you to your best story. That's what your process is for: to search for, discover, and develop what you *need* to know *about the story*, which is best done within a context of understanding *why*.

TURNING CRITERIA INTO INSTINCT

This whole notion of criteria-driven story development goes to the question of knowing what to write, where to put it, and why. It may or may not be a function of innate talent—most often it isn't. It may be the product of learning and experience. This is the universal question nonwriters pose to working writers with a strange look in their eyes, as if there is something mystical about cobbling together sentences and paragraphs into scenes that fill chapters which unfold in a sequence that makes sense. It is the question that plagues all writers, and all stories, from the moment of a declared intention to write. And yet, while most writers can't really answer the question, an answer does, in fact, exist. It resides in the contextual whole of the set of criteria you are about to encounter here.

And right there is our opportunity to raise the bar for our work.

Hopefully, the process we apply to our work embraces things we know and understand about the principles of storytelling. But when one's particular frame of reference is thin ice for a writer—either because of lack of experience or an absence of learned knowledge—then the story emerges from within a vacuum in that regard, in much the same way someone called to the cockpit in an emergency would be operating blindly as they try to land the airplane in a snowstorm using only the context of their experience as a passenger. Let us hope someone is on the radio speaking instructions into their headset, if they could even *find* the headset in that dire situation. If that ever happens to you, pray that whoever goes forward to help has at least been through ground school.

The key variable in story efficacy is not, by default, our choice of process, of how we prepare and plan and execute our stories. Lawyers and accountants and athletes and actors would agree, because once we put on the uniform and step onto the field or enter a courtroom or sit in front of our keyboards, we have, in fact, signed up for something in terms of the end product. To say you hope to sell your fiction is to declare that you seek to become a professional writer. Certain standards apply. No one in the audience cares how we got there, they only care about how well it works on the page.

And wherever there are standards, there are criteria that frame access to them.

There are unexpected realities that apply to novels today.

Below you will find six true statements about writing fiction today. Some of them will be familiar, some may challenge what you believe. Ignoring any of these might explain the failure of a project to reach its highest potential, including why it keeps getting rejected. These truths frame your work as an aspiring or even a working novelist. They also inform the development and state of your story instincts. These aren't hard-and-fast rules, per se, but they are realities. Exceptions can be found, but aiming to become an exception is not a good path for a newer writer. These aren't principles, per se (which touch on the specific craft of narrative exposition), yet they become context for the application of principles.

This is what smart writers have discovered as contradictions to what some consider and apply as conventional wisdom. Even if—especially if—you've never attempted to write a work of fiction before, this is the landscape into which you are about to venture forth.

1. NOT ALL STORY IDEAS ARE VIABLE AS THE BASIS FOR A NOVEL.

You really can't sit down and write *anything you want* without meeting certain criteria (which you may or may not know) and expect it to be saved by your brilliant prose. Rather, what might save the idea—by making it stronger—is the *premise*, to which you can apply significant criteria. While there is no data on this, it is the opinion of many folks who do what I do (write and coach fiction) that as much as half of the collective body of rejected stories owe their downfall to a weakness in the story idea itself as well as the premise that flows from it. As my colleague Art Holcomb recently said to me, "We need to find a way to help these people land on better story ideas." That statement, which I agree with wholeheartedly, was part of the impetus for this book.

Nobody is going to stop you from pursuing a weak idea. You are largely on your own to recognize the truth about the idea, which is challenging because in all likelihood you love the idea. It bears repeating: The purpose of an idea is to inform a premise, which has defined criteria to apply. Sometimes one of those criteria might be accessible from within the idea, sometimes not. In either case, those criteria become a vetting tool that can be applied at the idea level, helping to shape it toward a higher level of narrative appeal.

Among the common pieces of advice from the front of the workshop room is this: *Write what you'd like to read. Write what you know. Write for you.* It's hard to argue these points, until you realize that what you like to read or what you know might only reside within a small demographic. Perhaps *really* small. The enlightened commercial author knows that you need to write for *others*, for the marketplace. If writing for others is not your highest motivation, then it should at least tie for first place.

2. **A MANUSCRIPT CAN'T *FULLY* WORK UNTIL THE *ENTIRE* STORY IS KNOWN TO THE AUTHOR.**

When a writer begins a draft without an ending in mind—even as a temporary placeholder—that draft is merely an extension of the search for story. In fact, it is just that, because an ending discovered mid-draft is destined for a major, if not complete, rewrite. Everything that has been written prior to that moment in which an ending crystalizes requires careful analysis, which almost always involves massive, necessary rewriting. Because we cannot foreshadow a story in which the ending remains unknown, nor can we set up that ending. And because new writers may not recognize this disconnect (a case of not knowing what they do not know) or choose to cut a corner because rewriting is what they signed up for, this becomes a common explanation for story weakness and failure.

3. **GENRE FICTION IS NOT *ALL ABOUT THE CHARACTERS*.**

Writers and gurus who say this—and they are legion—are at best only partially right. For literary fiction, this is certainly true. But genre stories are about *how a character responds to a calling*, to the solving of a problem, via actions taken and opposition encountered, thus creating dramatic tension that shows us the truest nature of who they are. Genre fiction uses plot to illuminate character, while literary fiction turns that inside out, with the primary dramatic tension coming from within the characters.

4. **IT ISN'T A STORY UNTIL SOMETHING GOES WRONG.**

Carve this into the hard plastic that surrounds your computer monitor. Dramatic tension stemming from something gone wrong is the lifeblood of fiction, in any genre, including literary works (which tend to be driven by internal conflict versus the external focus of genre-based stories). Conflict is essential to fiction, to an extent you could argue that it is the most critical element of a story among a short list of other critical elements, all with available criteria to help us assess and optimize.

5. **A STORY ISN'T A SNAPSHOT. IT IS A MOVIE IN THE READER'S HEAD.**

This is critical context, and it speaks to one of the most common mistakes newer writers tend to make. Theme and setting and history and character backstory—all of which are common sparks for the original story *idea*—need to be framed within the unspooling forward motion of the narrative along a dramatic spine (drama stemming from conflict), in pursuit of a dramatic question, facing obstacles along the way, driven by things that *happen*—to, and because of, your protagonist—rather than a static snapshot of what is, which too quickly can become an essay or a manifesto about a specific condition or belief.

6. **STRUCTURE IS OMNIPRESENT IN A STORY THAT WORKS.**

Structure is, for the most part, a given flow of unspooling information rather than a unique invention. It is too often linear and episodic, to fit the story you are telling. Nor is it a formula, because you are free to do what you'd like within this given flow. The game of golf requires that you play specific holes in a specific order. There is no rule about which clubs you use at any point along the hole, though there are expectations and best practices that show you the common wisdom. As a professional, you concede that nobody has won a championship putting with a fairway wedge.

You may need to wrap your head around structure as an expectation.

Structure is the most often challenged tenant of fiction, and yet the most enduring and provable. Exceptions are as rare as true geniuses. People who argue against structure are actually talking about *process*, suggesting that stories are best developed without consideration of structure, which at some point will become a necessity that must be retrofitted into the results of such a process. And because, even more than applying criteria to the blank page, *revising* toward a standard is highly difficult. It is something newer writers often struggle with or skip altogether, only to find that they've just sabotaged their story for this reason alone. When a professional advises you to write your story however you feel the story should be written, this may be a write-it-now-fix-it-later proposition. The fixing, in that context, is inevitable, but it won't be as extensive if a proper understanding of structure had been applied as a form of criteria earlier in the process. Most professionals know that before the story will work at a professional standard for genre fiction, it will align with a specific flow, one that unfolds in four contextual parts (which we will examine closely very soon). And if they don't, they recognize that this may be the problem when they realize something isn't working.

There are as many structure-driven authors who enjoy a high degree of success as there are writers who believe structure should not be a consideration in early drafts, at least within the framework of process (the latter may or may not understand that story *is* structure regardless of the process employed). The real question is: Does the structure you've ultimately used work? In genre fiction there is very little latitude in this regard. Because when you finally get it right, whether through your own instinctually fueled evolution of the story as you apply criteria or through outside feedback, it'll most likely fall in close alignment with the principles of structure that are omnipresent within the genres—which we'll examine closely later in this book—which are there not because of a rule of engagement, but because this is the way stories work best.

These market-driven truths frame the mission of the commercially ambitious author.

Armed with these understandings as context for your initial story formulation efforts (the focus of Part 2), you are ready to delve deeper into the power of criteria-driven storytelling in the coming chapters, beginning with a hard look at where all the confusion comes from in the first place.

The Sound of the Writing Conversation

Context leans toward clarity.

This notion of being criteria-driven isn't a common way to think about what we do. In more than three decades of kicking around in this business, I've never heard it framed in these terms. This is why I know this is new territory and why I'm certain it can be a breakthrough mindset delivering the clarity so many writers are seeking.

Imagine taking your idea and expanding it into a premise that meets essential criteria, and then unspooling that premise across the arc of the story, applying proven criteria to each part and milestone, every twist and turn, as well as to the character and emotional arcs, and finally, the reading experience itself. All this in contrast to … simply hoping for the best, without complete clarity on what "the best" might look like.

What's new within this proposition is the role of *criteria* in the process.

When criteria becomes the target of story development, that's a deeper level of craft. It doesn't diminish the role of instinct in spontaneity—which is what some traditionalists might claim before they truly understand this approach—because a higher level of reader response is precisely the purpose of instinct and the point of spontaneity. It's adding a checklist and a blueprint to what is otherwise left to memory and sensibility, and for some, guesswork.

When was the last time you read a bestselling genre novel that wasn't set up, followed by the launch of a core dramatic proposition in a way that propels the hero down a new path or quest, or causes her to run from something or someone? Then the context of the story changes in the middle via new information. The hero steps it up because of that new information, the villain does the same. These actions lead to confrontation or a standoff or a lull, then into another twist, and finally the paths

Great Stories Don't Write Themselves

converge, confrontation and deception occur, the unexpected manifests, and eventually the problem is resolved.

None of that is formula. All of it is simply the *natural order* of how stories work.

So, if that is true, why would you *not* set out to shape your story in that fashion? To envision it unfolding in this manner? The answer is: because you don't *know* about this. Know it or not, you can be assured that if you don't unspool your story that way, feedback will push an inevitable revision toward that very form. Experienced authors find that this sequence of unfolding story is how they *think*. This is their instinct, sometimes after years of trial and error. Their stories tend to spill out of their heads and onto the page in a way that is already aligned with this criteria-driven paradigm. Not so much for newer writers—that's sometimes more like a textbook threw up on a printing press—but they can, nonetheless, get there just as quickly by applying the criteria, however learned, to that same process.

Thus our mission as authors emerges as evident and inevitable.

Stare at it long enough, study it deeply enough, and criteria become visible beneath the veneer of the words themselves. Like raising the hood of a car to behold an engine that powers the entire machine.

Nearly every novel that is traditionally published today is evidence of the pursuit of criteria. If you're looking for exceptions, try the self-published realm, where there isn't availability nor qualification of eyes laid on the story prior to going public. Self-published books that attract a readership do so, in great part, because they align with these principles. Because, once again, based on history and analysis and reader preference, this is how stories are best presented and experienced. Think of them as *best practices*, a term that applies to almost every profession in our culture. This could become your version of actually knowing what your favorite A-list writer knows.

Pick your source of writing wisdom carefully.

Folks dispensing writing advice are everywhere. Some have never published a novel and perhaps have never written one. Every blog post you read, lecture you hear, and writing book you invest in reflects value, if nothing else than as a mirror you can hold up to the truths you accept. In the end you may have cherry-picked morsels of value from various sources, all of it combining to inform your own choice or process.

Bestselling legal thriller author Phillip Margolin, for example—someone who delivers a killer keynote, by the way—creates outlines for his novels in excess of fifty single-spaced pages, and he won't begin the first draft until he's satisfied that he's in possession of the best possible story, beat by beat, after considering all angles and options. This works because he knows the criteria for the best possible story. He has the proven instinctual chops to make that call, which is a notable differentiation from most newer writers, and one we should learn from. He is most comfortable writing a draft when he knows the story in great detail. For him, the line between knowledge and instinct is not so much blurred as it is merged. He applies specific criteria at the pre-draft planning stage, leveraging a well-honed storytelling instinct in the same way it would serve a pantser doing it within a draft.

There are dozens of other bestselling authors who develop stories in an almost identical way. Just as there are dozens more who write their bestsellers completely by the seat of their pants, landing on story points as they go. In either case, when looking in at the level of skill from the outside, we should avoid the temptation to imitate, and focus instead on learning what they have learned.

Does outlining rob Margolin of the chance to seize better ideas when they arrive during the drafting process? That's the rap on outlining, usually voiced by writers who may have had that experience because they know no other way (again, we get to choose whose advice and opinion we value). For Margolin and other experienced outliners, nothing is compromised, including the utter creative thrill of spontaneous improvisation. The outlining process he uses considers narrative alternatives along an unfolding yet still pliable story road—

which is the same story road that a *draft* considering the same options would take—so it's likely that when he arrives at the drafting stage he's already landed on the best choices available, after considering alternative treatments during a given narrative pause. Truth is, the thrill of having a new and better idea during the brainstorming for an outline is just as intense and rewarding as having one that arrives during the writing of a draft. If a better idea pops up on Margolin's radar—which absolutely happens for outliners every bit as frequently as it does for organic writers—he only has to tweak his story notes that lead to the outline itself, rather than injecting a new idea into the full contextual length of an actual draft.

On the other hand, bestselling author Robert Dugoni begins his stories with a crisp premise in mind but says he's open to how the story unfolds as he proceeds through the draft. But we must take care in how we interpret that. Because Dugoni absolutely understands how a story must unfold within his genre (mystery)—in other words, the applicable principles of the structural dramatic arc—and his instincts are drawn to what works within that expectation, rather than a rookie's temptation to toss in the random backstory of his hero's favorite baseball player.

In either case, the author's path toward her final story is informed by criteria, whether that list resides in her experience-informed head or on a piece of paper taped to her office wall.

I'm not here to sell you on the notion of outlining as part of your process.

Rather, this about showing you how having *context* actually leads you to a form of outlining, if not in print then in your head in the moment of inserting it into a draft (which is exactly the same phenomena as it is when it is written into an outline). Rest assured, the more experienced the author, even if they decry outlining and claim to be a pantser, engage with their drafts with some form of outline, perhaps existing only in their head, which provides that context of emerging exposition. Either way, outlined or completed as an organically-written draft, for the criteria-driven author new ideas that arrive late to the party still have an opportunity to contribute to your vision for the story. Because the mission-driven author understands that it must be considered and implemented within the larger context of the unfolding story itself.

When Margolin stands before an audience of hungry writers, this is what he talks about. All of it is valid … for him. The same goes for Dugoni, who is one of the few bestselling authors actively teaching on the workshop circuit (bestsellers are more frequent keynote speakers than they are workshop facilitators).

The real question becomes: What is valid and empowering … for *you*? Who is right?

The latter is the wrong question to ask.

Rather, ask what context is being applied to fuel the choices you are making as the story develops, either in a draft with no plan or in a set of notes that will be become an outline. Is the organic thinker really more creative, as some claim, than the story-planning outliner who captures the moment on a yellow sticky note rather than writing an entire chapter?

Truth be known, most writers work in the middle of that continuum. Because both are outcomes of the same intention and the same conjuring of ideas and exploring them before adding another idea that moves the story forward. Both ends, as well as the middle, are equal expressions of instinct.

There is an A-list *product*, rather than an A-list process.

I submit to you that the latter doesn't exist. Because A-listers across the board create their bestsellers using both sides of the proposition, and everything in between, with no clear majority emerging.

I've seen this prove itself in more than a few keynote addresses by famous authors with bestsellers to back them up. Not long ago, one of them told hundreds of serious writers at a major conference that he composes a 100,000-word character biography before tackling a draft of his work-in-progress, just to "find the voice of the character." He contended that we should all do the same. That *finding your voice* always requires pain and suffering. Such a contention from the mouth of an A-list author proves nothing other than the circle I've just completed here: How they write *their* books doesn't matter. What matters, from a learning perspective, is being able to recognize what it is about their work—the end product—that succeeds.

Better to cull value from their product rather than their choice of process. And yet to acknowledge, at least for that writer, that this circuitous route was what it took to get him there.

Here's the footnote to that story: That 100K character sketch the author wrote? He intended it to *be* the novel. It wasn't ever a strategy or a tool; it wasn't even a story-development exercise. He thought it *was* the novel. He admitted as much. He sent it to his agent as such. The agent returned it forthwith, riddled with, well, ridicule. Because it wasn't just a bad novel, it wasn't a novel at all. It was hundreds of pages of character sketch and uneven backstory, with no dramatic tension (plot), no theme, no structure, and nothing to root for. Nothing *happened* in those pages. Which means this successful author, standing behind a podium at a major writing conference in front of many hundreds of other authors who are, for the most part also working or at least aspiring professionals, couldn't tell the difference as he typed.

This is what happens when you write your novel without reference to criteria, or even actually knowing the difference between a novel and 100,000 words of brainstorming.

This is not the common wisdom, nor lack thereof, among any category of author. It's certainly not a choice that the majority of A-list authors would make. It's just *that* guy. Trouble is, that guy is telling other writers that this *is* the conventional wisdom, that this is indeed how it's done.

The only truth in that is this: This is how it's done … *for him.* One of his books sold four million copies, so by hook or crook, he got to the finish line on that project. But I'll risk saying this: You can bet there is an uncredited editor out there somewhere who knows her role in that success story.

There is a better way to decide what to write.

Criteria-driven authors consider their story choices against the available criteria in real time. Once exposed to these principles, you may find yourself thinking about story development in the same way.

Whether they're assembling a beat sheet that will become an outline or they're writing an initial developmental draft, criteria-driven authors have a way to evaluate each narrative idea as they get to it, right where it inserts into the flow of the storyline, whether that be an outline or a draft. They apply criteria to their choices. They can tick off the criteria, for example, of a Midpoint story turn without hesitation (something many less-experienced authors cannot do and something you'll learn very soon in this book). When the criteria-driven author is alone in a room creating the sequence of his story—be it via planning or pantsing his way through a draft—and he reaches that critical Midpoint story milestone (half the battle is knowing that it is, in fact, a critical story milestone), those criteria are already a part of his thought process. Of his *search* process. Or if it isn't, he knows there is a list of criteria to apply to a midpoint story turn. Ideas float to the surface, and they either meet or come up short of the criteria and given context for the moment in question. If more than one idea is in play, the writer can more easily assess which is best because there are multiple criteria to apply to any given story moment, depending on its placement in the sequence of the unspooling story.

One of my esteemed colleagues, James Scott Bell, suggests we can find value by writing our stories from the middle. An interesting proposition, that. That's how important the Midpoint of a novel is, so important that you can begin planning the story from there, working backward and forward and adjusting on either side in context to what you come up with. This doesn't alter the criteria for any given story element in the least; it is simply, and perhaps brilliantly, a suggestion about the process applied. It is, in fact, a criteria-driven process, because it relies to a significant degree on the author's understanding of the purpose and criteria of the Midpoint itself.

Great Stories Don't Write Themselves

But it doesn't really work until the writer has developed and committed to a central dramatic premise. You can't land on a Midpoint until that over-arcing context is in play.

Right here is a teachable moment, so let's be clear.

The criteria-driven author understands where she is in the sequence of her story at any given moment, both in the development phase *and* the drafting phase. And that all of it is, in fact, in context to the premise. And eventually, to an ending, even if it exists only as a placeholder for the time being. Drafts are always better when they are heading toward something. These authors aren't guessing any more than a surgeon has to guess what is beneath the skin at any given place in the human body. Criteria-driven authors know the context of a given moment and that location within the sequence, the expectations of that blank space (much more on this to come), what came before, and where the story is going or might be going after that—which is critical to pace and exposition. Because all of this is an integral part of the premise itself.

The other way to go about it, the less-than-criteria-driven way, is to *just write* the moment without sufficient context in play. Without truly understanding what the mission of the moment is. This is like a SWAT team arriving on the scene without knowing what happened there or what they might encounter. Just get out of the van and start shooting. It's a simpler strategy, certainly. You don't have to think as much, even if the price is less assurance and possibly settling for a mediocre choice. Or, worst case, hitting the wrong target and not knowing about it until hearing it on the news later.

But avoiding deeper thought shouldn't be our objective as novelists.

The time for blind, random story assembly is at the premise stage, not the outlining or drafting stage. Premise is where you get to play with the idea, and you don't move on until you find dramatic chemistry that works within the vision for the character. That's why outlining and drafting are simply two versions of the same thing: story *implementation.* Or if you prefer, *bringing the premise*—which is more story *formulation*—to *fruition.* If something needs changing at a given point, neither process is more prohibitive of doing so than the other.

Of course, at the end of the day the results speak for themselves.

Margolin and Dugoni and our confused keynote guy each end up with a book that works. Their process works for them, and, at least for the first two, they are representative of how A-list authors go about their job. Neither is more or less conventional with their wisdom than the other. There are just as many writers who struggle with any process, which is an outcome of not writing in context to principles and criteria that are second nature to writers who don't struggle along the story development path, at least to that degree. For them, the story struggle is bliss.

There is truth within the noise.

The good news in commercial fiction is that common themes emerge from the differentiation between blind instinct and a principle-informed story sensibility, which is a higher form of storytelling. That good news is "process neutral." It applies to all processes with equal power and validity, once sufficient knowledge is applied.

As writers, we begin with a blank page, which must at some point, by whatever means works, be filled in with choices that are informed by a combination of experience and learning, filtered by instinct. That is always the root of the choices we make. The point here is that when neither your experience nor your learning is fully developed and functional, or if it has come from something you've heard that wasn't fully informed, the context of the choice becomes thin ice.

Out of the mouths of the anointed ...

Here's another cautionary tale lifted straight out of the collective writing conversation. It's my favorite famous author story because it shines light on both sides of the story-development proposition, which is an issue of precision and pain tolerance.

In a recent author profile in *Writer's Digest* magazine, an 11-million-copy bestselling author confessed that *she has no idea how she does what she does*. Those were basically her words, which at a glance sound humble and mysterious and perhaps romantic. But in any case, they translate to this: *I just go with my gut.* Clearly, after a hit movie adaptation and a few screenplay credits on top of her considerable book sales, the numbers prove her wrong, because what is a validated instinct if not knowing what to do?

Claiming to not know how she got there isn't saying she doesn't know what her story craft needs to look like when she does. Her numbers prove that, as well. And thus, the paradox is reinforced. Her contention that *she doesn't know* is simply proof that, as it is in many forms of art and athletics and academics, *doing* and *teaching* exist as different core competencies, only rarely shared within one practitioner. My guess is she'd make a terrific keynote speaker.

Beware the bestselling author interview. It can lead you straight off a cliff.

So, why is it not yet clear to so many?

Because the collective writing conversation, while touching on truth, is filled with well-intentioned noise and contradictory assertions, sometimes from authors who truly believe that nothing is certain, nothing is known, that nothing can truly be learned short of *just writing* and paying your dues. It's a congenial buzz that confuses and competes and digresses and wanders, and it would rather talk about how to find an agent or how to beat the odds on Amazon than it would talk about what makes a novel work at a high level.

It's as if everyone already understands this stuff. That the criteria are obvious. That such a focus is so entry-level in nature that you embarrass yourself and anyone within earshot if you get too excited about it.

That, too, is misinformation, and it is as toxic as believing that you can make it all up as you go, with no context, and you'll be just fine … if you *just write.*

This is a vulnerable moment.

It would be fair to ask, at this point, after I've held up the documented thinking of some bestselling authors as examples of equality across the scale of confusion we all face, why you should believe me after all that. Why you should buy into a contextual frame of reference for storytelling, one I contend resides at the very core of everything we know about storytelling that works, when I've acknowledged that it is barely on the radar within the writing conversation?

This isn't where I throw my résumé at you. Outside of my writing books, it wouldn't make a decent dent if I did, because starred reviews and awards aren't nearly as impressive as massive sales statistics. Rather, the reason you should pay attention is the possibility that this approach and these truths are already rumbling around in your head as you read.

I'm not suggesting *how* you should do anything.

Choose the process that best serves you. And, if the *experience* of writing is your highest priority—the pure bliss of putting words on paper, the vicarious escape of making up stories, the pure and noble suffering of it all, even to the point at which you value the experience more than success itself—then choose the process that's the most rewarding for you. All others, however, will probably want to choose a process that is more effective for them.

I get it, writing should be fun.

In my view, it's the most fun when it *works*.

If you choose to consider the criteria-driven proposition, it'll likely be because there's a gap in your full understanding of how storytelling works, and deep within your creative self you already know it. You quietly wonder if there's a better way. What you've heard isn't completely clicking for you, in part because it isn't taking you where you want to go. Maybe you're looking for something that suggests, perhaps at long last, *why* a story works, when it does. You want to truly understand how a story works and what may have gone off the tracks when it doesn't.

Your instinct is already engaged as you encounter and process this material. That's how you'll know if it's right for you, because like the secret to a story problem suddenly revealed, you'll know it when you see it. More accurately, you'll *feel* it when you glimpse the immense potential of what this could mean to your writing dream.

Even then, though, there isn't a straight line to the winner's circle, which is the focus of our next discussion.

5 Realities, Odds, and Other Inconveniences

Nobody ever said this would be easy.

This is simple. Just write. *If*, that is, you truly know what you are doing.

Of course it isn't actually simple. Ever. Trying to make it simple is the Big Lie within the writing conversation I've just exposed. That said, adopting a criteria-driven context for both your process—because it empowers *any* process—*and* the end product it creates renders whatever complications we encounter much more manageable.

The goal of the criteria-driven approach isn't to make storytelling *easier*. It is to make your story better. How? By putting your story development sensibilities on steroids, allowing a quicker and stronger assimilation of context and instinct, fueled with contextual *content*, within a framework of principle-based knowledge and criteria. If you know what you are looking for as you search for your story, and if you know what criteria to apply to your choices about what to write and where to put it, your odds of choosing well escalate significantly.

This is you becoming a student of story.

Being a criteria-driven author means you are interested in the infrastructure and chemistry of story. You understand that story is built upon a consistent blueprint that defines the path of a story and is fueled by dependable facets of the human reading and learning experience. Very loosely, that blueprint looks like this: story set-up scenes ... hero's response to a call to action ... hero's proactive attack on the primary problem she is dealing with ... scenes that bring the story to resolution.

All four blocks of scenes are written within different contexts that are unique to that block, and all four almost always come in this sequential order.

This is not a formulaic path, which refers more to the specificity of your choices rather than the functional mission of those choices. Rather, they prescribe an *expected contextual flow* of your story, based on best practices and expectations in the commercial market. You might ask, expected by whom? Answer: the genre, for one thing. Agents and editors, for another. Even then, that flow is pretty much identical between all the genres. If you leave one of those four contexts out, your novel might read like a short story that is too long. Just as the contexts are given, so too are the transitional milestones within them. You don't need to decide whether or not you need a Midpoint twist (you do), but rather, you need to decide what the very *best* Midpoint story turn will be. One that makes the reader sit back in their chair and say, "Whoa, I didn't see that coming!" That blueprint is a universal sequential model, one that calls for a Midpoint milestone, while not remotely telling us what it should be, other than prescribing how it shifts the story into a higher gear. This is always a good thing.

It's true, we sometimes must kill our darlings.

Time to insert a principle into this layer of thinking: Evolved writers tell us that at some point along the writing road, we will be asked, if not forced, to let go of things we were originally in love with. This refers to specific ideas, sometimes big ones, that no longer fit into the evolved premise, compared to the original version of the idea. Some writers, though, are hesitant to do this. So they rationalize a way to insert their beloved pet idea—in the form of a scene or a piece of backstory or a situation—into the story that has already moved on from it. I've seen this happen frequently among new writers, who say this idea they're now being asked to toss was what brought them to the story in the first place. It's like an adult bidding their childhood blankie goodbye. But as a professional who is criteria driven, which means we base our story development on principles and criteria, we must not yield to that overprotective instinct. It can be the thing that makes or breaks the story when it comes time to send it out into the world.

As a principle, this will always keep you on track: Avoid the temptation to take side trips, to expand and expound on peripheral focuses—including overwrought backstory—and in general demand that every scene in your story move the exposition forward through the contribution of something new or expanded.

The pros make it look so easy.

The examples and sources of the core principles and criteria of fiction are so common, in fact, that they begin to define the essential forms and essences of successful storytelling itself. Again, though, we need to know what we are looking for, and looking at, before those core principles may be recognized as such. If you've ever watched a professional athlete, such as a pitcher or a golfer or a tennis player, even a poker player (not really an athlete, I'll grant you), you'll notice that the competitors at that level all pretty much appear to be doing the same thing in the same way. Which is to say, to the uninitiated layman, all pitchers look the same, all golf swings seem alike, and so forth. But a true student of the sport notices and cares about the nuanced variances, the subtleties and the biomechanical physics that differentiate them among their competitors. They notice the habits and sensibilities that a winner has developed over time and may even seek to imbue their own game with those same repeatable instincts.

Then along comes cybernetics, which breaks performance statistics into smaller, actionable chunks of information, along with the application of digital video analysis, which does the same for the physicality of the athlete's role. The criteria that drive the criteria-driven storytelling proposition are the literary version of all that. It won't appeal to everyone, but it will be the answer to the prayers of analytical, frustrated writers in all genres who are looking for more tools to work with.

As students of story, we should always strive to notice what causes a story to work and why. Which means we should not only be avid readers, we should be reading *analytically*. We should be on a flaming crusade to discover that treasure. Trouble is, it seems like presenters and bloggers these days are talking about *their process* without much focus on the core essences of story itself. They get a lot more clicks writing about how to beat the system on Amazon than how to write character backstories that aren't overplayed.

Unearth the truth beneath the obvious.

But just like an avid tennis player watching Serena Williams, you have to know what to look for to benefit from the observation. As writers, we need to hunt down and capture the inherent nature of emotionally resonant narrative effectiveness versus the episodic mediocrity that defines and explains rejection.

While the principles that result in great fiction may at times seem obvious, and while I concede that good work sometimes doesn't get noticed, I can assure you that writers who truly own the craft are in short supply, especially if process and marketing have been the focus of the author's apprenticeship. Among those 96 percent of stories that are rejected, even if written with perfectly good sentences (a huge percentage are), there are many who have made impossible, unreasonable, or even questionable choices and glaring omissions within their choice of story and the narrative strategies employed within it. In other words, they were always going to be rejected, criteria or not.

I'm assuming you want to be *great* at this work.

Not just to blend in, not just to sit in the workshop audience and take notes, but to truly become the next Gillian Flynn or John Green. If, as an alternative, you quietly admit you'd settle for simply getting into the game and have your book on the shelf at Barnes & Noble or ranked on a page on Amazon, you need to know that shooting for the middle may not get you there.

The odds are better when you aim for the higher bar, because agents and editors and avid readers are looking for the next home run, not the next base on balls. Being good in this business is the same thing as being average, because the vast majority of pretenders *are* good. Good books by good writers are rejected as a matter of course. You need to swing for the fences, beginning with the story premise itself, for which there are specific criteria, listed herein.

Bestsellers and break-in books aren't always better written, but they are often—very often—built around a better *idea*.

Discover your personal writing truth.

This morning, I was skimming a popular writing blog, one where until recently I was among eight contributing bloggers weighing in on the stuff working writers care about. Today's post was one of a series of "first-page critiques," which is just what it sounds like: A writer submits the first page of his work-in-progress, then one of those eight resident authors imparts honest feedback from the front of the room, which is almost always an exercise in *this-is-for-your-benefit* torture. (I'm not a big fan of first-page critiques because beyond a sense of voice and a more intuitive sense of the writer's chops, you really can't tell much about the story as a whole—nor should you—from reading the first page.)

Today's entry was particularly flog-worthy on the *sentences matter* front—the writer had seemingly skipped the entirety of high school English Comp 101—which meant the ensuing stream of commentary from other reader-writers would be a pile-on worthy of an episode of *American Horror Story*, with a dash of writerly empathy. One of those contributing reader-writer-critics said this:

> I agree with (today's critic). But you can't write a good book without a sloppy first draft. So keep going.

And there it was, the obligatory passive-aggressive writerly encouragement. One writer slapping the back of another through the passing forward of what she believes to be conventional wisdom. A voice from the crowd, without a résumé, utters what seems to be an irrefutable truth, repeating something she's heard that makes her sound knowledgeable, and the other folks in the crowd nod and move on, adding this to their bank of collective writing wisdom.

But in this case, and many others like it, it's just *not* true.

Or it may be only half true, half the time, which is almost worse. There are imposters clanking around, watering down the efficacy and value of that knowledge about the form and function of story, as well as the process of getting to one.

You absolutely *can* write a first draft that isn't sloppy (assuming the comment wasn't, in fact, *sloppy* in its own choice of adjectives). The fact that too many writers misspeak the truth—the list of misnomers is long—says less about expectations than it does about how high the bar is and how many folks out there aren't ready to compete at that level. You *should* write a first draft that isn't sloppy in a *"me-write-good"* sort of fumbling way. If you can't achieve that much, if you can't punctuate, if you don't understand tense and if you jam thoughts together with the organization of a high-school freshman's closet, if your dialogue sounds like it been lifted from an elementary school play, then you aren't ready to submit the work in a professional context.

In the same vein … if you can't yet catch a ball, maybe you shouldn't attend this year's local professional tryout. Opt for a year of playing catch first. Value the feedback you receive, and begin your journey toward a higher level of craft at both the line and the story levels.

I'm not saying that all conventional wisdom is wrong or misleading.

But too often the memes you may have pasted next to your screen are outdated or were never true in the first place. They may, at some point, have been the belief of someone who is famous enough to walk away from a debate. Sometimes these assertions are issues of process (where truth itself is a moving target), but too often they take confident swings at core issues of the storytelling craft itself. For example, I know of one semi-famous author who swears that writing cannot be taught, in the same breath that he invites you to attend his next writing workshop. Hopefully that workshop is on the topic of irony, if nothing else.

Here's an example from the very summit of the literary pantheon.

The bestselling keynote speaker (now deceased) at the first writing conference I ever attended spoke for half an hour about his "Ten Rules of Writing," one of the first of which was to never begin a novel with a prologue. Okay, noted. All the panting acolytes in the hotel conference room were madly taking notes, because this guy was *famous* with a capital F. Because of that, I believed this ban on prologues to be holy writ for the next few years, until I encountered a prologue in a novel by an author I loved, and who was even more famous than was the by-now dead guy I speak of here. It was explained and confirmed to me by yet another legitimately famous author that this particular *rule* wasn't true at all—which I had suspected—not even a little.

Dennis Lehane, Michael Cunningham, Nelson DeMille, and J.K. Rowling, among many other A-listers, regularly use prologues in their work. Prologues are all over the bookstore. It doesn't matter what the keynote speaker says and it doesn't matter what your high school writing teacher once told you. That's all you need to know on this issue. You hear this about semicolons, too, at least within fiction (from me included), but that doesn't make it universally true. It makes it *a suggestion for your consideration*. It is a preference voiced by someone behind a podium. Conventional wisdom, even for that famous dead writer, may be true some of the time for some stories, and it may have been true for that guy, but nothing is always and completely true all of the time for all writers.

Here is where a cynic might point out something once said by Pablo Picasso, the essence of which I buy into, at least to the extent that it can be adapted to become a core theme of this book, and maybe your career:

"Obey the rules like a professional, so you can break them like artist."

Hear, hear. Exactly. Change a few of these words and we have our truth:

"Honor the principles and criteria of story like a professional, so you can apply and bend them to your will like a story artist."

Notice the translation doesn't say or imply the *breaking of rules*, which in our case refers more to principles. Rather, this refers to the molding of them to suit what your evolved instinct believes to be the best choices in context to the given moment at hand. Knowledge plus instinct, filtered through criteria, is the most efficient path forward in this or any other professional endeavor.

In the next chapter, I'll direct your focus toward the final piece of the contextual puzzle, one that will clear a path to your introduction to the layers of available criteria that just might turn you into the novelist you always dreamed you could be and already know is eagerly waiting inside you.

6 The Power of Storytelling Context

··

Behold what separates the wheat from the chaff.

By now you may be itching to encounter the first set of part-specific story criteria, which reside in the realm of *premise*. That material awaits in the next chapter, while this one is the final primer for that immersion (consider this a swimming lesson before you are thrown into the deep end of the pool), and it seeks clarity regarding not only the need for criteria as a writing perspective but the immense upside available.

Let's be honest. While there is indeed an abundant and exciting upside in store, perhaps the most immediate benefit of approaching our work from a criteria-driven perspective—it's *context*, actually—is the avoidance of failure and suffering. The cessation of avoidable mistakes. Too many writers are committing to tepid story ideas and making bad story decisions not so much because of poor judgment, but because they don't know what they don't know.

This final tee-up will show you why some writers make those mistakes and others don't. It is because they may lack the proper context for what, and how, they write.

None of this is *theory*. This is straight out of the reality of the writing experience. I have been on the receiving end of thousands of story pitches in some form, the majority of them from new and otherwise frustrated authors. With some exceptions, I can sense almost immediately if the story has the right DNA, the raw grist, to have a shot at the bright lights. I am not remotely unique in that capacity; virtually every agent and editor, and to some degree every working professional author and discerning reader can do the same thing. Why? Because the *context* from which the writer is creating the story is, for better or worse, always evident in the pitch.

What are you writing in context to?

That question almost always triggers a need for clarification, and even a challenge regarding why this question even matters. Shrugs and blank stares take over the room. And yet, by definition, we are always writing in context to *something*. Trouble ensues when that something is the wrong context, which is all too prevalent within today's noisy writing conversation.

Every story begins and unfolds from within two unique yet concentric categories of context.

- **CONTEXT CATEGORY #1: WE ARE ALWAYS WRITING IN CONTEXT TO WHAT WE KNOW ABOUT THE CRAFT OF STORYTELLING,** even at an instinctual level … as well as what we *don't* know. Which is just as strong a context, but in a destructive way. (When a student pilot crashes the airplane, it will not be explained by what the pilot knew, but rather, by what he didn't.)

  It is obvious that a writer like, say, Nora Roberts (over 500 novels written, with more than 200 million copies sold) does her work from within a very different context than does a newer writer. Does this flavor of context matter to Nora Roberts and authors like her? Certainly. Moreover—and when conjoined with context #2 below—it *explains* them.

- **CONTEXT CATEGORY #2: WE SHOULD BE WRITING IN CONTEXT TO A VISION FOR THE STORY WE INTEND TO CREATE.** The whole story. Not just the idea you began with, but what happens along the narrative-expositional arc of the story. This differs from the previous category in that it is entirely possible—and entirely too common—to have an idea for a story that seems very clear and promising, when in fact that writer knows absolutely nothing about the form and function of professional-level fiction and the criteria that maps it out.

  It is when we end up writing *about* the shiny object within the story idea—very often the first spark of inspiration, such as a compelling setting or story world, powerful theme, strong character, or a moment that is actually just a scene without actually being a *story*—that we can become stuck in a trap of our own making.

Nora Roberts isn't a huge success solely because of what she knows about craft. Her success stems just as much from her ability to land story ideas that work, that glow in the dark. New writers struggle within both realms. But even writers who wield a keen sense of craft can have trouble coming up with stories that stand out from the crowd.

Not all songwriters are professional level singers. Just as not all singers are songwriters. As authors of fiction, we are both when it comes to the music of our storytelling.

To clarify, allow me to flip this on its dark side.

Let's say you want to write a story showing what it was like to grow up in the Great Depression. That's a viable idea and a rich story landscape. But is it a *story* yet? If you think it is and you write about it episodically, even eloquently, but without a *dramatic macro-arc*, then you have a context problem. Because, based on a criteria, it is *not* a story yet, even though the word "story" appears in that statement of intention.

Imagine Tom Clancy's *The Hunt for Red October* without the plot, without the Russians, and without Jack Ryan and a looming threat of World War III, just a shiny object—the thing that fascinates the author and what the author hopes will fascinate the reader—in the form of a submarine. In that case, without those elements, it really isn't a story at all, at least not yet, because it doesn't meet the criteria for a fully-populated story.

As stated here, it's the wrong context from which to write. Shiny objects—a facet of a story idea that is dripping with appeal and intrigue and fascination, like a submarine, often the centerpiece of an original story *idea*—can be a tempting misstep, precisely because a story has many levels of criteria to meet, only one of which calls for a shiny object of differentiation (see the forthcoming discussion of *concept* in chapter 10 to fully wrap your head around this nuance).

In *The Da Vinci Code*, Dan Brown was obsessed with religion and artifacts and puzzles and mythologies, shiny objects all … but are any of those the core unspooling dramatic *arc* of the story? They aren't. Rather, the core arc (plot) is a murder mystery wrapped in an amazing backstory, within which his obsessions become the fuel that differentiates the story from others.

Shiny objects—conceptual ideas that glow in the dark—are absolutely the stuff of bestsellers and break-in novels. But what gets less credit, yet is absolutely essential, is the criteria-defined narrative vehicle that delivers it into the heart and mind and consciousness of the reader, in the form of a conflict-driven, stakes-fortified, hero-dependent dramatic story. Also known as *the plot*.

That singular misplaced belief—that you can write about your *idea*, rather than a fully-vested premise leading to a plot that arises from it— is responsible for more derailed dreams than perhaps any other.

Let's come at this from yet another angle.

Let's say you are a newer writer, and you have an idea about a story about an oil drilling platform far out at sea. That's a killer setting, full of opportunity and intrigue. That's your category #2 context, it's your vision for the story, and thus, it's the context for what you will write. But in that form—it's just an oil platform at this point—it is an *insufficient* context. It is only the first step toward a viable story *vision*. It's just an *idea*. Be very clear, there is no story yet. If you sit down to write about that idea, you may end up with a bunch of stuff that happens on an oil platform, without ever really landing on a compelling dramatic macro-arc for a novel.

And yet, your obsession with oil drilling rigs remains. They are your shiny object. If you haven't written a novel before and you know very little other than what you've gleaned from your experience as a reader, you might be tempted to just write a tour of an offshore oil drilling rig and the way of life on board, peppered with anecdotes and episodic stuff that happens to someone you believe to be your hero because he's *there*. (Often in this situation, it is because the *author* was there.) If that happens, you are in contextual trouble. You are destined for tough feedback and a major rewrite. Because that's a category #1 contextual problem—you aren't meeting the criteria for a fully-formed story that works. A shiny object is almost never a viable premise, though perhaps

Great Stories Don't Write Themselves

it's the pretty wrapping paper for one. The story won't happen until *criteria* become the *context* for the revision of the story you began with.

If you don't know the criteria, then you are writing from a context of not knowing what you don't know. And in this case, you are pretty much screwed.

To be honest, this happens all the time among newer writers.

Historical novels fall victim to this frequently because the settings can be astoundingly rich, as do stories set in an alternative story world. Just going there seems like a fun vicarious ride. But just going there isn't enough. Some writers don't bring a full awareness of the context of a *novel* versus that of a memoir, and that becomes a problematic roadblock that must be dealt with.

An awareness of what kind of context, and the completeness of it, is driving your unfolding story (plot) informs your ability to recognize when an idea is strong, or even viable at all. Because, at a glance, it must become the framework for a dramatic arc (which is precisely the thing that outs some story pitches as deficient, even in the presence of a glowing shiny object at its heart). It informs your ability to move forward from that idea into the actual beginning of a story-development phase, beginning with the fleshing out of a premise—where ideas become fully-vested dramatic arcs—elicited from the seed of the original idea.

If your answer, when asked about your story, is, "Well, it's kind of complicated," and then you can't un-complicate it quickly and clearly, then you may indeed have a *context* problem. Your vision for the story may not be working as well as it needs to. Because your vision for the story is clouded, probably because of the delicious toxic fumes of the original idea and its shiny object that started the whole thing.

This is where what we *don't* know bites back.

Nobody at the writing conference will ever tell you that your story idea isn't marriage material. That it is, despite its shiny object, not yet a viable *story*, at a glance. For some this feedback seems too intrusive.

Nobody wants to rain on someone else's parade. It's like telling a contestant in a bake off that their cake tastes like day-old oatmeal. Or, they might be of the belief that *any* story idea can be made to work—too often an attempt to pound a square peg into a round hole—which is true *only* when the author strengthens an original weakness within an idea through a stronger premise based on that idea. One that meets the given *criteria* for premise. They nod and smile as you pitch it, and you'll glean from that what you want to hear. Which is, "sounds terrific! All systems go!" And then, off you go to begin typing.

It is a problem—as well as an explanation for failure—when authors begin to write the story before that level of wholeness has been achieved. This is not to say that using a draft to find the whole story isn't a viable method; it remains just that for many. But such an approach—pantsing—is best undertaken when the context of a whole story is in place, in the form of a full and complete premise, per the criteria you are about to learn—even if only deemed a placeholder for that discovery draft. A complete placeholder story vision provides the value of context for a whole story, while allowing your drafting process the latitude to shift gears and add nuance along the way. In fact, writing in context to a vision for the whole story empowers your pansting efforts to evolve into something even better, much more so that writing in context to nothing at all.

Context embraces a *process-versus-product* realization.

Almost always, when experienced writers and teachers talk about storytelling, they are talking about *process—their* process, how *they* do it—rather than about the general principles of *story* itself. From this is born the divide between story planners (plotters) who outline and those who prefer to just write from the seat of their pants and hope that something good happens (pantsers).

But it's all just *process*. None of it, not a word of it, dictates the precise nature and nuance of what is actually written—better stated, what *should* be written—and the criteria that are available to apply to it once that happens. The application of criteria certainly can be the determinant of the nature and direction of the real-time creative decisions that a writer faces during the draft, but they are just as potent and empowering when applied retroactively across the arc of a story upon completion of a draft, no matter how it was written.

Of course, you can always revise what doesn't work.

But first you must be able to discern, to recognize, that something isn't working. Or more germane to our goal, to recognize when something in the story has not yet been *optimized*, which is often the case when the writer sticks with a first idea that manifested during the creative frenzy of pantsing a draft.

When you are revising you are, once again, doing so *in context to something*. Your context is the draft under revision. Which means that the broken draft itself is the dominating *context*, rather than *criteria* that await to be applied. This can be a paradox when the lack of satisfied criteria is the reason you find yourself engaged with rewriting it. Criteria empowers us toward an understanding of the mission of the scene or moment itself—the context of the scene—which in turn allows us to consider options and alternatives that compete to become the best possible execution of that story moment rather than the organic one that showed up in the nick of time.

This, too, is when revision is called for ... *if* the writer recognizes the opportunity for a better story beat.

The goal, then, becomes the empowerment of your ability to recognize and choose.

Either in the planning phase, the drafting phase, or the revision phase. The criteria will serve you at all points along the way.

You are about to encounter a collection of lists of criteria for the various parts and essences of your novel, including aspects of your writing process. This will give you a means of evaluating your story in the same way that an Olympic diving or gymnastics or skating judge evaluates a performance. Were certain requisite moves on display? Was it symmetrical and graceful and powerful? Were corners cut? Was something left out? Were the compulsory elements nailed or given an obligatory nod? Was it moving and memorable? Was the degree of difficulty high enough to qualify the contestant for a medal?

In this analogous case, the writer is both competitor and judge. In a field of endeavor that seems to defy precision and analysis, these criteria-centric checklists will allow you to evaluate your story with more precision than a general "well, it sort of works, I think," to a level that is more analytical. And, of course, honesty—essential to being a successful judge—is heightened when there is something to compare against the evidence.

Maybe you actually can write from the seat of your pants ...

... but, then again, maybe you can't. Not yet, at least. Maybe your process—*that* process—is what's holding you back.

This is the issue that challenges the collective whole of the community of new and emerging authors. They believe they can approach the craft of storytelling just like established, instinctually qualified authors do it, because they heard that they can—and perhaps *should*—in a keynote address or a book by one of those famous names.

It's easy and even valid to say that established writers, by virtue of their proven experience, are more talented than most. But what is even more true is that such authors *know* more than most, and that knowledge manifests in the form of instincts that are applied to the work.

It's time to start talking about *what* causes a story to find its wings.

When I started writing about writing, I ran into a guy on an online forum who made the following statement: "I never outline. It robs the process of creativity and the possibility of discovery. It takes the fun out of it."

So says ... *that* guy. Who has never published a word. So not only are famous authors seducing us with their process preferences, unknown authors from all corners of the online writing world are boldly echoing opinions framed as indisputable truth.

And it just might be true ... *for* him. Or a particular famous author. That said, this is absolutely not—it never has been—a universal truth you should apply to your own experience ... at least until you *should*.

The things we don't know become the learning we need to seek out and discover—and vet—and then understand before we can begin to truly wrap our heads around fiction as a profession.

Because while process remains a choice and a debate, the principles of effective fiction and the criteria that frames them remain universal and beyond dispute. Be careful who you listen to, and be discerning about your recognition of what is true and what is a chosen context from which to write.

And thus a paradox has been hatched.

So, if not everyone agrees, how then do we pursue the core craft we need to write a novel that works, whatever our process, even if the folks we admire and look to for answers claim they don't?

Take the common advice to *just write*.

Or better put, *don't* take that advice. It's a convenient answer given to writers who ask The Big Question about how to write a novel. This answer is true for some people, some of the time. Half-truths are hard to dispel and clarify, and are easily accepted by the half that seeks to take what seems to them to be the easiest path.

Depending on the degree to which the writer commands the core principles, telling a new author to *just write* may be like telling a medical student to *just cut*. *Just write* is half of the answer, for half of the question, applying to half of the writers who hear it, sometimes long before they should even consider it.

Because *just write* is advice about process, not product. And process is always fueled by what you know, even when *just write* seems to be the solution when you know very little. A paradox, indeed.

This seems to be how the writing conversation—blogs, books, how-to articles, workshops, conferences, keynote addresses, famous writer profiles, writing groups, critique groups, and writing forums—is framed. And yet, collectively, combined with practice and a seat-of-the-pants ability to assimilate skill and truth as it collides with what we would rather deem to be mystical and elusive, there are things that actually *do* define the journey of learning to write a professional-caliber novel.

Knowing where you stand relative to these core truths—the criteria—can save you years of exploration and untold buckets of blood seeping from your forehead. The writing conversation is a loud and largely imprecise place, drowning out what it is you may truly need to hear and understand. At some point—once you have the criteria firmly embedded in your instincts, rather than at the starting line of your journey—*just write* may become a viable option to take your story forward. Until then, without criteria being your context, it is like jumping off a building without a parachute, a choice that always begets major medical attention, or a body bag, when it happens.

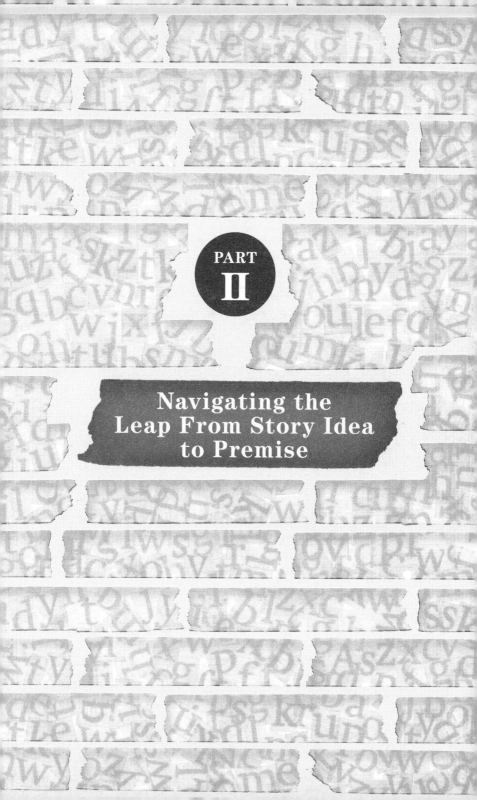

PART
II

Navigating the
Leap From Story Idea
to Premise

7

The Eight Criteria for Premise

....

Let the storytelling begin.

The definition of *premise* among aspiring and professional writers isn't exactly controversial, but it is less than precise. Especially if you consider the breadth of its context as it is applied within the writing conversation. Even professionals—agents, editors, gurus, and published authors—tend to use the terms *premise, concept, idea,* and *theme* interchangeably, when in fact each refers to a unique facet of story. This is like a surgeon using the words flesh, muscle, and skin interchangeably, when in fact each refers to unique and specific parts of the body.

Actually, *premise* has two different yet valid contextual uses. One tells the whole story in one breath. The other cherry-picks a lead aspect of the story—a hook, if you will—and delivers it like an appetizer. Those other seemingly analogous words—*concept, idea,* or *theme*—may be the flavor of the appetizer and thus the primary element of this teaser form of premise, but none of them are actually a full and functional premise, per se.

In the context of pitching a story and within conversation, that short log-line form of premise is perfectly and functionally appropriate. But for the writer seeking to land on a final form of a fully vested premise to assist with and evaluate the state of his story development, he absolutely needs the longer version, which is a full and functional story premise. The earlier he solidifies and commits to it in that form, the better off the drafting process will be.

The quick-pitch slug-line will always be the most common form of use. But if an agent hears your appetizer version and then says, "Very interesting, tell me more!"... *then* they are asking for the entire premise (not to be confused with the full manuscript), which expands on whatever singular slice of premise you delivered within the pitch.

Here's an example. For Robert Dugoni's bestselling mystery, *My Sister's Grave*, the quick appetizer premise could be this: The story of a woman's loss and a man who may have been falsely imprisoned for her sister's murder.

That works because it pushes buttons even before you hear the rest. It's very likely that an agent hearing this pitch would ask for more.

Here's the full premise. It touches all of the criteria bases for a complete premise and is told in Dugoni's own words via a clip on Amazon's "My Book in 15 Seconds" feature, which appears at the bottom of the novel's listing page. This is how the author describes the premise:

> To find out who killed her sister, Sarah, twenty years earlier, Seattle homicide detective Tracy Crosswhite must get a new trial for a convicted murderer, but she might just be opening the door to darker secrets, and even greater danger.

He delivered that in just over eleven seconds. Notice how he didn't begin with, "Well, it's sort of complicated ..." as many less-confident authors do. Notice how we meet a protagonist, how she is immediately positioned as a hero in the story, and how antagonism and dramatic tension are implied because, also implied, this hero is going up against higher powers. Both sides have a dog in the fight, which means there are stakes that drive them. You also see the inevitability of an escalating exposition full of twists and surprises. Notice, too, how the form and function of this premise pitch are different and more comprehensive than the appetizer slug-line version offered above. Both have a place in the process, but only the longer version is of service to the author at the story development and drafting stages.

You might argue that since the book is finished and in the market, of course the author knows the story well enough to pitch it that thoroughly. We don't know how much of this Dugoni had solidified in his mind in the early stages of visualizing and writing the story, but you can bet the skeletal essence of it all was the context from which the story sprouted and grew over the course of planning and drafting and polishing. This was the vision for his story, providing strong context for its development (per our look at *context* in the previous chapter). That's what authors at that level do. They apply instinct to begin drafting with a fleshed-out version of the story guiding them (context), perhaps still clinging to their nametag as a pantser all the while. The draft becomes a value-adding process rather than the blind search process it is for so many.

Now imagine what your first draft might look if you knew this much about *your* story. You absolutely can when you focus on a complete premise as the transitional tool that takes you from story idea (which is really the appetizer slug-line version) to actually writing a draft. It is when authors draft from *the idea only*, without a meat-on-the-bones, criteria-nailing premise, that the process becomes complicated and results in what a majority of writers believe to be the inevitability of a first draft that, for lack of a better word, sucks.

You can skip over the *it sucks* phase and begin writing a draft that executes the full version of your vision for the story by using the criteria for premise as context for what you are about to narrate with your prose.

There are eight specific facets that comprise a complete premise.

All of them are available to authors to contemplate prior to writing a draft and provide context for that draft, whatever your process. That said, some writers prefer to use the drafting process to land on each of these eight criteria. But make no mistake, the premise isn't complete and functional until those eight points have been defined, no matter how you go about doing so.

There are more pivot points to a complete story, but the story isn't functional until *these* eight elements are in place. In this form, the premise is not quite a synopsis, but you're getting to one. A complete premise is the integration of character and dramatic tension within the proposition of a story arc, which is what the eight points of premise seek to achieve.

Right here is where the debate shows up in the form of old habits and belief systems that may not be true at all, at least for you. The cynic asks, "Hold on, how can you land on a specific story point if you aren't writing the story yet? If you don't know what happens to get you to that point?" It's a fair question, but it's actually quite obvious. Whether planning or drafting, every single idea comes from your own thinking. Not writing, thinking. You have to think of it before you can write it. And you don't need to write blindly into a corner before you stop and ask yourself, *Okay, I'm in this corner now, how can I get myself out of it?* All of that happens in your creative imagination at the planning stage, no differently than it does within the drafting stage. Using this, you can actually "write" the novel in your mind (a few notes will help) to completion before you even begin a first draft.

You do that by applying criteria to the process.

Beginning a draft without having a solid premise in mind is like going to college without any notion of what you want to do with your degree, which is a factor in what you eventually must declare as a major. Sure it's fun, you party and hang with new friends. But really, is that why you're there?

Writers face the same decision ... eventually they have to declare a premise. When it's in place on the first day of class, all of your choices going forward become more germane, less random (like that basket weaving class) and more likely to get you a job when you're done. You won't have to add an extra year of classes before you qualify for the career you've decided on somewhere down the line, when it was too late to make those first two years of school actually matter.

Some never do make that declaration. And too often, they find themselves less than happy and fulfilled with their default career—taking whatever was available at the time—as compared to the professionals who were working toward a destination all along.

The complete premise brackets the *entire* story. All eight of the major criteria for an effective premise are culled from a character quest and the source and nature of dramatic tension along that path, leading to resolution. This is true in literary fiction, as well, because those protagonists also require a quest, often through an internal darkness, that resonates with stakes and emotional empathy. It becomes invaluable context for everything that comes next.

There's that word again, *context*. The deeper you go into craft, the more value you'll attach to context as an essential story development tool.

Welcome to day one of spring training, where the first thing on the agenda is to see what kind of shape your story is in before you get to put on a uniform.

Lest you think this is all there is to it, that you need only to come up with those eight parts of premise and you'll be good to go, know this: Each of these eight criteria for premise are categorical headers for lists of related standards and expectations that are subordinated to the category in question. Among the collective whole of those lists there are literally dozens of things the writer needs to ultimately consider and know and implement, and each of them are qualitative in nature.

It is in plumbing the depths of this substrata of criteria where writers might discover the true potential and heart of their stories—as well as in assessing the degree to which your story idea makes those reader outcomes available to you. It can lead you to a moment of epiphany upon realizing that these are things you have been taking for granted all along.

INTRODUCING THE EIGHT CRITERIA FOR PREMISE

This is what you need to *know* about your story, with specificity about how it unfolds within the narrative, before your premise can be considered complete. If you begin writing a draft before the premise is complete, then you should understand that the objective of that draft is to discover and flesh out a complete premise, stated in these terms.

The story idea itself, the one to which what you started with might have been attached or was tangential to, could be any one of these eight criteria. This is often the case, but the criteria-driven author understands that this singular idea, even though it resides on this list, isn't remotely enough to fuel the whole story.

Either way, this is what you need to nail down before the story will work:

Great Stories Don't Write Themselves

- **PREMISE CRITERIA #1: WE MEET THE PROTAGONIST (HERO),** whom we will root for on a specific quest after being introduced to the reader within a forthcoming story framework. While the protagonist may be embroiled in a problem when we meet her, that problem isn't the core story proposition that will become the narrative spine of the novel's exposition. Something new and bigger awaits down the narrative road, after we've come to know and care about this character to a degree that will allow us to *care* about what is about to happen to her.

- **PREMISE CRITERIA #2: SOMETHING HAPPENS THAT CHANGES EVERYTHING.** After a group of scenes that share the mission of setting up the story, this critical moment launches the core dramatic arc of the story—it could be argued that this is the most important moment in the novel—giving your hero a problem to solve along a path of response. It's called The First Plot Point, as well as other nomenclature within the writing conversation. But whatever you call it, it is a non-negotiable story beat that is best placed with specificity within an awareness of structure (see chapter 17).

- **PREMISE CRITERIA #3: THE HERO IS COMPELLED TO REACT** to and engage with that problem or need—often running toward safety, or at least seeking more information—thus fully launching the hero's story journey, going deeper into its darkness.

- **PREMISE CRITERIA #4: THERE ARE STAKES IN PLAY,** put in place in the prior set-up scenes, which pose an urgent win-or-lose pressure and threat.

- **PREMISE CRITERIA #5: SOMETHING OPPOSES THE HERO ON THIS QUEST** (a villain or force), creating conflict and dramatic tension. This, too, was likely glimpsed in the opening scenes, but now functions as who or what threatens the hero in this new responding context. This is the source of drama and conflict within the story, which are both essential criteria for efficacy.

- **PREMISE CRITERIA #6: THE STORY ESCALATES AND TWISTS,** as do the stakes and the level of intensity, frustration, need, threat, and urgency on both sides. (This simple bullet embraces the entire complexity of the story's ultimate structure.)

- **PREMISE CRITERIA #7: THE HERO'S STATE OF PLAY ELEVATES** as contextually defined by structural flow (discussed here in the Part 3 chapters), leading to a final confrontation that pays off everything the reader has been asked to consider and root for thus far.

- **PREMISE CRITERIA #8: THE STORY IS RESOLVED**, primarily at the hero's hands, moving the character back into her life, perhaps in an altered form, or not, which could involve dealing with the consequences of the story just told, because things may be different now.

If you are writing a series, take note: All of these criteria apply to *each book in your series.* You need to have engineered a macro-arc for the series strategy, which leverages the ending of each book as a means to propel the reader forward to the next novel.

This list is introductory in scope. There is still much to understand within each of these eight points, but before we take that deeper dive, we can benefit from exploring the relationship between premise and the core story idea from which it springs.

These eight points of premise are not yet the specific structure of the story, though they are the elements that will become critical to the turning points within that structure. We will examine story structure in more depth in Part 3 of this book, after a closer look at the story idea itself in the next chapter.

At the premise level, we have only eight specific things to create within our vision for the story. But it is almost inevitable that deeper thinking into what transpired from these things will be part of the thought or writing process. Even if they are placeholders, easily swapped out for better dramatic renderings discovered during the process of drafting, this creates an empowered context for all that follows. These are targets, and all of them are essential to the story *working.* These are what pull the reader deeper into the story while giving you something to write about, rather than something to randomly explore without a clear connection to where the story is going. Like climbers taking a first look at the mountain before them, this model allows us to grasp the extent to which premise influences everything about the story-development process.

An absence or weakness of any single element on this list renders the story weaker for it, maybe even dysfunctional. Because if you didn't recognize these eight story facets as essential at the point of origin, you may not even notice their absence and the risk that creates. It's like those climbers forgot to pack water. By the time they collapse on the trail, they may never understand what took them down.

These elements are always available to you.

You can turn to these elements before—actually, you need to have considered them before you move forward—during, or after an actual draft has been written. Which means this is not only a story planning and vision tool, but a set of power tools for revision, as well.

The same is true of the subordinated criteria under each of the eight categorical headers. Some of them, by definition, will only emerge once you get to the drafting stage, while others quickly become integral to the initial stage of story development. Enlightened pantsers almost always have a strong vision for the story in mind. If they don't, that's the contextual abyss discussed in the last chapter, much like Dugoni's fifteen-second pitch, and use organic writing during the draft to discover opportunities to fill in the blanks and engineer transitions (what I like to think of as connective narrative tissue between story points).

You can't set up that which you do not yet know will be important to the story, so you have to find those elements and either plan for them or incorporate them into drafting at some point. In either case, the efficacy of applying these criteria as standards is exactly the same regardless of where you fall within the planning-pantsing continuum.

Story development, however you do it, is a criteria-dependent exercise.

Too many authors begin writing an *incomplete* story—often unwittingly, because they don't know what constitutes wholeness, while at the same time rationalizing that this is normal, this is how it's done. Too many of those writers end up not actually finishing the draft, at least to the point of intended and necessary efficacy. Without the long game of the story being even somewhat clear, writers are tempted to settle for a first-choice option for a scene or a story point. Or, they move organically from scene to scene in a way that made total sense at the time, yet later seems indefensible (explained by some form of, "Well, it seemed like a good idea at the time ..."), some of which could be improved upon, some of which you might be stuck with unless you're willing to rewrite the whole thing.

That difference—optimal versus settling for the first or most obvious solution—is the stuff bestsellers are made of.

Or just as true, it is the nuance—the secret sauce—that can get you published.

Welcome to the storytelling party for aspiring professionals. This is where it gets real.

It all begins with an *idea* for a story, one that leads to rich and fertile ground from which a compelling story premise can emerge. But that said, there is more opportunity at the idea stage than you might realize at first glance.

Great Stories Don't Write Themselves

8 The Mission of Your Story Idea

This moment may strike you as backward. We're about to move into a discussion about your story *idea*, when the prior chapter was about a *premise* that is culled *from* that idea. Don't jump to a conclusion too quickly, though, because there is method in this seeming madness. Because it is your understanding of the criteria for premise that becomes massively informing context for searching for and committing to the story idea that will fuel it.

Sometimes writers begin with a story idea that is totally flat. If they don't understand what the idea must *become*—the criteria-meeting premise—they may never sense and acknowledge that flatness. They write a novel from it anyway. Unless the drafting of that novel turns up more dramatic and emotionally resonant opportunities, the story remains at risk because it too may end up reading as flat.

Rare is the story idea that meets all of the criteria for premise. In fact, usually the idea in its original form usually hits only one of them, sometimes none at all. This is why the evolution of the idea toward a fully-informed premise is so important to understand.

For example, if your idea is to write *a romance novel set in 1940s New York during the war years*, you can easily make the leap to a hero with a problem, something she must achieve, something blocking her path, and a big pile of emotional resonance to be mined within that framework. But it's not there yet within the idea itself, as stated, even if it is implied. You can easily make the leap (a massively dramatic leap, in this example) to adding a layer to the idea that shows your heroine falling for someone while her husband is away at war, after discovering evidence that he had been cheating on her. When you add that layer to your idea, you are actually engaging in the development of a premise, one that owes its DNA to the nature of the idea in the first place.

But if your story idea is *a love story set in 1979 Topeka, Kansas*, because that's when your parents met, it is less clear how this will grow into something infused with the criteria-summoned compelling specifics that will become a novel that works. It's possible, yes, but the story emerges quicker and better when the author has more in mind than just this idea before they actually write a draft.

If being published and finding readers is your goal, then your idea must be on fire with dramatic and emotional *potential*. If you are writing a purely literary story, then you should proceed without sweating these criteria all that much, simply reaching for the pearls as they surface along the way. But if your story is a romance, even a love story that doesn't qualify as a romance, or a mystery, thriller, or fantasy, or if there are paranormal elements involved, if you want it to be more than biographical and episodic, then the connection between idea and premise becomes your guiding context going forward.

This idea-premise dependence is a game changer.

Part of my work is to evaluate and coach submitted story plans and manuscripts, as well as story pitches and writing samples at conferences and workshops. By definition this includes story ideas and premises, as well as scenes and finished drafts. This is why I have developed and honed lists of criteria that are specific to all of these phases of the process. I have seen firsthand the carnage that results when these criteria have not been considered.

I didn't invent any of this or make it up to suit my process and preferences (which is exactly what some writers do, they make up their own rules and principles as they go). Rather, these are universal principles, well proven and widely practiced among the best authors on the planet, even though they may speak of them using other terminology, if they speak of them at all. All I've done is cull them out, dust them off, and develop an explanation and a context to be applied, positioning them as tools instead of just theories.

After working one-on-one with close to a thousand writers over the course of three decades—considering the same story ideas pitched to agents and editors, and to online buyers via a slug-line on the digital bookstore page ... after fielding opinions on this topic from colleagues who also hear pitches for a living, some of them as agents and editors ... after considering the number of submitted stories that are accepted for representation (less than 20 percent) or the much smaller fraction accepted for publication (less than 5 percent) ... and after considering the sheer volume of self-published titles (nearly a million books annually and growing) against average sales of less than one hundred copies per year per book (a consensus of several online sources) following an investment of over $1,000 per title for editing and design (an average that includes a relative handful of mega-selling self-published authors; here's a reality check: The odds of succeeding as a self-published author are slimmer than finding a traditional publisher and hitting pay dirt there) ...

... after juxtaposing all these opinions and percentages and sources against the dreams of millions of writers who are willing to put in the time and effort to defy them ...

... I have come to a sobering conclusion. It may discourage some, but hopefully will summon you, the criteria-driven author, to a higher level of aspiration. It is this:

You need *a better story idea.*

Just as true, you need to know when an idea becomes viable and ready to pitch, which is synonymous—it *should* be synonymous—with ready to write. Because at the back end of this discussion is this dreary truth: Too many writers don't get there. And yet they begin writing anyway. And that's the problem. Any idea pitched before it meets certain criteria is, by definition, a thin or weak idea. This is not a good thing in either context where the idea matters: as the heart of a pitch in the form of an appetizer, or the seed for a story you are about to develop.

The latter can be saved—that's precisely what *development* means. But at the pitch level, the idea may or may not be the thing that gets the listener's attention. Too many times it becomes the very thing that gets you rejected, even before you've written a word of it.

This truth should get your attention.

It means, at the professional level to which you aspire, you really cannot, with great confidence, sit down and write just any old thing that appeals to you. You need to consider what will appeal to prospective readers, who are already buying and reading books that have factored reader appeal into the decision to commit to an idea.

It should make you salivate to learn the criteria that can be applied at the idea level to make sure you are submitting pitches and ideas that are competitive at a professional level, and launching stories that lean in to the criteria for a viable premise.

A secret weapon mitigates this risk.

The people issuing those rejections won't tell you that it was because of the *idea*, by the way. They'll say some variation of a dreaded shallow cliché: "It's just not what we're looking for at this time."

This happens for roughly nine out of every ten submissions.

You thought this was all about the *writing*. Your sentences. Your character arcs. Your very serious thematic intentions and literary gifts. Which may be largely true if you are writing in the literary fiction genre, though many of those nine out of ten are not. In the genre-fiction game, it's about the *idea* at the center of your pitch.

The idea excites *you* ... what can go wrong?

Ideas reside at the core of what you pitch to agents and editors and readers. Before anyone will agree to read your pages, they will have heard your pitch (prospective readers get it on the back of a book cover or on the online listing page) and, because they hear or read something that appeals, they've agreed to consider more of the story.

Besides simply being unskilled at the art of pitching (something for which you can find vast resources online), the more common problem is that writers are *pitching the wrong thing*, at the wrong point in the story-development cycle. Which means when it comes time to write the story, they may literally be writing a story that is burdened with mediocrity out of the starting gate.

All story ideas arrive in our heads as a finite slice of something bigger. Maybe it's a sudden intention to work in a given genre, or mashup of genres. An idea for a setting (such as Vietnam, Paris, or the moon), a timeframe (any historical novel), a meaty social issue to break down (such as *The Help* or *The Cider House Rules*), or a character that will give Holden Caulfield a run for his money (which is a high degree of difficulty to aspire to) … all of it can seduce the writer to an extent that she believes an agent or editor will jump at this much only.

And he just might, because anything can and does happen out there. But in genre fiction the agent or editor is usually looking for something more precise. Something that hooks. Something fresh while tapping into known lanes. Something that poses a question so intriguing—often in the form of a "what if?" proposition—so dripping with dramatic and emotional potential that they can't wait to hear more. Agents know that story ideas are a dime a dozen, while writers capable of executing across the array of part-specific story criteria are rare. Within a pitch agents are looking for a sense of that, as much as they are evaluating the potential of the story.

Here are some sample story ideas that, while perhaps are compelling at a glance, actually are not enough to hook a weary agent hearing your pitch in the elevator after ten hours on the floor at the writing conference hotel. You may see a story in each of them, but chances are the agent will feel like she's heard this pitch before.

- Street life in Detroit in the 1950s.
- A story set on a space station as aliens attack Earth.
- A story about a gold medal–winning soccer team.
- An alternative history story about what the world would be like had John F. Kennedy not been assassinated.
- A love story about forbidden attraction and parental judgment.
- A YA story about a foreign exchange student at an elite private school who claims to be the reincarnation of Adolf Hitler.
- A speculative novel about what would happen if we received news that a massive celestial body is headed toward our sun, with a col-

lision and certain apocalyptic consequences calculated to be two weeks away.

- A spy thriller about war in the Middle East.
- A historical novel about love among hippies in 1968 San Francisco.

These are valid frameworks for a story. But they do not stand alone as the promise of a story that the agent would largely have to accept on faith. They are not strong enough … yet. The best outcome with any of these, pitched with this level of brevity, would be a request for more information—right there in the face to face you are having—an expansion of the pitch just offered, including the eight points of criteria for a robust premise, which you experienced in the previous chapter.

The problem is this: Too often the writer does not have a bold response when asked for *more*. They aren't in command of those eight criteria for premise, some of which might be just the thing the agent is listening for.

These story ideas are primarily generic propositions. They are single-element promises. There may or may not be a story within them; the pitch doesn't really say either way.

There is no hero yet, no plot. Thus, no dramatic tension. Maybe the idea, on its own, is inherently compelling, maybe not. But in each case, it could be rendered *more* compelling. And, in terms of the premise that becomes the next step in the development of these ideas, there are up to seven other story elements that aren't visible or even implied within these ideas.

There is more work to be done here. It all depends on not only the writer's ability to complete that work, but their level of awareness of *what* must be done, and why.

THE CRITERIA FOR A SOLID STORY IDEA

The idea proposition is framed with significant context. All of it oozing with ways to cull a solution from its assorted parts and implications. To seize this opportunity, we need to learn to recognize what about our pitches and ideas is deficient or hits a wrong note and how this initial idea-refinement effort adds value to the entire story-development process that follows.

The unspoken truth is this: Agents, editors, and readers really *don't* want to hear your story *idea*. Rather, they want to hear the best, strongest part of the *premise* that the idea inspires. Also, this isn't about the pitch so much as it is about the author's readiness to actually write the novel at a level that competes in a commercial marketplace.

The universe sent you the idea in ways that defy explanation. But the rest of what is required is yours to conjure, evaluate, and place in context to the larger proposition of a story. The best pitches and ideas are retrospective, they consider the whole story—even if you haven't written it yet—and harvest from it the aspects that would merit mention in a headline. Because that particular aspect is glow-in-the-dark compelling.

A quick example: Imagine if you were pitching a story featuring Superman as your hero. In fact, that's your story idea: *I'm going to write the next great Superman story.* The end. Your pitch probably wouldn't even need to get into the plot of your story, because the plot isn't the thing that stops traffic. Rather, "This is a story about an alien child discovered amidst the carnage of an alien spaceship crashing on earth. The child, who is secretly taken by a couple living on a farm in Kansas and raised according to the highest human values, begins to exhibit superhuman strength and feats of heroism. He grows up to be a hero who will save the world from evil in all forms."

Now *that* is a pitch (it happens to be the pitch for the original Superman mythology; yours would need to bring something fresh and exciting to that baseline). But it is only the backstory of a novel or film or graphic novel written from it. The form of the pitch (idea) is the author's call, and in this case, this might be the most compelling framing of the idea itself, because it glows in the dark. (Of course this is an example of the raw grist of a pitch that works; make sure you aren't pitching something that has already been done.) *Many* actual plots might emerge from this single idea. (If you don't agree, you are in a minority;

this core story idea has proven to be one of the most beloved and enduring of characters in all of fiction.)

Part of the art of committing to and pitching an idea—which are largely the same thing when done right—is isolating the most compelling facet of the story it might become. That realization, in turn, fuels the writing of the whole story with context, one that shows us where the real opportunity resides. A good agent can shred you with unanswerable questions, all of them reasonable, if the idea is too weak or too thin.

Ask yourself if your story idea glows in the dark, or if it depends on an emerging story to reach that level, if it ever does. From there you can apply criteria to the idea to shape it into something that begins to promise more than what it is on the surface.

The highest purpose of your story idea is to evolve into a premise.

That pitch for Superman falls short of a criteria-meeting premise that can be used as tool for creating the story itself. But it has enough to create a vision for what could be. A premise has eight parts; that pitch is only a fragment of two of them.

So if the idea doesn't need to clearly state all eight of the criteria for premise, then how many of them need to be at the heart of an idea that works? Good question. The first phase of idea development should strive to meet four high-level, idea-specific criteria, which includes *four* wider, categorical facets of the story you'll eventually need to cull from the seed of that idea. For now, you are building the foundations of the story that will support the weight of the full story further down the development line.

In other words, you step up *from* the idea into the realm of *premise*, one step at a time. Four steps for the idea, followed by eight steps for the premise, four of which came from the idea itself. This is followed by dozens of ensuing steps that move you from premise into the realm of writing a draft.

THESE STEPS BECOME CRITERIA FOR YOUR STORY IDEA.

And they also suggest what needs to be clear within any pitch of that idea. The bar your idea must reach is high, as defined within these four criteria. Ideally, one or more of these, applied to your story, should glow in the dark to become the primary hook of the story proposition. Superman flies around in a cape, and *that* has been hooky enough to capture the imagination of generations of readers and moviegoers.

- **IDEA CRITERIA #1:** A notion of dramatic intention (plot) that gives the hero something to engage with (a need, a purpose, against opposition) in the story.
- **IDEA CRITERIA #2:** A vision for the nature and worldview of the protagonist, something that is unique and will be worthy of reader trust, that becomes someone the reader will root for in the story.
- **IDEA CRITERIA #3:** A sense of thematic and emotional relevance to the reader. This is what connects the story, whatever the genre, to real life.
- **IDEA CRITERIA #4:** A high-altitude sense of how the story will structurally unfold—what the hero will be called to do or accomplish in the story—including major twists that point it toward a satisfying ending.

In addition to filling the blank space when someone asks you for more about your story, they are also your entry points to complete a more robust fleshing out of the idea toward the realm of premise, which has those eight specific criteria to check off, all of which relate to these four pitch-level criteria.

This is your story, one step at a time, beginning with a first step that glows in the dark.

Notice what this *doesn't* say.

It doesn't say that writers who understand those criteria shouldn't stick with what seems like a thin idea as they begin the process of story development. Rather, you should recognize that weakness and use the story-development process itself, infused with criteria, to strengthen it. You just might come across the saving grace layer that isn't yet clear. Move forward, whatever that means to you. Do further story planning and vision work. Or start a draft, with the understanding that this is still just a means of finding your whole premise and the whole story that rises from it. Just don't pitch it yet, or commit to it as *the* story. Because if it doesn't scream compelling answers to those four idea-specific criteria, it's not ready.

If your story is *literary* by nature—something John Irving or Donna Tartt or Jonathan Franzen might write—make sure the agent understands this (indeed, make sure that *you* understand this, and that this is your intention) and listens for the right notes within your pitch. Because the notes are subtly different in this particular genre. Character trumps plot in literary fiction, though plot remains the essence of structure and narrative arc. And structure, the key to genre fiction, has softer edges in the literary genre, with conflict often stemming from the characters' internal issues rather than external sources of villainy.

Here's your job in navigating these steps.

Within the process of fielding and vetting story ideas, the writer should seek to understand the following:

- Understand the difference between an intention or a slice of a story and a criteria-meeting dramatic, conflict-driven, stakes-dependent story idea.
- Be able to articulate the difference between an idea, a concept, and a premise. All three are required, because all three bear upon the story in unique ways.
- Understand the mission and role of a story idea within the story-development process, beginning with premise. Understand pitch versus plan.
- Know and apply the criteria for a promising, fertile story idea.

- Consider how well, how richly, your idea leans into the eight criteria for premise, which you have in your head or at your fingertips. They won't all be there at first, but they all need to be in play when you are writing a serious draft. For a keenly astute criteria-driven author, this might just be the first draft.
- Avoid the traps that can take you down from that intention.
- Study and practice the unique skill of pitching your story ideas.
- Be on top of what must be done to an idea once it lands.
- And finally … read chapter 10, The Criteria for Concept. That secret weapon awaits you there.

This is where the criteria become your best friend. Because they might save you a year in the life of your writing apprenticeship, chasing an idea that was never there in the first place.

With that in mind, let's turn to the joyous work of turning our glow-in-the-dark ideas into premises that soar.

The Idea-Fueled Premise

We've had a look at premise. We've been challenged to find and commit to stronger story ideas. Now it's time to connect those two realms and discover how, when regarded together, the whole suddenly renders in excess of the sum of both.

You've been introduced to the eight requisite elements of premise. But now, with a high bar for the story idea fixed in your head, there is value in revisiting those eight criteria for premise in an expanded way, because now we can more clearly make the connection between the idea that birthed it to the premise that will live and breathe on the page.

Bear in mind that more is involved once you get to the manuscript stage—such as specific structural manipulations and narrative milestones, as well as scene-building criteria and how to optimize both character and dramatic arcs. Collectively, these are the weight-bearing foundations on which the story will stand or fold.

Which is to say, your story—after you've arrived at the four criteria for the story idea, because *that* becomes the raw grist for this premise stage—should have these eight facets strongly in play:

1. **A HERO TO ROOT FOR** … if not upon introduction, then later, after the hero has been given a problem to solve, giving the reader something specific to root for. Introducing your protagonist in a way that launches a character arc and sows the seeds of reader empathy are the primary mission, among several other jobs, of the scenes that appear within the set-up block of the story. Here is where you establish your hero within a *story world,* with a hint of foreshadowing and a sense of emerging stakes and approaching antagonism. The highest goal of this introductory block of scenes is to give the reader someone, and something, to root for once the sky begins to fall.

    A critical differentiation here: *rooting* is different from simply *observing.* Many new authors compromise their story at the starting gate because their proposition is to "*observe* my protagonist on *a series of adventures.*" Versus a *dramatic* objective—a plot—wherein the hero has *something specific to do* and accomplish (which may include evasion and survival) under the pressure of antagonism (usually a bad guy), with something significant at stake. For example, a thriller in which the hero must find and disarm a bomb before it takes out an entire city. Or, lovers who must find each other before one of them makes a decision that cannot be reversed.

2. **A STORY-CHANGING MILESTONE MOMENT** that launches the core dramatic arc. This is called the First Plot Point (FFP), though it's also identified using different terminology, depending on which writing guru you are referencing; James Scott Bell coined a term that applies here: "a doorway of no return." This story moment is the transition between the novel's set-up scenes and the launch of the hero's story quest, which commences with #3 below. (If you like movie trailers, you can spot the FPP in almost every trailer that you can find, because it's *that* important to the story being told.)

    This is arguably the most important moment in the story, because it puts the core dramatic unspooling thread (following a setup for this launch) into play. This is also the most difficult story point to get right if you are still searching for your *core dramatic story* as you draft (pantsing), because right here is when you need to *know* what that core story is and how it takes center stage in the story. If you plan only one thing ahead of time, it should be this moment: when the core dramatic story moves front and center as the focus of your hero, and your reader.

3. **FROM THAT POINT FORWARD, THE HERO BEGINS TO MOVE DOWN A NEW PATH IN RESPONSE TO THE CALLING OF THE FPP.** Soon he begins to struggle for something, which the reader has been moved to root for. Your protagonist now has a goal to reach, a battle to win, or something that must be done, and thus begins a quest that wasn't fully in play before the FPP that just changed every-

thing. There is now a problem to solve. Someone to save. A threat to elude. The FPP has kicked the core dramatic arc of the story into motion, and this launches a series of scenes that show the hero getting deeper into darkness, long before success comes within reach or reason, all while under pressure or threat from a source that may be known or unknown or something in between. Confusion and chaos reign while the stakes escalate.

4. **STAKES GIVE US A REASON TO ROOT FOR THE HERO AND EMPATHIZE.** This is what the hero is playing for: the consequences of success or failure. They may not have been clear at the FPP moment, but they clarify and the hero's quest moves forward. Those stakes have been foreshadowed or set up prior to the FPP, but now that the hero is in motion, with a goal driving her decisions and actions. Those stakes become clearer, they escalate, and they may even change at some point. Often the hero is running in the dark here, metaphorically speaking, or at least in the shadows of what can be only partially seen and understood. Stakes that at first seem to be simple survival may grow into something infinitely more complex.

5. **SOMETHING BLOCKS THE HERO'S PATH (USUALLY A VILLAIN).** This is the main source of conflict and dramatic tension in the story. This leads to evasion, realization, and confrontation, all of it escalating as the story picks up pace moving forward. The reader may or may not understand the source of the hero's obstacle early on, but they soon will.

   The villain (or antagonistic force) is usually at least partially visible after the FPP, or earlier in the set-up chapters in some partial or implied form, or perhaps veiled behind a false identity ... or even right there in front of everyone. But if the agenda of the villain remains vague, it will emerge as the story develops, getting darker as it goes.

   Stories that unfold episodically (often the case in literary and slice-of-life novels) are also fueled by antagonism, though in this context it may take the form of a series of emerging situations and people that stand in the hero's path toward a goal. In this type of

Great Stories Don't Write Themselves

novel (a saga, or other episodic tale), it is the sum of these episodic one-act plays that create momentum toward the story's macro goal, which is often some realization or epiphany awaiting the hero. For more genre-specific stories, there is usually one primary macro story arc and one primary villain (or natural force, like a storm or disease, or a social or political construct, which is best presented with the face of a singular villain), giving the reader, in essence, someone or something to root *against*.

6. **ESCALATION AND PACING VIA STORY TWISTS AND TURNS.** This refers to the structure of the story. When done right, it follows an unspooling path largely prescribed by genre, thus creating story logic. The stakes of the hero's quest might shift with these changes, as can clarity of the source of antagonism, all of this causing the hero to regroup, escalate, become more strategic and creative and courageous as the villain ups its game as it moves forward. Specific twists divide the story into rough quartiles that allow a specific contextual flow of the hero's quest, all of which align with given principles of narrative structure, including a context-shifting Midpoint turn.

7. **THE STORY BUILDS TOWARD AND ARRIVES AT A CATALYTIC FINAL CONFRONTATION.** In the first half of the story, the hero struggles. In the second half, the hero begins to create a path that will lead to resolution, with many contextual shifts and twists along the way. The hero is always the primary catalyst in the story's resolution. He should never be saved, nor should he simply observe that which resolves the story. Rather, he has his finger on the trigger of it all. After learning lessons and processing newly acquired information, the hero summons courage and cleverness to arrive at this climactic moment, which can be a face-to-face square-off with the villain, or a bird's-eye view of how the hero has outsmarted and outplayed the villain to trap her into an inescapable position of demise and defeat. Or not ... that's your call as the author.

8. **RESOLUTION ENSUES.** Because of what the hero decides or does, someone wins, someone loses, or there is a surprise in store for both

sides. The goal is emotional gratification for the reader, sometimes unexpected, which is in part dependent on how the story resolves. Happy endings are not required of a story (depending on genre, some of which demand that justice be served, that evil be thwarted, and love endures), but always, the reader needs a sense of closure and some emotional resolution as a result.

It is incumbent on the evolved form of the core story idea itself to create the stage on which all of this plays out. A setting or a theme isn't enough. Rather, a proposition of some kind within those more contextual factors becomes the idea that will empower a premise that can tackle each of these formidable narrative incumbencies.

It should be noted that this is not an exact sequence of the story's structure.

All of these criteria for premise, with the exception of #2, are composed of groups of scenes—including *sequences* of scenes—that tee up, pay off, and transition the story as it moves forward. There are indeed specific story milestones within the principles of story structure (a topic we will cover, via criteria, later in this book; we will deal with scenes, as well), all of which are *embedded within* these eight points and will be extracted and placed in context to one another once the mission of these blocks of scenes is understood.

When all eight of these story essences are in play within your story plan or draft, then all of the structural pieces are in the game, available for your placement and fine-tuning so that the effectiveness of their relation to each other is optimized. When one or more of these is missing, the novel has not effectively been completed. The whole becomes a machine with a wheel missing.

If something about your story glows in the dark, it will reveal itself within your meeting of these eight criteria. If you can't find it, that's a signal that maybe you aren't done searching for such an element, or even for a core story idea that works at a higher, more conceptual level.

When you find that nugget within your story, you will also have found the core of your pitch. Which means if you're working at the premise level, you need to retrofit the key element back into the "story idea," as presented within the pitch. Either way, it could end up being the thing that will sell your novel, to whoever feels that energy, whatever context for that delivery applies.

There's a high probability that what's working within your idea is that glowing element and a degree to which it is *conceptual* in nature. Keep reading to discover what that means to the story.

10   The Criteria for Concept

If you're waiting for a magic pill, a secret sauce, or a steroid shot for your story-making efforts, this could be your chapter.

If there's ever been a word, a term within the lexicon, swirling about in the collective writing conversation that is at once ignored, misunderstood, misused, and undervalued, it is the word *concept*. Some folks, even agents and editors and a few story coaches I've encountered, use the term interchangeably with *premise*, which is like a chef using the words *recipe* and *spice* as synonyms, which they are not. Recipe is a snapshot of what elements are involved and how to cook it all up. Spice is the way you make that combination of substance and preparation memorable, delectable and, when you nail it, downright amazing. Dishes without spice rarely make the cover of a magazine about food, even if they were technically well-prepared.

This confusion is unfortunate, because *concept* is perhaps the most liberating, differentiating, and ultimately empowering story essence a writer can understand and apply. It is available to all, and yet rarely shows up in the discussion of what a writer must understand and execute. This is like leaving the part about anesthesia out of a grad school class on surgery.

Concept is the stuff of which special sauce is made. And every writer should want to imbue their story with the special sauce that will make it stand out in a crowded genre.

Let's begin to define what *concept* means, in the context of storytelling.

Concept in stories is most simply defined as the presence of something *conceptual*. It can manifest in many facets and elements of the story and is usually a proposition, focus, or an assumptive *state* that lends compelling energy to the story around which it will wrap itself. It is often the core of a story idea or a driving sub-text of premise. It is the part of the idea that glows in the dark, that differentiates, that seduces and promises something vicariously exciting.

Concept isn't necessary. But it is almost always enriching.

A love story between two people living in Walla Walla, Washington, with nothing more to say about it at the idea level, is conceptual only in the alliteration of it (because *Walla Walla* rolls off the tongue nicely). You could build a criteria-meeting premise on that idea, and it will quickly sink to the bottom of the story barrel in the publisher's mail room. Why? Because as stated, nothing about the idea is remotely *conceptual*.

Beyond that bare bones idea—writers too often begin drafting stories with only this much on the table—there is nothing that differentiates this love story from any other and nothing that screams to be written or read. Because two people meeting cute and falling in love, without something more, is simply boring. Agents will either pass or demand more of you, and it, before they let you off the elevator. Because if you can add something to it—such as, a love story between an advisor to the president of the United States and a political pundit with nothing nice to say about his wife's boss ... that *is* compellingly conceptual. That idea promises a love story that plays out like an MMA championship bout unfolding in the lobby of a Midtown hotel. There is a context, a framework, and a special sauce involved, all of which create an exciting, energized expectation about the story to come. It is perceived as *conceptual* at first glance.

The story of a county sheriff fighting evil in rural Kansas? Fine. But as a crime novel, not very conceptual. There's really no reason for someone to buy the book, unless they are looking for stories set in rural Kansas. But put a cape on that character, make him a mild-mannered reporter for a metropolitan newspaper, give him a backstory that shows he's the orphaned child of parents from another galaxy who sent him here alone so he could survive their planet's demise and the adopted child of wonderful human farmers who teach him American values ... and you have a story that is not only conceptual but is actually the real bones of one of the most successful fiction franchises—graphic novels, television, and movies—in modern history.

Of course, where examples are concerned, I've plucked the rose to make the point. The more conceptual the idea, the greater the chance someone will love the story, whatever that story might be. Notice in this Superman example there is no story described, not even a little. It's all concept, consisting of backstory and the nature of the protagonist. From there, wonderfully compelling hijinks ensue.

It's fair to ask a question at this point that goes like this:

What if a story about a small town sheriff in Kansas is the story *I want to tell*? Fine again. But here's the deal—if your expectations are that such a story will launch your career as a bestselling novelist within the crime genre, and if that's truly the basis from which you choose the raw material of your fiction, then adjust your dreams accordingly. Because concept, whether at a high level or simply as a nuance imbued to an otherwise pedestrian story, is the ingredient that may get you published and draw readers to your work.

There's nothing at all wrong with writing small stories. Just don't expect them to break big because of your command of the art of prose. Give that sheriff in Kansas something conceptual, or frame that small town within something unpredictably conceptual. For instance, it happens to be the location of the most toxic chemical plant in the nation, which happens to be the family business of the folks who are running the state—even if it's not from another planet. Do that and your odds go up by orders of magnitude.

Concept is the answer to this question: What about your story will make me, a weary and cynical reader who is hungry for something that will challenge and capture me, believe in life again? What about your story—not your writing—will do *that*?

It doesn't have to be a cape and a backstory. Rather, it can be the relevance of the problem being addressed (which is theme) or the crisp dissection of the politics and emotions and the vicarious ride it all delivers (which is intrigue) that render it worth the time on both an intellectual and emotional level.

Sometimes it's the villain that is conceptual. The hit TV program, *Killing Eve*, is a great example of this. As is author Jeff Lindsay's *Dexter*, the ultimate antihero.

Great stories are special. Not just because they are well written, which is where so many authors are placing their bet. Add a fresh and compelling conceptual layer to the story idea, and then render it with sparkling prose and incisive narrative execution, and suddenly you are working on a different level. Suddenly you are in the game ... you are in it to win it.

The secret weapon of storytelling is about to unfold before you.

Conceptual appeal isn't restricted to the paranormal. It can be a proposition that infuses any genre with compelling energy. The proposition is built on a singular, even peripheral specific idea infused into the mix of a story. A concept doesn't need to be extraordinarily huge or contrived or even random; it can simply be a defining paradigm within which the story unfolds. For example, a story about a dog returning home after running away three years earlier. That's a conceptual *idea*, a conceptual *proposition*, simply because it meets the criteria for concept that you are about to experience. The fact that it is also the story idea—it plucks the heart-strings from square-one—illustrates that ideas are the richest ground from which conceptual seeds might be culled.

This is where criteria, applied to the idea that resides at the core of your story idea, can keep you centered on the sweet spot of this opportunity.

Some of you are blinking right now.

We've already discussed story *idea*, and we just covered the criteria for *premise* ... and now we're going to look at the criteria for *concept*? Isn't all of this the same thing? Or at least overlapping to the extent that it creates confusion?

I hope you can see, via this introduction to concept, that it is not at all the same thing as premise. Rather, it is the wrapping paper within which your premise is delivered.

Certainly, idea, concept, and premise absolutely can, and perhaps should, be somewhat concentric circles. The mission here is to make sure *you* are not among the confused. Something *conceptual* may indeed already be part of your story idea, and when that's the case it carries forward to create a conceptual context for the premise that follows it.

If you're looking for the obvious, here's an example: the defining nature of any genre, all of them in fact, is a conceptual commonality. All time travel stories have a conceptual centerpiece in the proposition that one can travel through time. All romances have a conceptual centerpiece promising that people will fall in love in this story. People can't get enough love stories. All crime novels have a conceptual centerpiece, wherein a crime has occurred and justice must be sought. And we love it when justice is served. Notice how all of those centerpieces are the reason readers flock to those genres. Because those centerpieces are inherently appealing and compelling to a certain slice of the broad readership demographic.

The real trick, though, is to add your own conceptual twist to the framework defined by genre that allows your story to claim its own ground.

It's actually more than a nuance. It's more like an opportunity.

Not grasping concept is like a baseball pitcher not understanding the need for and the consequences of *spin* on the ball, even if he understands that *spin* makes the ball curve in midair. Success requires more than *just throwing*. At higher levels than Little League, *spin* is well understood. It is the sum and substance of what makes a pitcher effective. In that same analogous way for writers, *concept*, or the lack thereof, explains why some novels become bestsellers and others, which may be just as well-written by the same author, do not.

Remember that novel by Alice Sebold that sold seven million copies, called *The Lovely Bones*? It was the unraveling of an unsolved murder of a young girl. A murder mystery. But Sebold didn't stop there; that was not the extent of her conceptual approach. She chose to narrate the story in *the voice of the victim*. Even then, she went to yet another conceptual level with her narrative strategy. The story is told by a fourteen-year-old girl from her residence in heaven itself, of which the reader gets a vivid glimpse.

That is conceptual. And illustrative of just how wide a lane the challenge to be conceptual can be, including the narrative strategy employed by the author.

Concept is like good looks for an actor, or a five-octave range for a singer, or an Ivy League degree for a job applicant. Because all of those things imply a promise of things to come. They are differentiators. Those qualities aren't always necessary, but they always get you noticed, and sometimes they are the thing that gets you hired. Of course core skills—*premise*, in this analogy—remain a prerequisite for landing the gig. But when both concept and premise are present, a higher upside is perceived.

Concept is the secret sauce of story selection.

A compelling concept is, in fact, what that agent might be looking for in a genre story.

Something that hasn't been seen before, in quite that way. It is as close to a magic pill as we're ever going to find. There's nothing magic about it, of course, and yet, despite its obvious omnipresence within commercial fiction, it is something that is rarely spoken of or taught as a specific target strategy for authors looking to break in or write a *breakout* novel. Or, more germane here, simply to make what they start with, or have at the moment, stronger.

Examples of conceptually driven home runs are everywhere.

In Paula Hawkins's 2015 bestseller, *The Girl on the Train*, the concept is stated this way:

> A woman whose life is not going well allows the world to believe she is going to work every day, when in fact she is simply boarding the train and riding around all day [this is conceptual]sitting in the same seat looking out at the world, wondering what the people inside those houses are doing, until it's time to go home. One

day, while staring out at the passing scenery, she witnesses someone she thinks she recognizes on the balcony of the house three doors down from the house she lived in with her husband, until recently, when her life went over a cliff. She sees the woman every day, watering flowers on the balcony, or through the windows as she moves around inside. She envies this woman and her perfect life. Then one day, months later, she sees the woman in the arms of a man she knows—because she's seen who the woman is married to—is not her husband, engaging in what appears to be a intimate moment. The next day the woman she saw is in the news. ... she's been murdered.

Very little of that is premise. There is so much more to the actual premise, all of it contextually framed by what you've just read about the story, which focuses on the *concept*. Concept is what sells this story.

The conceptual element here is the notion of the train itself, as the means of escape for this troubled, unreliable narrator protagonist. It is a proposition delivered with a metaphor, one that intrigues while it becomes the pivot point on which the entire story tilts and then goes off on an unexpected tangent. It's almost as if this woman is invisible, which is a more obvious example of a conceptual proposition, and within this comparison we learn that we don't always have to go that far out on a limb with our conceptual idea. Without the train and this vicarious experience of voyeuristic envy, the story is more traditional and predictable. This concept opens up the narrative to the introspective narration, unreliable as it is, that is its hallmark.

One of the great things about a conceptual layer within a story idea is that it begets other conceptual ideas. In *The Girl on the Train*, the story is actually narrated by three first-person voices—another example of conceptual narrative strategy, which is one of the six realms of story physics—each of them unreliable in that they are giving us their version of reality, which don't completely align with each other.

An important initial criterion is this: Concept is *not* premise.

Rather, a concept *frames* a premise with a contextual focus and essence. It becomes the stage on which the drama of the premise will unfold. This is more natural law than it is criteria, because this gets you into the right arena to even begin considering conceptual elevation.

Consider this example, which hasn't yet been written as a novel: *A little girl claims she's been told something specific by a famous but recently dead feminist, which stirs up trouble, because there are people with secrets to hide.* That's the concept, in a nutshell. This leads toward the premise—it informs the premise, but it's *not* the premise—that the dead feminist was actually murdered, when it appeared and was thought by all to be an accident. This expansion of the idea—which is a concept, pure and simple; it is a conceptual *proposition*—into something that is inherently dramatic as it leads to the all-important level of *premise*, because it is the *story* that will be developed *within* the framework of that particular concept. That story, as described above, becomes the abbreviated pitch version of a premise that implies all the criteria that it doesn't directly address, imbued with a highly conceptual proposition.

When that conceptual framework is judged as inherently appealing, to the extent it generates interest *even before a plot or a character or a theme is added to the mix*, we witness the power of concept in play. The premise works because the concept appeals.

Is concept always necessary?

To clarify, a highly conceptually fused premise is not *always* necessary. Literary novels are known for not leveraging a specific concept (a high concept usually labels a story within a genre, which is something literary authors don't want), which is precisely why, in a nutshell, a certain (large) percentage of the collective readership out there aren't drawn to the literary genre. There are plenty of examples of great, iconic stories that aren't all that conceptual, but they end up being magnificently resonant on an emotional level and are usually found on the literary fiction shelf.

When you are writing in what is more commonly thought of as a commercial genre, then concept will always help you infuse your story with inherent reader appeal. Again, because the highest context of the genre itself is already conceptual, which means there are levels of conceptualization that give you infinite choices within your story planning.

Sometimes a concept isn't recognized as such because it is a situation that *could* happen—*To Kill a Mockingbird* comes to mind—and yet, in retrospect, you could say that the story becomes a classic precisely because of the *theme* at its core. The theme was, in fact, conceptual in nature because of its universal emotional resonance.

It's fair to say that concept is a proposition that pushes buttons and draws interest, regardless of its nature. It's not always a plot proposition, per se, but a framing conceptual proposition. In *To Kill a Mockingbird*, the conceptual element is the theme of racial tension (apply this to the forthcoming criteria to see why), with a respected white man, Atticus Finch, defending an accused black man of a crime he did not commit, set in the deep South where this was unheard of at the time. It pushes a button that draws readers to it at this core conceptual level ... even before we know any particulars of the story (which is the hallmark of a strong concept). John Grisham leveraged what is almost the exact same conceptual proposition in his first novel, *A Time to Kill*.

A reliable way to improve a premise that seems flat or obvious is to inject it with something highly or even moderately conceptual. Doing so will shift the premise to some degree. Maybe you set the story in a conceptual place, like a resort or in the executive suite of a huge corporation. A change of setting can inject new energy into an otherwise flat idea. Imagine if *To Kill a Mockingbird* wasn't about a trial with racial overtones but was merely the trial of someone accused of stealing someone else's mail. The difference is obvious, perhaps, but the lesson is not. The themes are completely different: one highly compelling, the other not so much. When we infuse our stories with something big, a strong theme or a provocative proposition, that becomes the conceptual element that fuels the entire story.

There can be a fuzzy relationship between concept and premise.

So, what is the problem when someone calls their idea a story when it is, in fact, *only* a conceptual proposition? When there is no premise yet? This happens all the time, especially when organic pantsing is the process of choice for that writer. Within a pitch or a conversation, no harm done. "My story is about a boy who hears dead people." This is a good pitch, if not derivative to the point of killing it, but it's not a story yet, because it's not a premise yet. It is conceptual ... which may not be enough. Because while concept is optional, premise is not.

What if the writer takes that concept and begins writing a draft from it—which is by definition the telling of a story—*as if* there is a story there, but without actually *having* the story yet? Without an understanding that certain criteria-requisite elements have not yet entered the picture—a hero, sent down a story path in search of something, seeking answers, safety, justice, or a return to a former state of being, all with something huge at stake, and with a threatening antagonistic force standing in the hero's way, complicating things. If there is no premise on the horizon when the draft begins, then the worst kind of pantsing situation ensues. Which is, a writer who doesn't know what he doesn't know, in this case, which is the essential nature of the premise.

This is why you need to *know*. This, in large part, explains why more than 96 percent of submitted novels remain, in fact, unpublished.

Embrace the power of the *What If?* proposition.

When Suzanne Collins had the initial idea for *The Hunger Games*, she was watching *Survivor* on television (or so the legend goes; she's not returning my calls to confirm this). This led her to a *what if?* proposition, which is perhaps the most powerful and common of tools that lead writers to a conceptual idea. Her *what if*, inspired by *Survivor*, was this: What if this game was played to the death? What if, instead of being voted off the island, players are carried off the island in body bags?

Even if she had stopped her conceptual vision with only this much, she already had a highly conceptual proposition.

That was the story *idea*. But she didn't stop there. The author's imagination manifested the rest of what made The Hunger Games series the iconic YA phenomenon it was, adding a backstory to the origin of the Games, a despotic villain, and a love story angle that actually became the primary structure mechanism of the narrative. All of it the product of a *what if?* notion that she explores. None of this is an entry-level expectation of new authors, but all of it is on the table no matter where one is on the learning curve.

It was the same with Harry Potter.

We don't know if J.K. Rowling started with Hogwarts as the originating idea or if the first spark of vision for the story was Harry himself. Which, in a more generic context, is to say that after-the-fact we can't know whether the author began with a conceptual idea or added conceptual layers to a more premise-based idea. But we do know that it is the combination of the two that appeals to readers, that hooks them into a vicarious and emotionally resonant story proposition that leverages a vivid story world as the primary conceptual framework. It is the story world that appeals, and without it there would be no Harry and no Hogwarts. Without Hogwarts, the conceptual centerpiece of those stories, and the vicarious experience it delivers to its target YA readership, Harry Potter doesn't work. Notice that Hogwarts is not a story. It is a setting. A framing device. A highly conceptual one, at that.

Consider the highest and most powerful criteria for concept of them all.

There are several key criteria for concept. But all of them support one objective, and when that happens, you'll know it when you see it. It is this:

- **THE SUPREME MISSION OF CONCEPT IS ALSO ITS #1 CRITERIA:** When someone hears a story idea that is imbued with a conceptual proposition (as a pitch or a written description), even when it doesn't yet have a plot or a character (which it will have when the premise is complete), the conceptual element at its heart renders a reaction that sounds something like this: "Wow! That's so cool! That is a story I want to read. Tell me the rest of this. I'm already hooked!"

When an agent says or thinks this—or just as wonderful, when a reader has this first reaction upon encountering your story—you've just hit pay dirt at the highest level. The idea level. The conceptual level. The premise level. You've differentiated your story. You've anticipated the desires and tastes of readers. You've set your own bar higher, which is precisely what you want to happen. This occurs only rarely in response to hearing a premise, because premise requires execution to shine. But concept strikes between the eyes, and when it strikes hard, the premise is already fueled with something special.

Earlier you were presented with a list of sample story ideas.

There is a difference between those ideas and the list you are about to encounter now. That difference, while sometimes subtle, is this: This new list offers ideas that are more *conceptual* than those listed in chapter 8. They more organically lean in to dramatic tension and character arc. Not that those earlier ideas were unworkable or that there wasn't a fragment of conceptual proposition at their core. But certainly, you could bring something more compellingly conceptual to those stories at the premise stage. You may need to do just that in order to satisfy the eight criteria of premise.

This is how criteria and concept serve the author, coming and going, at the idea stage, or the premise stage, or both. Even within the revision stage, when richer ideas may enter the dramatic proposition.

Here is a stronger list of story ideas, which are also more pitchable than those on the last list, because these are more conceptual in nature:

- "Snakes on a plane." (*A conceptual proposition, with terror built-in.*)
- "Two morticians fall in love." (*An arena-setting rendered conceptual because it is forbidden and uniquely fascinating, perhaps terrifying.*)

- "The world will end in three days." (*A conceptual situation, a conjecture, a* what if? *scenario that immediately asks the reader to consider what they would do in this situation.*)
- "What if you could go back in time and reinvent your life?" (*A conceptual proposition, literally a* what if? *every reader would contemplate.*)
- "What if the world's largest spiritual belief system is based on a lie, one that its church has been protecting for 2,000 years?" (*A speculative proposition with thematic specificity, already pushing buttons, and already having sold well over 100 million copies in various forms.*)
- "What if a child is sent to earth from another planet, is raised by human parents and grows up with extraordinary superpowers?" (*A proposition for a compellingly conceptual hero.*)
- "What if a jealous lover returned from the dead to prevent his surviving lover from moving on with her life?" (*A conceptual proposition or situation, allegorically powerful.*)
- "What if a paranormally gifted child is sent to a secret school for children just like him?" (*A highly vicarious paranormal proposition that is highly conceptual.*)
- "A story set in Germany as the wall falls." (*A historical landscape, conceptual because of its historical significance. Already more conceptual than a story set in Detroit, from the prior list.*)
- "A story set in the deep South in the 1960s focusing on racial tensions and norms." (*A cultural arena, also conceptual because of the social construct it explores.*)
- "What if a renowned black musician tours the deep south in the early 1960s accompanied by his polooka tough-guy bodyguard with much to learn?" (*Hello, Oscar.*)

These ideas are more *conceptual*. Some of these are only *concept*, without a premise attached. Concept is something that can boost the appeal of the story idea, because a premise and dramatic arc stemming from it will be more easily imagined and expected.

There are more empowering criteria for concept to consider.

We've looked at the *mission* for concept, which is when someone who hears about it gets excited about reading the story itself. Here are other key criteria to apply to a conceptual proposition, whether it was there from the start or something you've retrofitted into the heart of the story intention. These, while numbered, are in no order of importance. They are all valid and useful.

- **CONCEPT CRITERIA #2: THE CONCEPT DOESN'T TELL THE STORY.** Rather, it frames a story to come. It is a landscape for an unfolding story, the stage on which a dramatic arc works through its sequence. It has no plot, it doesn't rely on a character in a normal, real-world context. It is the *contextual framework* for story that unfolds within it.

- **CONCEPT CRITERIA #3: THE CONCEPT IS GENERICALLY STRONG AND CAN APPLY TO MANY STORIES.** The idea is so compelling, so universal in appeal, it could launch many different story premises. It could become a *series*. (In fact, almost every series you can name is built on a conceptual proposition rather than a specific premise. When someone talks about the *premise* of Harry Potter, for example, they're getting the nomenclature wrong—*concept* is what they mean when referring to a series as a whole entity, because in the seven books within the series there are seven *different* premises.) This is true because concept creates a story world proposition (like The Hunger Games books), a context that applies to everything in the story or, in a series, the stories (zombies, for example), or a character-capability proposition that can be repeated (like an amazing detective or superhero). Vampires, rich bachelors, vigilantes, revenge stories, historical worlds, serial killers ... any proposition that can repeat itself with the same characters and contexts and story world is because those things are *conceptual*.

  Consider the various medical examiner novels that have become a successful series: the Rizzoli and Isles books by Tess Gerritsen, the Kay Scarpetta novels by Patricia Cornwell, or the Temperance Brennan novels from Kathy Reichs. The story world of forensics, medical examiners, morgues, and postmortem evidence are the conceptual elements of these novels, and any movies or television shows based on them. Reichs's books leverage a concept so strong that not only are her nineteen novels and their spin-offs all bestsellers, they have inspired the hit TV series *Bones*, which over twelve seasons has delivered 245 episodes, each with a different premise. And each leveraging the same identical concept: the scientific, investigative world of the dead.

When your story idea can fuel 245 separate stories, you'll know you're on to something. The great news is the number doesn't have to be nearly that high.

- **CONCEPT CRITERIA #4: THE CONCEPT, WHEN ISOLATED, DOESN'T REVEAL PLOT.** And yet, it *frames* a plot. Or as criteria #3 prescribes, it could frame many plots. It may imply a central dramatic story proposition (another way to describe premise), or the nature of the story, which is a good thing. When that happens, you have already captured the reader's interest.

A concept might describe a hero that shows conceptual abilities. We are drawn to the story because of those abilities (we read the Jack Reacher novels because we anticipate the butt-kicking that will befall a deserving lowlife). It could also be a conceptual villain or antihero, or even a scary disease or a frightening storm. Even a dark social construct (which is what The Hunger Games series and *The Help* leveraged as their conceptual cores). But concept doesn't define a specific hero's problem or quest or caper—the story itself, the *plot*—nor does it define a specific unfolding dramatic proposition. It only suggests a contextual framework for the story—or many stories based on this concept—within which a story will unfold.

- **CONCEPT CRITERIA #5: CONCEPTUAL CHARACTERS BECOME THE STORY'S CONCEPT.** Heroes and players that aren't inherently conceptual—they are real people—can actually become conceptual when they rely on an exterior conceptual proposition. They *become* heroic, and heroism, in retrospect, is highly conceptual (because we love our heroes). Buyers will flock to the next Katniss Everdeen story, no matter what the plot might be, because it's all about Katniss in the context of heroic quests.

Certain characters *become conceptual* by virtue of what they do and how they do it, often depending on rare gifts or abilities that separate them from the norm. By definition, when you create a character with a rare gift or ability, superhuman or not, and apply that gift to the story journey before them, you have injected the story with someone *conceptual*. Beloved detective and spy heroes may or may not apply special gifts or abilities, but they achieve special outcomes. They rise to a conceptual level through performance. In a first novel, people don't line up to buy because the character sounds so intriguing … unless the hero is amazing, in which case the hero is *conceptual*. Those novels earn a growing readership through execution, and down the line, readers begin to attach a conceptual attraction to those heroes. "I'm down for the next Jack Reacher novel," is an example of how conceptual heroes attract readers.

It behooves us to fully understand the nature and limitations inherent to the genre in which we are working. Some make us reach deeper to land on something conceptual that fits. Not all stories are a good match for a conceptual character, a fact that doesn't diminish the potential of such a story. But something conceptual, even a little, in terms of theme and setting and culture, can make any story with the most regular of players something special.

Just this morning on television, which I was watching prior to coming back to this chapter to polish it off, George Stephanopoulos was interviewing Julia Roberts about her new holiday-release film, *Ben Is Back*, a story about regular people facing regular, yet highly dramatic, challenges. It was already conceptual in a real-world way, depicting a son with a drug problem coming home to face a mother who feels helpless to heal him (it's conceptual because it's not a normal day in the life of a normal person). She said something that punctuates the point about adding a conceptual layer—*another* conceptual layer, in this story—to make a story stronger: "Here we are with all these real issues and high family drama, and then they decide to set the movie within a twenty-four-hour time window, the morning of Christmas Eve through Christmas Day. As if that isn't stressful enough, on either count."

That's a conceptual add by virtue of this narrative strategy—a powerful way to tap into the upside of concept—a new layer of ambiance and context lending urgency and poignancy to the whole thing.

If you are writing detective or crime novels, or romance novels, or even adult contemporary—genres that at a glance seem to defy high concept (unless you are leaning into the superhero genre)—you can still tap into the conceptual realm, even though the story world is realistic and nobody is wearing a cape. Just as the writer of *Ben Is Back* did, see if your story landscape might lend itself to something more conceptual to make the story more vivid, if only a little. A fascinating job, a dark backstory, a weak link that will hinder them ... anything that strikes a reader's fancy as compelling even before the story is layered over it is, in fact, a conceptual essence.

- **CONCEPT CRITERIA #6: CONCEPT SETS YOUR PREMISE APART.** Even when your story taps into familiar dynamics, often because of the tropes of the genre, ask yourself what you can add that will set the story apart. Familiarity can be an asset—people buy romances, for example, because they know exactly what to expect; it is what they come for—but something fresh and edgy within a familiar framework is a powerful strategy, one that taps the power of conceptualization to raise the bar. (The *Ben is Back* example does just that.)

    This is what Michael Connelly does so well in his crime novels set in Los Angeles. His books usually offer up something deeply thematic, disturbing, and compelling in a way that sets him apart. In *The Closers*, for example, the story revolves around a sixteen-years forgotten cold case saturated with racial overtones and police corruption, which was a real issue in the days of the backstory. It pushes buttons as it unspools a detective mystery, giving the hero more than one layer of antagonism to deal with. This was Connelly's strategy all along.

    In the Twilight series, we have vampires. Conceptual, yes. Unusual, no. People buy vampire stories because they enjoy the tropes of that genre. But Stephenie Meyer's vampires are different. They twinkle in the sun instead of exploding. They live with and interact with humans. They even attend the same high schools and experience the same teen trials and challenges. They are young and hot, and they fall in love, for real. They are capable of choice in the face of temptation driven by bloodlust. They are divided among themselves, creating a tribal rivalry. All of this is layered onto the expected appeal of vampire mythology, thus adding to the conceptual proposition.

Concept is everywhere in fiction.

And yet newer writers, perhaps confused on the subtle differences between commercial and literary novels and films, tend to lean toward the nonconceptual with episodic, meaning-of-life story propositions. Professional authors understand that we can explore the meaning of life through any genre, and indeed, any conceptual proposition that imbues a premise with more compelling energy than does a diary-like documentary of a year in the life of a fictional character who is *just like you*.

Series television is nothing if not the extended exploitation of a concept. *Castle*, for example (which lasted for eight seasons), is built on *one* concept, without a shred of supernatural context: A successful novelist is allowed to shadow detectives in a local New York City precinct so he can lend his creative insight into actual cases and find inspiration for his novels while he's at it. That's not a plot because it's not a premise. Rather, it's a terrific concept. Over seven seasons, there were 173 episodes built on that single concept, each of them bringing us 173 different story *premises*.

Virtually any enduring television series is built on a singular conceptually-fueled foundation, in the form of a conceptual proposition.

The question becomes: What is conceptual about your story idea and premise?

What about your story idea, or your premise, if anything, will cause someone say, "Whoa, now *that* is the story I've been waiting to find!"

When they do say that, it will likely be because of a conceptual layer within what you've described.

If you struggle to find an answer, consider opening yourself to shifting the story toward a premise that has a more conceptual layer in play, something that will attract readers to your story world and your character and your plot, because the *context* itself is compelling.

When you recognize that you do, in fact, have a winning conceptual idea on your hands, you may actually be more vulnerable to the common misstep of the new writer. Which is to set out to *write the concept as* the story—a bunch of episodic scenes that show various facets of the concept in your story world—without ever truly landing on a rich premise (a macro-arc) that is *fueled* by that concept.

- **CONCEPT CRITERIA #7: THE CONCEPTUAL LAYER OF AN IDEA FOR STORY EXISTS AS A PROPOSITION, A SPECULATION, A NOTION, A SITUATION, OR A CONDITION.**

  Such as, *what if a brilliant law student ends up practicing law before he passes the bar, based on his need to change his life and the fact that he is a prodigy that is already better than all his lawyer peers?* Yes, this has a character, but it is the conceptual nature of this character that drives the proposition. It isn't just *the story of a young lawyer,* which, while true, is flat and less than compelling. This is the concept of the TV series *Suits,* which has lasted for nine seasons (to date).

  A proposition can be to deliver the story in a unique, unexpected way (as we've seen in some of these examples), which can inject massive conceptualization into an otherwise real-world story.

  Go back to that list of story ideas shown earlier in this chapter, and notice how each of them is either a proposition, a notion, a condition, or a context, and that they have their own level of appeal even before you add a specific premise (plot) to the proposition.

- **CONCEPT CRITERIA #8: CONCEPT CAN BE A TIME OR PLACE, OR A CULTURE.** Consider the Outlander novels by Diana Gabaldon and the TV series based on it. There are dozens of premises fueling each episode of the four seasons (to date) of the program based on those novels, which include eight titles, all of which (episodes and novels) launched from the same singular conceptual idea: *a time-traveling heroine doctor in a love story that spans centuries*. In this context, there is a macro-premise and an episode-level premise in play, which describes the essence of a series in any media.

A love story set in ancient Rome is going to be significantly different than a love story set on a space station. Both are conceptual, by virtue of where they are set. Both are places that are fascinating, places readers will never experience in their real lives. Both offer a vicarious experience that isn't possible in the real lives of readers. Even if the essence of the love story itself is the same, it is the *setting* that is conceptual, defining, and differentiating. You wouldn't think of not describing these settings in the pitch for either story, because those settings are what fuel and differentiate the stories at a glance. Both of those ideas glow in the dark ... but neither of them are *stories* yet.

- **CONCEPT CRITERIA #9: PERHAPS MOST OBVIOUSLY, A CONCEPT CAN BE AN IRRESISTIBLE *WHAT IF?* PROPOSITION. WHICH IS SUBTLY DIFFERENT THAN A SITUATIONAL PROPOSITION (SUCH AS SETTING).** Dan Brown mined this niche to write the second bestselling commercial novel in the modern era, *The Da Vinci Code*. It has sold more than 80 million hardcovers and dozens of millions of various editions of paperbacks, and it has led to a series of movies, not to mention the subsequent bestselling resurrection of Brown's backlist, which are equally conceptual in nature. The Harry Potter series sold more than 100 million copies, but Brown's feat was for a single title, which is the tenth-largest-selling novel in history. (In case you're wondering, *Don Quixote* is no. 1, with more than 500 million copies sold. Notice that all the novels mentioned here leverage a conceptual idea at their core.) There are at least a dozen *what if?* propositions at the heart of Brown's story, the most provocative of which is this: *What if the largest religion in the Western world is based on a lie, covered up and protected with deadly force by a secret organization that knows the secret dark truth and the disruption of power that would ensue should it ever be exposed?*

That's killer stuff. There's a blurb from iconic author Nelson DeMille on the first hardcover edition of *The Da Vinci Code*, simply stating, "This is pure genius." Which is the goal and common theme of concepts that work.

Engage in a *what if?* exercise, either with yourself or someone else who won't steal your story.

A *what if?* exercise can lead you to a powerful premise, as well as an originating story *idea* infused with conceptual energy. In *My Sister's Grave*, Robert Dugoni's series-launching novel that has sold millions of copies and is still going strong, he arrived at this *what if?* proposition after working through options, never settling until his instinct told him he had arrived at the best possible premise. That premise was, as an expansion of that fifteen-second version shown earlier:

> What if the body of a young woman who died twenty years earlier suddenly turns up in the wilderness of a bitter Washington winter, revealing new evidence that calls into question the small town rush-to-judgment identification and conviction of a killer who has been locked up the whole time. The victim's sister, Tracy Crosswhite, an underachieving police officer in her own right, sets out to discover the truth about her sister and the man convicted of her murder, but is met with resistance from the citizens and the police who are embedded there, leading her to discover the truth about what actually happened, who actually did it, and why, while seeking to quiet the troubling guilt and voices from the past that have tormented her each day since her sister disappeared.

Compare this to the author's eleven-second conceptual pitch and you see just how much the concept has informed the premise, as stated here. Only now we have a hero and a quest, with implied antagonism lending drama, and the very essence of justice itself emerging as stakes, all of which are premise issues.

In a genre in which it's all too easy to sound like the last mystery you read, that's a killer premise, one with an internal landscape that is as vivid and compelling as its stark external setting. It is conceptually rich by virtue of how it taps into the hot buttons of readers. These are real people in real situations, but it searches for those hot buttons as the criteria for its premise in its final form. Just as the film *Ben Is Back* added a context of the family holidays for Julia Roberts's character's struggle to save her son, Tracy Crosswhite faces additional layers of conceptual challenge in the form of an emerging love story, family doubt, and distrust of the very police officers and court officials with whom and for whom she works, all in a bone-chilling ice cold setting (story world) in the dead of a Washington winter. Readers relate to it, beginning with the premise itself, as embodied by the title itself.

The Da Vinci Code also rides the wave of a highly conceptual thematic intention, via that focus on the religious culture of the Western world (which pushes the buttons and challenges the beliefs of hundreds upon hundreds of millions of potential readers). Theme is a rich arena for conceptual power. *The Help* by Kathryn Stockett, *The Cider House Rules* by John Irving, and *The Fault in Our Stars* by John Green, are all bestselling, thematically strong stories leveraging the power of emotional resonance through the human arenas within which they are set. These are stories in which the theme is *conceptual*, but by virtue of theme becomes the means of meeting the criteria for concept: It is something that, before plot or character is added, compels interest. Many examples of conceptual success owe their storytelling efficacy to the power of theme.

Maybe you should consider, or reconsider, your premise from this enlarged view of the power of a conceptual layer. It really is the secret sauce of genre storytelling, and in its way it becomes a secret weapon when proactively applied to a story that is already propelled by a solid premise but isn't getting the response you'd hoped for.

Consider putting a cape on it (I offer this metaphorically), and see what happens.

11 Context for Criteria-Driven Drafting

If this journey was a freeway, we have just exited one interstate and are about to merge onto another. A rest stop is on the right, so we're pulling over for a moment to add a critical awareness to all that you have just discovered and hopefully taken to heart. It has to do with process and the manner in which these product-centric criteria become part of it.

We are between two stages of the story development process. There are three such stages, actually, but we're not yet ready for the third. They are as follows:

- **STAGE 1: THE *SEARCH* FOR STORY** ... wherein you have a story *idea*, and you pound on it and add layers to it until it finally becomes a story *premise*. Hopefully a premise that is infused with *conceptual* appeal. Or if not, it is saturated with heart leading to empathy, and the potential for intrigue leading to drama.

   When the premise is ready, when you've nailed all eight of those criteria, your job becomes the fleshing out of that premise using expositional scenes, which are subject to a long list of part-specific criteria when they work fully and optimally. But that can't happen until the macro-arc is known, allowing it to become the context from which the scenes that populate that arc are envisioned and developed and written, which is the focus of the Stage 2 work described below. Stage 1 is all about the discovery of your optimal macro-arc in a way that satisfies all of the stated criteria for it.

- **STAGE 2: THE STORY *DEVELOPMENT* PHASE** ... wherein one of two things apply:

   1. If you are a story planner, you begin the process of working toward a *detailed* outline that tells the whole story, or a beat-

sheet that does the same, or some other method of identifying scenes and key story milestones, whatever suits your preference. You've fleshed out the premise, now it's time to flesh out—using scenes and transitions—the arc of the story itself. When you are satisfied that the story works and that it has satisfied the criteria for each of the various elements of a story, it's time to write a first draft from a rich context of all you have already created. Or …

2. If you are a pantser (someone who writes organically, literally composing the story in real time as you write), or even a hybrid writer (one who plans to some degree and writes organically to some degree, as well, which is a description of a huge percentage of working writers), you may not actually have finished your *complete* premise prior to beginning a draft. Your placeholder premise (if there is one, and I highly recommend that you create one even if you're not sure where the story is going) may not yet satisfy the eight essential criteria for a premise that works. What's lacking remains to be discovered as you write that first draft. From here, you don't stop writing drafts until you've accomplished the same two things that a story planner has put in place back in Stage 1: a complete premise that includes a specific ending for the story, in your case (as a pantser) within a draft that fleshes out a series of scenes that meet the criteria for the flow of context and exposition of a story that works.

- **STAGE 3: THE OPTIMIZATION AND POLISH OF STORY** … wherein you do just that to a completed draft: plug holes, trim as needed, add where required, elevate the dialogue, and generally make sure the story reads at the richest level of experience possible. The iconic author James A. Michener once famously claimed he was only a mediocre writer, but he was an astute and artful rewriter. He was referring to the efficacy of his labors within this third stage when he said that.

Here's the value in understanding this story development model.

The goal is not simply to be aware of your process leaning either way, toward planning or pantsing. The goal is to apply the value in doing so. A less-than-aware pantser is prone to accepting real-time story choices as a draft unfolds in a way that doesn't afford the same vetting tools, in the form of criteria, that a criteria-driven story planner has available. Both options bring opportunities to either succeed or realize that you have already thrown yourself under a bus by writing yourself into a corner. At which point your job is to crawl back out and fix what needs fixing.

Further forward-moving exposition is rarely the cure to a story problem. Which is to say, it's almost impossible to write yourself out of a corner of your own making, precisely because that toxic corner remains for the reader to encounter. It's like taking someone in a 12-step program out for drinks mid-program, just to see how they're doing, a decision rationalized by the notion that you can get back on track later. Sometimes the corner into which you've written yourself can kill a story altogether. The best option is to erase all traces of a toxic moment in the story altogether by rewriting from a point before it occurred, erasing it and burying all traces of it under the better options you've manifested within the rewrite.

The roots of that kind of problem extend backward from that place where you've realized you made a wrong turn, and you can't just cut across a field to get back onto the right road. That's the technique too often applied by unaware pantsers, who are *too* trusting in their story instincts, and it is what will explain the story's rejection if this isn't properly fixed within a criteria-driven revised draft that never makes that fatal wrong turn.

Here's how this awareness is best framed:

You are always working within *at least one* of those three realms of story development. It is entirely possible—it's very common, in fact— that you are working in two of those stages at once, either concurrently or toggling back and forth. For example, if you are drafting away without an ending in mind and then a cool idea for an ending pops into your head, you are by definition working concurrently in the search phase as well as the development phase. You are already executing expositional ideas, for better or worse, as if you have committed to them. That moment when the new idea for an ending pops into your head is critical, because it may not work if your solution is to simply alter the direction of the story at that moment. Most likely, you'll need to go back and optimize the narrative path that leads to it.

It's all *just writing* when we are up to our chin in it.

But criteria-driven writing is a higher calling, one that allows us to benefit from the subtleties of *knowing*, allowing us to benefit from an avoidance of drafting mistakes when that draft is without the context of a completed arc toward a known destination.

This is where those who might view all of this as restrictive or formulaic are proven wrong—the battle cry of the hard-core pantser who *just can't do it any other way*—but in a way that doesn't serve us. Or that particular pantser. Because you can still write your story—your novel or your screenplay—any way you prefer, in any order you prefer. As long as, when you arrive at the third stage of this story-development sequence, you have applied and will continue to apply given criteria for the parts and parcel of your narrative. As long as the context of the optimal form and architecture of story is what guides you to the finish line. Whether they exist at the core of your instinct or as some form of external checklist you have at the ready, they remain available to vet your story and bring it to a higher level at *all three* of the stages of story development.

This has been the goal all along.

To fuel the substance of your instinct not just with experience, which is an imprecise long-haul proposition, but with the principle-based fruits of the labors of those who have come before and left us with examples of what stellar craft can manifest. Like someone discovering an alien spacecraft, when you retro-engineer and analyze something that glows in the dark, functional rationale and criteria of performance is what you find.

As a story coach I've seen this tendency to settle for an incomplete premise and a resultant wandering draft happen again and again. I've seen manuscripts in which nothing at all happens for the first two hundred pages—which is full of character anecdotes and backstory, without a core dramatic plot having surfaced—and then suddenly, when the author had a wake-up call in the form of a sudden inspiration to take the story in a more dramatic direction, an actual plot enters the picture. To defend this is to say you can write your story any way you please (you can) and still have it work as a publishable piece within its genre (which is where you would be wrong … if, that is, your way differs significantly from the final outcome as contextualized within the collective criteria at hand).

That tendency to over-write the setup section of a story, because they are in love with the backstory, is tragically quite common among newer writers, who aren't aware of why it doesn't work. An awareness of the criteria for story arc explains why, as well as shows us what will work, but many writers aren't there yet. They don't know what they don't know, so instead they just guess and imitate what they think they've read in published novels but has actually been misperceived.

This is the great challenge, and the great plague, of the newly minted novelist and screenwriter. Not only aren't the criteria evident in their story choices, but the arc of the story itself is too flat, or uneven, or illogical, because—even if the core idea is compelling—they didn't know how to shape and unspool a narrative arc. They weren't empowered to recognize that they hadn't yet finished the search for their best story, or hadn't applied any standard of criteria to what they ended up selecting. They aren't clear on the core macro-arc of the story, in a dramatic context, before they write a draft that is intended to become final. Instead, they settled on "a" story as it arrived on the page after spilling out of their head in the organic moment of drafting. A head that was not yet ready to command the ship of story.

Which is why we all must experience a period of discovery, growth, and apprenticeship to know what must be known at the most basic level of storytelling. This doesn't mean you shouldn't actually write novels during that time—though it does explain why those novels won't ever leave your desktop—but it does invite the newer writer to concurrently seek out the knowledge that will empower him to the level required before those stories will work. Because there are no guarantees that you will stumble upon them, at least as a succinct context for your work, by simply writing. Enlightenment is *not* inevitable. I've known writers who have struggled for decades without sufficient awareness regarding how and why a story works, and I've seen their faces when they realize there is a better way forward. The various categories of criteria are perhaps the most concise and effective window into that knowledge.

A word about alternatives and odds

Some of my colleagues on the workshop circuit won't agree. They advocate just getting the story down on paper, as soon as possible, working from some shred of an initial story idea. To *just write*. This is the default approach for those 96 percent who will end up being rejected, because either the idea or premise weren't strong enough, or the execution wasn't on point. The difference among the 4 percent that break through, as compared to the 96 percent that don't, is connected to their discovery of what they didn't know before. Timing and a bit of luck notwithstanding. If their breakthrough owes itself to coming up with a better story idea than those they'd written before, that, too, is a manifestation of what they have learned about the criteria to apply to a new story idea.

Clearly, drafting prior to a solidified, criteria-crushing premise is an organic approach, one that assumes the writer is equipped with the requisite knowledge to understand what about a given draft isn't working as well as it could. In this case, that isn't possible until the draft is done ... *unless and until* the writer embraces the power of criteria as they make decisions along the story path. A draft undertaken without knowing what you need to know about it, *including* a clear notion of how it will end—which is precisely what the criteria shows us—is likely doomed to significant revision. This is why the so-called conventional wisdom claims, without much push-back, that all first drafts will be a terrible mess. If so, it was because it was a Stage 1 search draft all along, rather than a Stage 2 working draft that the writer assumed it to be, one that never met the criteria for moving beyond that initial search stage, one that could not impart nuance and details, or foreshadowing, to story elements because that author had not yet realized them within a vision for the story.

This is where that paradox unites pantsers and planners on the same page.

Because a vision for the story, one that is complete and criteria satisfying, is essential before the story can work. That can happen via trial and error, or it can happen via instinct that is already imbued with a criteria-driven sensibility. And because stories developed and written from either source can work—success stories abound from both paradigms—then the inescapable conclusion is that any and all processes face the same challenges, against the same criteria, toward the same height of the bar they must reach. It's a preference, a choice, or an emulation that isn't serving you.

It's just that when trial and error and endless revision finally does take you where you need to be with story, you might not readily recognize what has just happened. That being a story that finally meets the criteria for effectiveness, which were there and available all along.

Certainly, choose the process that works best for you.

But a factor in that decision should include an understanding of which process works best for the *story*, as it resides in your head, and how it reflects whatever level of knowledge you possess. Maybe, just maybe, you don't *know* enough yet. But the knowledge is at hand. In fact, it is everywhere if you look closely enough.

As a goal, regardless of your chosen process, try to frame the story within a working premise that meets all eight of those stated criteria

Great Stories Don't Write Themselves

before you set out on a first draft. It doesn't have to be final, but you should understand when it isn't, and specifically why. Even if you're not completely sure about it, use it as a placeholder. Because writing a draft from a placeholder premise is vastly more efficient and effective than writing a draft with no premise at all. This is precisely what famous pantsers do, even if they claim they had no notion of a destination when they started. In that case, their instinct quickly leads them to a premise, and from there, their drafts emerge from a more empowered context.

Some will conclude that I've just made a case for story planning, to the exclusion of pantsing. Not true. Because this isn't a black or white, all or nothing proposition. Outcomes show that pantsers who understand the criteria for story do quite well, as well as story planners working from the same criteria. Which brings us full circle to the understanding that process is not the determinant of success. The criteria, however, *are*.

Creating your premise before you write a draft does *not* mean you must turn in your pantsing card. You still get to flesh out the story organically from that premise, whether final or placeholder, creating scenes and making story decisions in the moment of drafting as opposed to adding scenes to a skeletal dramatic outline prior to a first draft. The truth is, you may end up doing a little of both, and to your benefit, because in this instance you will be pantsing toward something specific—in context to something in a craft sense—rather than swimming blindly in a sea that has no landfall on the horizon.

This is exactly how famous pantsers do it, even when they claim from behind a microphone that they had no idea what the story would be when they began. A lack of knowledge holds you back, it takes you down, regardless of what your chosen process. The same three stages of story development apply to all writers and all processes, but without consistency of sequence. The same is true for a successful story planner at the moment of transition between idea and premise.

Nobody knows, at first. Every author who succeeds does *know* at some point. The earlier that point arrives, the better any ensuing drafts and new story ideas will be.

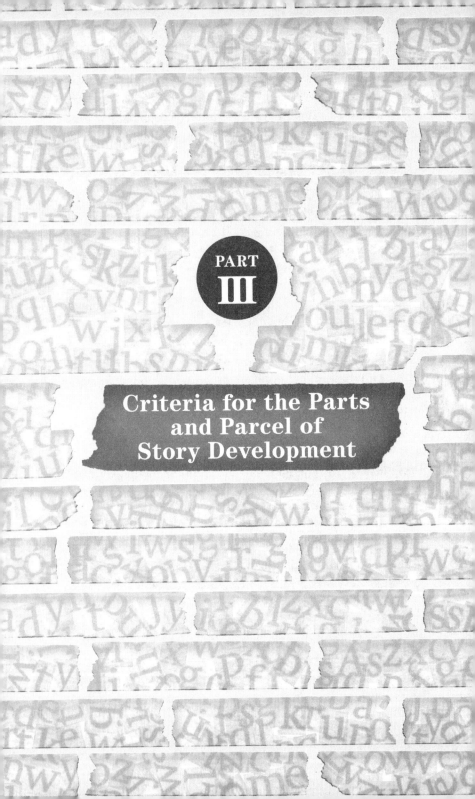

PART
III

Criteria for the Parts
and Parcel of
Story Development

12 The Functional Mission of Story Structure

Welcome to the deep end of the pool.

Not only will your premise serve you here, it may end up being the life preserver that keeps your head above water. This is where it gets serious, and also where it gets fun. Because this is where your story springs to life.

It is also where you choose sides.

There is a loud and credible contrarian view about story structure that is alive and well within the writing conversation. There is also a quick and unassailable explanation for the variance, one that you should apply when anyone, including well-known author-guru types, tell you that there is no default structure for genre fiction (a case better made, yet still dubious, for literary fiction), that you should tell the story the way your instinct tells you it should be told.

Great advice when you know what they know. Confusing and even toxic when you don't.

Two things about that.

First, they are referring to process.

They are advocating for a *just write* approach, and if it comes out as something that doesn't align with the given principles and criteria for structure, then be your own artist and do it your way.

Allow me to again paraphrase the wise words of the ultimate artist, Pablo Picasso:

Learn the principles like a professional, so you can violate them like an artist.

Fine when you are an artist, but risky when you are still in an apprenticeship, which is the first half of that quotation.

Thing is, those gurus actually do reflect those very same principles of form and function in their own work. I've read their novels, and they read like workshops for the very story structure presented here, that apply everywhere. They're only confused about the context of the advice they dispense, because they may find a free-form story discovery process more productive than engaging with the search for story from within a specific paradigm. Even though, sooner or later as the drafting process becomes more precise, that paradigm will present itself.

They are talking about *process*.

They are telling you to write the story from a process that best *serves* you. And for some that best choice is to indeed write—or however you develop your story arc—from within the common form of structure, shaping the flow and content of the narrative into those prescribed lanes or by dumping the story out onto the page in whatever way it naturally happens for you. The latter may produce something that looks like the artist, in her quest of a portrait of her family, has opened a can of paint and splashed it all over the garage. She'll get there, if she knows what getting there means and requires, but it requires a lot of reworking that original mess.

Those gurus are telling you to just let it rip. You can clean it up later.

Fine advice, if you actually *can* clean it up later. If you know enough to clean it up properly. If you can't, or even if you can and prefer not to spend a year rewriting things, there are criteria relative to how a story optimally unspools when it works. And—the best news of all—nearly every published genre novel follows that form.

The gap in that logic of a *you-be-you* approach is this:

If your gut is already sufficiently informed, either through experience or learning, then indeed, your story may emerge from your head onto the page already aligned with the principles of structure within which it will optimally work. And if it doesn't, then feedback and revision will lead you back to that very format, and readers will never know that you didn't do it your way, because at the end of the day, you actually did.

Structure is not in the eye of the beholder.

The structure conversation becomes challenging very quickly, because not every writer understands what structure actually means in this context. In fact, most would be surprised to learn that it is more simple and universal than they thought. When you hear a writer say something like, "I still need to work out the structure for my story," there are two possible implications in the air, neither of them entirely valid. They may be saying they don't yet know what follows what in their story in terms of expositional story beats, or they may be saying they need to pour their premise into the given paradigm for structure that they've been taught (and which you will be presented here, though perhaps in a way that is fresh and more empowering that you imagined it could be). Or, worse case, a paradigm of their own creation.

Once you know the premise, you are halfway home where structure is concerned. Which means when you develop your premise with structure in mind, things tend to fall into place more naturally. The notion of making up a structure of your own to fit the story you intend to write is like someone building a bridge claiming that, in order to do so, they need to reinvent the core engineering and infrastructure principles that are applied to any and all bridges built in the modern world, even within a massively wide spectrum of architectural shapes. It's the *foundation* that matters, and the degree to which the primary anchors of the bridge—or your story—are equipped to handle the weight and stress that the premise will place on them.

It is when *your way* reflects the optimal principles of the craft will you have arrived and have a seat at the table with your professional peers. Some of whom might employ a process that looks more like finger painting, at least at first. Nobody ever knows the extent to which editing, chaos, confusion, and multiple passes have been part of the journey of a title to a place on the bookshelf, or even a bestseller list. But the less-spoken-about bottom line is this: Beneath the surface of every story on the shelf, the structural foundations look pretty much the same.

And that is great news for new and struggling writers. It means there is truly a valid conventional wisdom, even if it is challenged by some, into which you can integrate your storytelling core competencies. They still remain your core competencies, but even a concept car at the auto show needs a conventional set of wheels to make it work.

Suffering is optional in this business. It's still hard, and you still may encounter frustration, but at least you'll know you are aiming the story in the right direction when the criteria for story structure have been applied.

This is what professionals know and understand, and practice, while newer authors either don't know, or struggle with. In part, because they hear mixed messages about it.

The following is universally true.

Structure is unassailable and inevitable, framed here as an analogy for writing long-form fiction.

When a bullet is fired from a gun, it goes through phases along its path toward ultimate stillness. There is structure to that path, defined by the natural phenomenon of physics. It literally explodes from the firearm into the environment, igniting a chain of events. The bullet accelerates for a short time while the force of the explosion exceeds the force of inertia. It then glides for a very few nano-slivers of time before beginning to decelerate and then descend at a rate calibrated by original velocity, air pressure, wind, and any obstacles it encounters. All this before it falls to the ground or lodges within a foreign object, in either case arriving at a state of stillness. It leaves a path of evidence of its power—carnage, in most cases, unless the target was in a gallery—and sometimes its origin, which can be assessed and analyzed to clarify information that can affect the world itself, often in major ways.

This is the journey of a bullet: explosive launch, acceleration, direction, gradual deceleration, confrontation, impact, complication, change, sudden deceleration, followed by stillness. And then, consequence. Whether for good or evil ends, or something as inconsequential as shooting a skeet clay target out of the air, is up to the shooter.

Stay with me here, I'm taking you to clarity.

Each of these states is a natural and expected evolution. This is science. Physics. These are forces of nature at work, harnessed by human intention or carelessness. They are variables in the calculation and calibration of the act of shooting. The bullet doesn't know or care about your strengths and weaknesses or experience, or even your preferences, and it doesn't forgive or compensate for factors such as poor eyesight, trembling hands, the failure to properly consider wind, poor judgment, or the presence of other variables. As the shooter, these factors are yours to manage and work around.

Now let me rewrite that paragraph, removing it from metaphor to position it as the natural order of things within storytelling:

> Stories play as a natural and expected evolution. This is science. Story physics. These are forces of nature at work, harnessed by human intention and proven over centuries of experience. They are variables in the calculation and calibration of the act of writing a story, all designed to optimize the reading of a story. The story doesn't know or care about your strengths and weaknesses as a writer, or even your preferences, and it doesn't forgive or compensate for factors such as the brevity of your experience of the state of your knowledge, for poor judgment or naïve choices, for rambling narrative, the failure to properly consider genre and the nature of human emotion in reacting to what the story puts forth, the bad advice that you've been given and believed, or the presence of other variables. As the writer, these factors are yours to manage and work around.

Our bodies, our minds, our health, our relationships, our careers, our interests, even our possessions, start out as one thing, and then depending on our decisions and the fickle randomness of fate itself, end up as something different. All of it changes as it goes. The one consistent inevitability at the end of the path is stillness, and the potential to leave something behind as consequence.

In that way, stories are life itself. And life itself becomes fodder for stories.

The shooter doesn't get to make up the course of trajectory of the bullet. The only available control over it is to take *aim*. Intention, leavened with skill, is all the shooter has. The same with writers, who aim their stories in a certain direction, taking into account the inevitable evolution of the character and dramatic arcs along the way.

All of that is story structure, which can be reduced to principles and criteria that focus the story along a forward path, achieving specific states of being along the way. Stories are about *change*. They evolve as they unspool. They are about encountering obstacles. They are about something that goes wrong as they move toward an *ending*.

A story is rarely, almost never, a snapshot. Rather, a story is a motion picture.

A story that isn't moving forward, that examines stasis, isn't a good novel. It may be a textbook, or a memoir, or journalism, and within those contexts it may be fascinating. But in fiction, things need to change and evolve. The path of that evolution is the mission of the criteria for story structure.

When we view our stories as a series of changing states, which can be described as a sequence of evolving contexts—four of them, in our case—we are guided toward the management of that expositional unspooling and what it leaves in its wake. We get to fill in what happens within those given spaces. All this *rather than* thinking of the dramatic arc as one gently swooping curve connecting beginning to end, which—while perhaps making for a beautiful rainbow—results in a story that may be missing some of the inherent opportunities at hand.

A good story bounces off things as it goes, changing shape and velocity and direction. The fun is in the twist, and the meaning is in the emotion.

There is a shape and flow to structure.

What you see below is a big-picture overview of story structure, presented here as a simple graphic. For some, this alone could be life changing. Because within the meme, *you don't know what you don't know*, this is a significant game changer if this is news to you. Once you internalize it—which means you stop trying to work outside of this truth—you'll see it in play everywhere, in all genres. You can't *not* see it when you know it's there.

And thus, structure becomes inevitable. And as shown here, quite simple and accessible. This is something you should immediately recognize from your experience as a reader of published novels.

As complicated as it may seem at first, structure really boils down to four major elements, unfolding sequentially within your story:

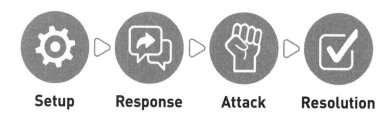

This isn't formula. In application it is more accurately thought of as *flow*. This is the sequential, contextual flow of a story that works. Skip one, and the story stumbles. Mishandle one, and it won't flow as well as it might otherwise. It boils down to this: From a structural perspective, commercial fiction unfolds as a series of four unique contexts, all leveraging what came before.

Even the folks who bristle like a porcupine confronting a service dog at the mention of structure can't push back on this fact of storytelling efficacy. If you're outlining, this is what you outline. If you're pantsing, this is what you pants. You still get to make it all up as you go, but when you do so within these lines—by making up whatever scenes you want in alignment with the assigned context of that part—you may actually be shortening an inevitable revision draft cycle by landing your early drafts within a structural format that works.

Writers who are structure deniers, who find it antithetical to creativity, bristle when they are shown how their own finished work, when it meets a professional standard, presents a core story arc that follows this four-part flow and its proportions almost exactly.

Because, when written and edited well, to a professional level, it will do just that.

These four blocks represent, and are defined by, a context that applies to each part (block of scenes) of the story individually. This renders the scenes that appear within these boxes *contextual*. It defines the mission of those scenes, which is to align with that assigned context. These assignments are organic, rather than random, even rather than optional. This is how stories work. Because this is how stories unspool: across an arc consisting of these four blocks of context.

1. All of the scenes and chapters in the first block (roughly, a quartile) share the context of serving the **SETUP** of the story.
2. All of the scenes and chapters in the second block share the context of showing how the hero initially **RESPONDS TO A CALL TO ACTION**, creating a new path for their story experience. Everything that precedes this quartile is setup for it.
3. All of the scenes and chapters in the third block shows how the hero has moved from a responding context (in Part 2) to a more proactive context of **ATTACK**.
4. All of the scenes and chapters in the fourth block show how the story levels as points of view converge to an ultimately confrontation and denouement that **RESOLVES** the core story problem and proposition.

Setup ... response ... attack ... resolution. It's really that simple, at its highest level. Look for this in the novels you read and the movies you see—it's always there.

The even better news for writers who see the immediate value of this—and if you don't, I'm betting you will when you encounter the criteria that justifies it all—is that there are specific mission-driven transitions, with specific placement between these respective quartile blocks, that create the evolution and shift from one context to the next.

It's like driving from Point A to Points B, C, and D on a freeway, with signage along the way. Except you get to create the view, the weather, the vehicle in which the characters are transported, and the core essence of what the journey is all about, emergencies and unplanned stops included. Even the music that plays along the way.

I'm hoping you already recognize the universal nature of this. Because almost all of the novels you've read and the movies you've seen are strapped to this contextual rocket ship of narrative exposition. Even most literary novels unfold along this contextual path, driven by the evolution of an inner landscape as much as genre novels are propelled forward by what happens external to the characters involved.

A story is the sum of these parts.

This four-part dramatic arc and character engine is fueled by yet another principle, one that we confronted back when we were dissecting premise, and it hasn't gone away here: A story is about something *happening*. It's not a slice of life or a documentary of a moment in time. It's a linear unfolding of action and reaction in response to something that has *gone wrong* for your protagonist, who responds to a calling or an opportunity or a need through an essential course of action (which the hero seeks and struggles to define), with something at stake and something opposing the hero's intentions. Conflict, which is an essential element of genre fiction, arises from this collision of objectives.

Genre-driven commercial fiction requires a *plot*. You can't get away from that fact of storytelling life. This—expressed as a structural model—is how plot unfolds.

The criteria for each of the four parts are analyzed in the next chapter.

This is best comprehended in detail after first encountering it at the highest level of functionality, which is what we're doing here. Sort of like understanding the anatomy of a human body before you start tinkering with the biochemistry that makes the parts tick and interact with each other.

As we go forward, know that you should regard the descriptor—*quartiles*—loosely, because the exact proportions among them have some wiggle room. But not to the extent that any of those percentages become single digits—and certainly not to the point of omission, because leaving any one of these out can spell disaster for a story.

If you shut down an essential organ, chances are the patient would not survive.

13 Contextual Application of the Four Quartiles

As a helpful context for seizing the inherent potential upside of this model, you could think of the scope of the work as the writing of four shorter pieces—four novellas—that become installments in a four-part series. But instead of four separate books, it's all one novel. Each "novella"—in this case, a quartile block of scenes in a specific order—has a different focus for the same set of major characters (in fact, each block has its own beginning, middle, and end), while becoming a unique part of a fictional whole.

Which is to say, each part tells its own story, which is a sequential subset of the marco-arc of the novel. Here are the four blocks of scene, each with its own unique contextual mission.

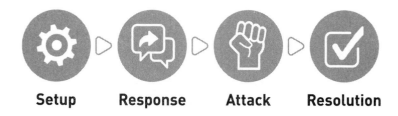

Setup   **Response**   **Attack**   **Resolution**

 Hero introduction; story arc and stakes foreshadowed; B-story seeded; tee-up FPP

 Hero thrust onto story path, driven by threat and stakes

 Hero more proactive, conflict/tension escalate; villain escalates

 Ultimate confrontation; various arcs resolved by virtue of hero taking action

We will view these contexts twice in this chapter. First we will examine each quartile in terms of its overall contextual mission:

- **PART 1** is the story of how the characters and the machinations of a situation converge and collide, allowing us to come to at least partially understand the stakes and the impending threat, while setting the stage for a path that the hero must follow.
- **PART 2** is the story of how the hero initially navigates that path, running into unexpected obstacles and complications, as the weight of the stakes and the pressure of a looming threat become clearer and more urgent.
- **PART 3** is the story of how the hero must up her game to reach the goal, to succeed or survive, in the face of an antagonist doing the same, each bringing new strategies and effort and passion to their respective pursuits of opposing goals.
- **PART 4** shows how all of what has happened has led the hero toward a final effort to do what must be done, who is now more clever, stealthy, and requiring more courage and wits than had been available before this, because the hero is no longer that wanderer or victim. The hero confronts the antagonist and becomes the primary catalyst in the resolution of the entire story.

If each of these sub-arcs has a beginning, middle, and end—which refers to the *transition* from one context to the next—then those beginnings and endings are the *scenes* that shift the context from part to part, from setup to response, from response to attack, from attack to resolution through heroism.

Why is this thought-model helpful?

Because it's easier to wrap your head around a 100-page story segment with its own context and ending-transition beat than an entire 400-page story. It's not feasible if you don't know the macro-arc, but becomes a way of establishing exposition and pace within each part when you do.

Each of the four blocks of scenes (quartiles) has its own contextual mission, meaning every scene within a given quartile needs to align with that assigned context (which is a universal principle and is not something the author should attempt to alter). When you get the first quartile right, the next one becomes more accessible because within the nature of each quartile is a context of teeing up the one that follows. And so on, until all four are in place.

This next overview of those same four quartiles dives deeper into the specific sub-missions of the collective block of scenes within the quartile. These become criteria-based prompts which ensure that the story is building and expanding the dramatic arc at the right pace, and in the right way:

- **IN THE FIRST "NOVELLA"** (the contextual Part 1 of your novel) we meet the hero, living her life, with nuances and other points of view that serve to set up the forthcoming story journey, which kicks off with something going wrong at the end of this segment, propelling the hero through a dark door toward an unknown navigation of this threatening situation. In doing so, we see what may be at stake later, when the First Plot Point (FPP) changes everything. Also, any mechanisms and foreshadowing for the FPP, while not yet clear to the reader, are shown here, so the FPP doesn't play in a vacuum. The FPP—which is the final scene of the first set-up quartile—calls the hero into action via some kind of response, thrusting her down a new or altered path in pursuit of safety, answers, help, or some other form of response.

- **THE SECOND "NOVELLA"** (the contextual Part 2 of the whole novel) picks up from this new context for the story and shows how the hero responds to being sucked into the story (a call to action via the FPP), now with the presence of stakes (as implied in Part 1), and with either the direct or implied proximity of an antagonist (villain) that will further threaten and hinder whatever the hero desires and needs to do. That pressure of threat and stakes is what forces the hero to continue to evolve this response. The hero is more victim than hero here, in that she may not fully understand what she is up against, or why.

- **THE THIRD "NOVELLA"** (the contextual Part 3 block of scenes) plays off new information injected into the story at the Midpoint—often clarifying the motives and clearer identity of the antagonist—which facilitates a sort of empowerment of the hero, resulting in a more proactive attack on the problem. In this quartile, the hero leaves Part 2's victim context behind and begins to push back, developing strategies and summoning courage. But the villain responds in kind—the hero doesn't fully succeed in the quest in this quartile because the bad guy is upping her game as well, which increases tension and stakes through confrontation and proximity.
- **THE FOURTH "NOVELLA"** (the concluding contextual Part 4 block of scenes) shifts from a Second Plot Point story turn (which offers more information that the hero may act upon, while also perhaps complicating things) toward an inevitable confrontation leading to resolution, satisfaction, or perhaps gasping emotion, perhaps even an epilogue moment that foretells what lies ahead as a consequence of it all. The hero is the primary architect of the story's resolution and should not be saved or passive as this comes about.

It's like driving from Seattle to Miami in four days, stopping to rest, refuel, see some sights, and regroup at three roughly equidistant points along the way. Stuff happens during the journey, not all of it according to plan (though it should not include a side trip to Canada). Something goes wrong: The car breaks down, there's a health emergency, or weather forces a detour. A story is a series of challenges for the hero, so this part of the analogy applies, as does the advice to avoid a random side trip that departs from the core spine of the story journey. Regardless, it's all one trip, divided into four parts, experienced in four contexts, all leading to a singular destination, driven by a goal, complicated by obstacles, with the view and the weather changing as you go.

All of this is big picture. For authors, more specificity is not only required, it is also what validates the claim that this model shows you what to write, where to put it, and why. Here's another pass that culls further specificity from these four evolving separate contexts.

Great Stories Don't Write Themselves

EXPANDING ON THIS INTRODUCTORY VIEW

1. **THE SETUP QUARTILE (PART 1)** ... Wherein the story establishes the protagonist in a pre-plot context, teeing up the forthcoming launch of the core dramatic arc. This is where we meet the players, get a sense of what will be at stake, including meeting or foreshadowing a villain or antagonistic presence, and we see the mechanical alignment of factors and elements that will soon launch the hero down a specific dramatic path, with a specific need and purpose, under pressure and threat, with something significant at stake and something standing in his way.

   Then something happens that changes everything—I call it the *First Plot Point* (FPP), as described earlier in the book, but it's known by many names, including *the doorway of no return*, and less specifically, *the inciting incident* (prior to the FPP a setup inciting incident often appears, not to be confused with the actual FPP), which launches the hero down a path—which is perhaps the most important scene in the story.

2. **THE HERO RESPONSE QUARTILE (PART 2)** ... With that FPP having changed everything for the hero, summoning her into action or re-action, a new quest has begun. She transitions from whatever she was doing prior to the FPP, within the setup quartile scenes where we first meet her, and dive head first into a response to whatever the FPP demands of her. Often, it's running for her life and/or an urgent need to learn more about what's happening. The protagonist is in trouble here, things are urgent because something has gone wrong. Perhaps more than she knows. Now your hero must run, hiding from a threat, leading to the seeking of more information and clarity. The hero's second quartile quest is to escape danger and uncover the truth. To fight back. Find help. Or go to the authorities. All while an antagonist looms nearby, getting closer, the threat becoming more vivid and growing closer, with peril now in play. Things get worse, long before they will get better. The hero doesn't

fully understand, and yet she is perfectly vulnerable to whatever antagonistic agenda is working against her.

Then the story changes again. It shifts, it escalates, or both at the Midpoint.

3. **THE PROACTIVE ATTACK QUARTILE (PART 3)** ... Wherein the hero becomes more proactive (rather than the purely reactive context of Part 2), buoyed by learning from previous failure in combination with new information via the Midpoint exposition. He becomes more strategic, more wary, more courageous, more clever. Acting as a victim didn't work, so in this quartile the hero becomes bolder and more strategic, leveraging what he knows and what he's learned, summoning new courage along the way. Stakes rise, tension elevates, the clock ticks faster. Even though his efforts won't completely work—yet—the hero becomes proactive to attack the problem. The villain, meanwhile, is responding to the hero's new moxie, making it all even more difficult and dangerous than it seemed. We learn more about the hero's motivation, perhaps seeing the method behind the madness. Things get complicated, more intense, more urgent. There may be a moment toward the end of Part 3 in which all seems lost, known as *the lull moment*. (This is true for love stories and relationship-driven stories as much as it is for thrillers and crime novels.)

Then something happens *again*, or is revealed or clarified—new information, or a consequence of things that have already transpired—that changes nature and pace of the hero's course of action.

4. **THE RESOLUTION QUARTILE (PART 4)** ... Wherein the hero goes all in, and we see the villain react to this new framing of situation and stakes. There is no turning back now. It's do or die, literally or figuratively. The joust, the dance between hero and villain, is on. A showdown is inevitable. Both sides become desperate, limits dissolve. We are heading toward a confrontation or culmination in which someone will win and someone will lose. Surprise lies in wait, either for the hero, the villain, or even the reader. Because of all that we have read and felt, we care deeply about how this will resolve, because the stakes are something we can relate to. The reader may not see how the hero

plans an ingenious surprise to win the day, but when it happens it will make sense in context to the partial glimpses they have seen of it. The story then ends by virtue of the author's choices. No rules here. The ending may be a surprise to both sides, but it must occur without anything that remotely leans into deus ex machina (which literally means *God in the machine*, which is a fancy Latin way to say *fortunate coincidence* and is almost always a story killer). It ends how it ends. That said, take note of the tropes of your genre, which may in fact, present an expectation of how your story should resolve.

When the dust settles, the hero returns to life—or she's dead, that's your call—either as it was, or as altered by the consequences of this journey. If the story is an entry within a series, this is where the transitional hook plays out, pointing the reader toward the next installment. In that case, even though the macro story continues and the hero lives to fight another day, you must resolve the core dramatic arc of the installment itself. It doesn't work if you leave the reader hanging and demand that they buy the next book to see what happens. That works in episodic television and in medieval saga stories, but not in a series of books.

Four parts—each with its own mission and context and specific criteria, defined within these descriptions, with further analysis to come—separated by three major transitional milestones, also serving a specific purpose within the story and driven higher through its own criteria.

This is how the pros do it.

Read a bestseller and see. In any genre. The author may claim he doesn't pay any attention to structure, that he just writes the story the way the story demands to be written, according to his gut. But guess what? This is how stories demand to be written. The experienced author's gut—perhaps after a form of apprenticeship that may have been as painful as anyone else's, and perhaps while in denial of these structural principles—knows that this model is universal and natural, and therefore inevitable. They also realize it is a *somewhat* flexible application. Read their novels and see (this being the best way to cement the principles of structure in your head, observe them working in the real world). Watch this very structure show up in these exact same four sequential contexts. For a quick crash course affirmation, rent a few movies and watch the absolute precision with which this model is exemplified. That's because it isn't really an option, it's more like the natural law of fiction, to some degree omnipresent in any literary long-form genre.

Chances are you've heard of the classic three-act structure.

What you've seen described here is an expansion of that natural law, with that "second act" having a natural separation into two halves of roughly the same length, each with its own contextual mission, and therefore leading us to a four-part story model. This four-part sequence is the most simplistic, deepest interpretation of story structure. It is the form beneath the surface, which is composed of scenes and narrative connective tissue. In reality it can get much more specific than this (as the ensuing chapters and diagrams will show, as there are specific criteria to apply to each of these four narrative parts, each of which has its own contextual mission with the story), but you could say this is what you need to know at a fundamental level, in a nutshell.

Notice that virtually all of the story gurus buy into some version of this. Even when they break it down into more parts and steps (one noted story guru uses twenty-two parts), it's actually from the same categorical four-part macro-structural flow. The only pushback comes from actual authors who, ironically, end up executing it, but can't quite bring themselves to acknowledge the omnipresence of it, favoring the notion of their own gifted instincts instead.

This *is* the instinct you've been striving to develop.

It makes total sense, too.

We really shouldn't have our heroes vanquishing villains in the first half of the story, at least in a way that resolves the core dramatic question. Avoid spending too much time introducing your hero—certainly not two hundred pages, as in those rookie examples I cited earlier—as if the focus of the story was, in fact, the life story of that character. Within genre fiction, it shouldn't be. This awareness harnesses what I like to call *story physics*, enlisting reader empathy and emotional resonance while delivering a vicarious experience from the page. This flow pulls us away from an episodic, life-story-centric, overly characterized premise, and points us toward a balance between character and something that *happens*, the consequences of something gone wrong and putting the hero under pressure and threat. This model prevents us from writing about a still photograph and delivering a living motion picture of a story.

Something must be engaged and something must be accomplished within the story. The hero's role is to get it done. That's what these four parts facilitate.

Obvious? Perhaps.

I can tell you from experience that in the real world, the only place this is obvious is on bookstore shelves. Among the unpublished—and even a significant percentage of self-published work—it isn't obvious at all, to some extent because it remains a somewhat forbidden, or at least imprecise, conversation. Despite my own efforts to the contrary, it's not even a foundational tenet of how the writing of a novel is framed and presented at workshops and other learning venues. Such a contrarian view is like teaching tennis without paying attention to all those silly white lines. *Just hit*, and all will be well.

If you are writing commercial, genre-driven fiction—thrillers, mysteries, historical novels, romances, science fiction, fantasy, mashups, and all the subgenres that splinter off these categories—to choose to ignore structure or leave it on its own to somehow manifest amidst your own construction of how the narrative will flow is to choose the long road, at best. Or to fall off a cliff, at worst.

I'll say it again: When someone tells you to not worry about structure, as if it will work itself out if you just listen to your own inner writer, they are actually speaking from within a context of process. The end product is as dependent on structure as a car is dependent on wheels.

The *high* road, the one with guardrails designed to keep you from driving over the edge of a cliff, is always the better bet.

Success is a fifty-fifty proposition with novels.

When you get rejected, it's highly likely you won't understand why (because you liked the idea enough to write a novel from it), and nobody on the other end is going to tell you the actual reason, at least with the detail required to take action from that feedback. That reason, if it isn't the writing, will likely be a less-than-compelling premise half the time and faulty execution the other half of the time. When that happens, it *can* be because of the writing itself, but just as often it is because of a structural issue.

But they won't tell you that. They'll say this:

The story is too slow ... that's structure.

I just couldn't get into it ... that's structure, provided the story idea itself has legs.

It sags in the middle ... that's structure.

It was too predictable ... that's structure, too, with less-than-original story choices manifesting within it.

It jumps around too much, I had trouble following ... that is structure, as well.

It just didn't work for me ... which almost always includes a structural misstep.

Can structure resurrect a less-than-compelling story idea or premise?

In one sense, it can. Because if you apply the criteria that reside within this structural model, beginning with the unique macro-criteria applied to each of the four contextual quartiles, you may be able to— you should be able to—quickly discern what is missing or is at least underpowered.

But without that realization, you can absolutely render a mediocre story idea across the arc of this four-part contextual model, and unless you elevate those ideas as you go, the end product will still fall short. There's a reason that almost all of the thousands of singers trying out for *American Idol* don't make it through to the top ten, though the great majority of them are perfectly fine singers. The finalists have an X factor, a secret sauce, a compelling essence that can be explained. The two-pronged call for higher ground you are studying here—1) the elevation of your story idea and premise through the injection of something compellingly conceptual into the proposition, and 2) the dramatic discipline of effective execution that these structural principles and criteria deliver—become the tool set that can take you to that ten-out-of-thousands level of differentiating excellence. Those, and the culmination of wisdom gleaned through experience, embrace the entirety of what is available to make the happen.

Other than those tools, we are left with guesswork. With not knowing.

Structure becomes a powerful tool of revision.

When something doesn't work, half the time it is because of a structural issue. When you apply the higher principles of structure to your completed drafts in need of further work, you seek to align with what amounts to part-specific criteria along the spine of your story. When you succeed in the revision, you will have remedied those criticisms through a structural adjustment. That's what structure *is*, in a nutshell: It is the flow of your story and the nature of the reading experience (context) within each part of the unspooling.

Structure is like gravity itself: inevitable, omnipresent, and rarely acknowledged within the art forms—dancing, running, athletics, architecture, even just walking around—that it defines.

Like someone jumping out of an airplane—analogous to starting a novel—there are effective means to a successful ending along an inevitable direction of motion. If you ignore gravity along the way, it just might end you.

Parachutes are not optional, and because survival trumps the bliss of falling unencumbered through space, they certainly don't compromise the experience.

14 Structure-Enabled Characterization

The following is not an accident. Nor is it coincidence. If this is your first glimpse of the forthcoming principle, you may believe this is too good to be true, but it is both (good, and true).

The author Carol S. Pearson is credited with bringing forth a modeled flow of characterization in literature. In other words, character arc. This was first presented in her 1986 book, *The Hero Within: Six Archetypes We Live By*, with influences from the likes of Joseph Campbell and Jungian psychology. Pearson is a psychologist, but she has a background in the academia of literature, as well as her work in the arenas of management and branding, so her model leans into an application within storytelling in a way that has fascinated writers seeking to understand what makes stories work.

It is no accident that her character model aligns almost completely with the four-part structural model we've just studied. That's because nobody is making this stuff up. We are all coming at the same truths from different directions, landing on a singular yet flexible model for the natural phenomenon at its core.

Story is always a coin with two sides—one a dramatic arc, the other a character arc—so this parallel shouldn't surprise. Exposition within a story exists as a platform on which character manifests. Action through plot is the window into character, the alterative being an essay-like vignette of a character, or in a more story-centric context, a literary novel.

Setup		Response		Attack		Resolution
Orphan (Innocent)		Wanderer		Warrior		Martyr/Hero (Magician)

The literary application looks like this, with the character contexts overlaid on top. Notice the symbiosis between the contextual missions stated within each box and the subtitle that appears above it relative to character.

The literary parallel of Pearson's model leverages the middle four of her original six archetypes—orphan, wanderer, warrior, and martyr—as mentioned in the title of her 1986 book (she's written many others since). But those are flanked at either end with two more archetypes, which actually lean in to embellish the entries that follow in a way that beefs up the literary parallel itself. Her first archetype was *innocent*, and the last was *magician*. All six should be viewed more as adjectives than nouns, or as analogous to an applicable human state.

As you review the criteria for the four sequential parts, as provided in the previous chapters, you'll notice that the language of character permeates all of it. The action (dramatic context) is hero-centric. It deals with what the hero knows while contextually leveraging, for dramatic effect, what the hero doesn't yet know, as well as referring the hero's intentions in interacting with the threat while in pursuit of the goal along the way. This is where character arc comes in, because the hero's decisions and actions reflect a shift from an original state toward a more evolved state.

THE CRITERIA FOR CHARACTER ARC

- **PART 1: ORPHAN (OR INNOCENT):** This first part of Pearson's model is the biggest stretch of the four phases, because we tend to interpret the word *orphan* literally (and of course, she's not suggesting that your protagonist is literally an orphan). *Innocent* is the better label here, but even then it isn't meant literally.

  Pearson is suggesting that the hero of the story is presented in a pre-plot context, unconnected (at least directly, or if at all, only partially) to the forthcoming plunge into darkness, which fully launches at the intersection of Parts 1 and 2 (the FPP). Here in the setup, the hero is doing other things, with other priorities. We see who he is in this context, including any weaknesses or demons that will plague him once he's facing a problem to which he must respond and with which he will ultimately engage and resolve. This is where we meet the hero untested by the forthcoming story, though perhaps battle worn from living a life that has, until now, dealt with other challenges.

- **PART 2: WANDERER**: Part 2 commences with the arrival of a problem or threat (or situation or opportunity) that calls for the hero's response. Which is less than informed or fruitful, through the entirety of this Part 2 quartile. The hero is, almost literally, *wandering* through darkness while reacting to pressure and exploring options. Here is where the hero flees, hides, seeks comfort, confronts fear and outrage, and he often senses or sees at least a partial presence of something that threatens (antagonist or villain) with an increasing proximity. There is a sense of urgency and threat. Because we've come to know the hero from Part 1, we empathize with this somewhat helpless, victim-like state. Soon there will be specific things to root for, but here in Part 2 we are feeling for the hero, rooting for him to find hope or opportunity as he stumbles through this darkness. He is wandering, and the reader wanders with him.

What seems to be an exception to this is common on bookshelves and on Netflix, so let's take a pause to consider it. Sometimes stories open in the heat of conflict, using flashbacks to fill in the blank spots of our understanding of how things arrived at that point. We see the hero embroiled in conflict, and we aren't sure why. The flashbacks tend to lead linearly to a full explanation of how and why, which is, in fact, a First Plot Point function moment, usually arriving within its assigned target placement (at the 20 to 25 percent mark).

Here's an example from the terrific film, *(500) Days of Summer.* I highly recommend that you see this film, and not just because it was a Golden Globe best motion picture nominee but because it is an example of how the structure unfolds behind a surface non-chronological narrative flow that seems to defy the principles, but actually becomes a workshop on applying them perfectly. In the film, Summer is the name of the hero's girlfriend, rather than a season. The story opens with them deep in a relationship that is less than perfect, yet vicariously promising. It jumps around in time, forward and flashback (to a point you can't be sure what is *present day* in this story), filling in a clearer picture of the path that has led them to this confounding place together, which is the focus of the chronologically later scenes. It builds toward something … which is, in fact, the First Plot Point (FPP).

At about the 20 percent mark, there's a scene in which the guy makes a reference to the future, and the girl, Summer, casually says that he shouldn't count on it, that she's not sure if she'll still be around. That's the FPP not only because of placement but because it fulfills the mission and criteria for a FPP by thrusting the hero down a new path, by changing everything, by giving him a specific problem and goal to work toward, and by showing us what is at stake and who is behind this threat and antagonism (Summer herself). It clarifies all those time-jumping scenes that comprise the story's Part 1 set-up quartile, even though the actual exposition of some of them is after that FPP moment chronologically. It's genius screenwriting, leveraging a complex and risky narrative strategy (part of the conceptual essence of the story), yet remaining solidly within the contextual four-part flow of story, as described here, and found virtually everywhere you look in the storytelling world.

- **PART 3 WARRIOR:** The word says it all: This is where the hero begins to engage more proactively. He attacks the problem at hand, and thus, the source of threat. (In *(500) Days of Summer*, we see that the hero has his work cut out for him to win this girl's love.) This may not be immediately fruitful, but it closes the gap. The hero is more informed as new information is leveraged, as well as lessons learned thus far. This is where we really root for the hero's forward movement, because our level of empathy, in proximity to hope, is even stronger.

- **PART 4 MARTYR (OR MAGICIAN):** In this final quartile, we bear witness to the hero's summoning of courage and the conquering of inner demons that may have hindered the path thus far. This leads to an ultimate confrontation, fraught with danger and often riddled with stealth and deceit, within which the hero seeks to survive, by (as the reality television series, *Survivor*, says) outplaying, outwitting, and outlasting the elements and the threatening villain.

Here in Part 4, *martyr* and *magician* are metaphoric descriptors. These labels don't remotely imply that the hero must die for the cause or rely on surreal powers to survive, but rather, they suggest that she is willing to pay a high price to attain the goal at hand. Often it may feel magical in terms of how out of the ordinary it may indeed seem.

This becomes a guide toward evolving your hero across the four-part arc of the story. It's intuitive and natural, leaving you the latitude to plug in any other facets of characterization—often through sub-plotting and the use of subtext—that you feel adds depth, dimension, and emotional resonance to the story.

In a mystery, for example, the detective is assigned the case—setting out with personal baggage they cannot shake, but perhaps will get in the way—with or without a full awareness of the reality he is about to confront. He is alone at this point (the *orphan* context), relative to the story. He is *innocent* of the darkness into which he is about to descend.

Then (in Part 2) things change. The case is now fully before them, and it is more daunting and complex. The victim deserves justice, and truth demands its day. This touches the detective at his core. This is important. But nothing comes easy. The detective *wanders* through options and negotiates deception and danger.

Then new information comes into play at the Midpoint, shifting the hero's path from a Part 2 wandering sense of urgency (sometimes clueless and even victim-like) into a more informed Part 3 sense of pursuit. After the Midpoint, he becomes a *warrior* who attacks the leads and the obstacles and gets closer to the truth.

And then, earning a break through courage and ingenuity and perseverance (the transition between Parts 3 and 4), the hero accelerates toward a confrontation, both with the truth and with the object of the investigation. The story resolves as the hero does what must be done (*martyr*), achieving at a high level of skill and courage and wit (*magician*).

OTHER CRITERIA FOR CHARACTER

In the journey of most emerging writers, character is the story essence first and most often assumed and recognized. At a glance it may seem like an obvious opportunity to imbue the players in our stories with certain qualities and issues that mirror real life, while adding to the complex responses and emotional weight of what we, as authors, are putting them through in our fiction.

All of that is well and good. But it's easy to go too thin or too wide with our characterizations, creating stereotypes and leaning too heavily into archetypes, which absolutely do weigh into how we cast our stories with characters of all stripes.

These high-level criteria might help you remain in the proper characterization lane.

- **CHARACTER CRITERIA #1: DON'T CONFUSE TRAITS AND TICS WITH THE TRUE MEANING OF CHARACTER.** If you stop with showing the surface eccentricities of a character without a deeper exploration, you are missing the opportunity to connect with the reader at a deeper level. Not maintaining eye contact, stuttering, not being able to sit still, massive ego, and insecurity issues … all are the type of surface anomalies that paint a picture but don't necessary show us who the character is at his core, or deep in a dark corner of his psyche.

  The real opportunity to show us the deeper core nature of a character is in the moment of decision or action. Is he courageous or timid? Does he act selflessly or selfishly? Does he hesitate or dive right in? Does he see the big picture or is he impulsive to a fault? This presents the opportunity to show a character arc across the four structural contexts of character (orphan, wanderer, warrior, and martyr/hero) by having the character decide and react to the moment of decision action differently as the story progresses. The timid become courageous and strong. The selfish suddenly value others, and so on. When the reader notices these types of changes, character arc is in play.

- **CHARACTER CRITERIA #2: THE OTHER DEEPER TOOL OF CHARACTER IS BACKSTORY**, which is the life experience that has created and shaped the character we meet within the story. This is an example of the past becoming prologue, if not literally, then as a context for the character we see in play within the story.

This becomes a tricky proposition—it is the place where many new writers show themselves as such—because in genre fiction our stories are not *about* backstory, per se, but they are forward looking. The life story of a fictional character or the saga of a family over a span of decades is a literary novel perhaps, but is really not the stuff of a commercial genre novel. But you can harness the power of backstory through reference, implication, or short flashback. You can show just enough backstory to fill in the blanks—explaining why a character is shy, hesitant around the opposite sex, wary of power and societal structure—and build reader empathy as you do. A kid who grew up in a series of orphanages probably ends up a different breed of adult than one who was raised in a loving traditional home. When you use backstory correctly (think of that facet of the story as an iceberg, and as you know, we only see about 10 percent of an iceberg while the rest remains beneath the surface, hidden yet dangerous omnipresent), the story remains on the rails and in its lane, moving forward with a deeper understanding and emotional resonance (rooting for the hero) on the part of the reader. Which is precisely the point of it all.

These models and principles, which if anything are criteria driven—both for structural exposition and character arc—apply with powerful contexts that work within any genre of fiction. In an endeavor in which context is critical, this becomes a flight plan and a touchstone that will fuel the journey with the right things at the right times, while keeping you in the proper lane that allows you to avoid driving the story off a cliff.

Criteria for the Part 1 Set-Up Quartile

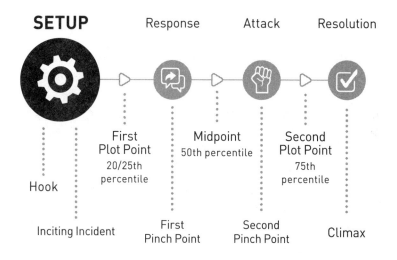

SETUP Response Attack Resolution

First
Plot Point
20/25th
percentile

Midpoint
50th percentile

Second
Plot Point
75th
percentile

Hook

Inciting Incident

First
Pinch Point

Second
Pinch Point

Climax

Introduce hero; set-up, foreshadow stakes and forthcoming quest (arc); inciting incidents

Hero reacts to the change resulting from First Plot Point; antagonist presence felt or observed

Hero proactively reacts; villain ramps up, too. The story moves faster, goes deeper, but isn't resolved.

Hero steps up, steps in, confronts, resolves; ultimate confrontation; post-story state (consequences) are shown as final beat.

Consider, if you will, the classic roller coaster. Stories that work are sometimes described as such—"a real roller coaster of a ride ..."—and any story in any genre is obliged to give the reader that ride through a vicarious experience that engages, entertains, intrigues, and is both meaningful and memorable while imparting emotional resonance.

For this analogy, imagine the very first part of a roller coaster ride. The moment when the cars are loaded and begin a steep ascent toward the first peak, all to the clanking of the chain mechanism beneath the tracks that tugs the car at an upward angle along that path. That angle is *setting you up* for a big surprise once you get to the top. You could argue that in those moments before the car reaches the crest, and before that instant of seemingly being suspended in air kicks in the ride actually hasn't started yet. The core experience hasn't yet fully kicked in. The rider isn't yet experiencing what she came for—even though the view may be wonderful and the anticipation exquisite—but you can sense or even see it coming. With each moment and each vibration, the little chain of cars is taken higher toward an inevitable moment of engagement, where the thrill and the terror take over, a moment from which there is no return.

The ride doesn't really begin until you go over that edge. Until then it's all set up.

You have to take the rider to a certain emotional place before the ride itself—going over that precipice so she can feel the rush of the fall—begins to deliver her money's worth. If we know that someone is afraid of heights or about to throw up, if we understand how the forthcoming ride will challenge them, that setup becomes all the more dramatic.

Your story has a similar but much more robust *set-up* segment that opens the novel and lasts until the moment when everything changes, when a *moment of no return* kicks in for the hero following those set-up scenes. The core dramatic arc fully goes into play at that moment, which is a turning point in the story, even if it has been partially experienced or glimpsed during the set-up quartile. This is the

First Plot Point (FPP), the doorway into the story, the commencement of the hero's core dramatic journey, as well as the reader's.

The setup contributes to the core emotional and character arcs by putting them into motion, or at least, pointing them in the right direction. But the arcs—both emotional and character centric—are still on the slow ascent and build toward a moment when everything changes, thrusting the hero down a path (or pick whichever direction suits you) into a cycle of reaction and action, change and adaptation, confrontations and resolution.

The author's job in these set-up scenes is to cover certain bases, sparking the reader's emotional connection to the hero, the story world, and the approaching dramatic ride itself. Also, plots often require that a mechanism be put in place, that certain facets and conditions and dominoes align, ready to kick into motion as it carries the hero forward, thrusting her along the dramatic path you have in mind.

If you shortcut this set-up block of scenes—which is a series of scenes that all share this same context (that of setting up the story) but stop short of actually forwarding the dramatic arc beyond the tipping point that it delivers—you are depriving the reader of a full and robust context imbued with emotional engagement. The ride is all the more vivid when you understand just how terrified and vulnerable the riders are.

There are specific opportunities for the front end of your novel, presented here as criteria.

The mission of the opening block of scenes is to create context for what follows, both at the major turn that thrusts the hero through door and down a pathway of dramatic arc, and later, when another door opens into the second half of the story. The more the author knows about that entire arc of story, the more effective the opening block of scenes will be.

This is why writing without a clear understanding of what lies ahead—the very definition of the pantser's process—becomes problematic ... unless the pantsing takes place within the context of applicable criteria. Which means the writer knows what the scenes that lie ahead must accomplish, even if they don't yet know what those scenes will consist of. But at some point, the author needs to *know*. And once he knows, the set-up quartile may need to change if it was written prior to that enlightenment.

How *you* get to that point of knowing isn't the point, because your process is your process. Just understand that if you are discovering the novel as you write it, once you do have clarity regarding how the story evolves, especially the ending, the more critical it is that you revisit your opening block of scenes (prior to that major FPP transitional moment) to make sure the requisite bases have been covered.

The forthcoming criteria provide specific targets for this first quartile narrative.

CRITERIA FOR THE PART 1 SET-UP SCENES

It's not wrong to regard the set-up quartile as the most critical terrain of your novel. It's like meeting someone new; if the first impression doesn't work, the reader is less inclined to stick around. And just so we're clear, there may be no warning signs that something is wrong or missing. This is where the story idea and the premise sink their roots, and perhaps their teeth.

The most common misstep occurs when an author isn't completely clear on what the novel is (premise) and where it is going (a sense of dramatic arc imbued with structural integrity), leading to a macro-arc as context. This lack of knowing can result in an opening sequence of scenes that is overly imbued with characterization and backstory to the exclusion of much else. In addition to establishing characters, foreshadowing is a critical mission of the set-up quartile. In genre fiction, a lack of what should be there and an overplaying of other elements will get you rejected quicker than having food in your teeth during a job interview.

Right here at square one, what you know about your story as well as the craft of how a story is developed and assembled means everything to the likelihood of a positive outcome.

- **SET-UP QUARTILE CRITERIA #1: ALL THE SCENES IN THE SET-UP QUARTILE SHARE THE SAME CONTEXT.** This is the core awareness of the criteria-driven author and the end game for any author once the story works without compromise. Every scene in this opening block of scenes has a contextual mission, which is to serve *the setting up of the story*. Which is not, directly, the telling of the actual core dramatic arc of the story (in the same way that a pre-op protocol is not yet the surgical procedure itself; everything within the pre-op serves the setting up of the patient and the medical staff for the operation to come, even when medicines are involved). In this initial quartile your hero isn't yet in pursuit of a solution, at least in context to the dramatic proposition of the story, because the proposition that requires resolution doesn't fully emerge until the very end of this quartile.

And yet, other story essences and facets do emerge early on, and they are critical to the creation of an optimal reading experience.

- **SET-UP QUARTILE CRITERIA #2: THE LENGTH OF THE PART 1 SETUP (NUMBER OF SCENES, MEASURED BY PAGES OR WORD COUNT) FALLS WITHIN AN OPTIMAL RANGE.**

The optimal length of the setup is roughly the first 20 to 25 percent of the entire length of the complete story, as measured by pages or word count. This goal becomes *part* of the story-planning process, as well as the pantsing process and a revision cycle that follows. Because if you get too far past 70 or 80 pages before the story turns the page from setup to actual dramatic arc exposition, then you know you are at risk of an over-written front-end. Consult the graphic at the opening of this (and forthcoming) chapters, which shows you the sequence and proportions of these contextual missions. You are shooting for 70 to 100 pages within this quartile—which should consist of eight to twelve scenes, give or take—depending on genre and the specific density of your story proposition.

The percentage in relation to the whole trumps the page count or number of scenes or chapters. If your name is James Patterson, your set-up quartile might include up to thirty or more scenes. The most valid thing we can say about that is that it works for him, and you need to discover what works for you. But the 20-to-25-percentile optimal location range pretty much works for everyone.

- **SET-UP QUARTILE CRITERIA #3: THE STORY OPENS WITH A HOOK.** This can manifest in many ways, including a prologue (a seemingly unrelated dramatic moment that asks the reader to stick around if they want to understand what it means to the story). Simply stated, a hook is the immediate putting forth of something that causes the reader to engage at either an emotional or intellectual (intrigue) level, or both. To want more. To seek answers. The hook doesn't launch the core dramatic arc itself, per se. Rather, it either helps set the stage for it, or it can be a sort of preview to a moment down the road within that arc.

- **SET-UP QUARTILE CRITERIA #4: YOUR FIRST PARAGRAPH ON PAGE 1 SIZZLES.** You may rewrite it dozens of times, including the final moment of polishing your final draft. Fiction has always been a first-impression, browser's market; as soon as someone sees something they like on either of the covers, they flip to the first page for a taste of your writing voice. Make it something that gets their attention. Conversely, you can sour the water by overwriting it, in the same way that meeting someone who won't shut up can be off-putting.

As a cautionary note, try not to begin that first paragraph with dialogue (cutting into the middle of an ongoing conversation) or something descriptive to the point of cliché. Rather, write an *introduction*. Deliver a moment of action or a flash of irony or wisdom, something that frames who the hero will be or how the story world will become a factor. Avoid mentioning the weather or how the trees bend in the wind, unless trees bending in the wind is, in fact, germane to the story. You want the reader nodding here, glad that they came and eager to read more. This first page is, of course, part of your hook, which is more than the first page alone. But like meeting someone for the first time, it's good to make a solid first impression.

Here is the opening paragraph of the novel *The Horse Whisperer* by Nicholas Evans.

There was death at its beginning as there would be death again at its end. Though whether it was some fleeting shadow of this that passed across the girl's dreams and woke her on that least likely of mornings she would never know. All she knew, when she opened her eyes, was that the world was somehow altered.

Legend has it that when a Hollywood producer read this first paragraph, he put down the manuscript and instructed his minions to offer three million dollars for the movie rights. Of course that's an anomaly, but the truth is that first paragraph is gorgeous and promising prose that is very introductory in tone, meter, and context, which may or may not suit your taste and style.

My favorite first paragraph is from the novel *Manhattan Nocturne* by Colin Harrison (shown below). It is stunning in its power, with only three adjectives used, two of them in one sentence. This is a high bar that may inspire you.

I sell mayhem, scandal, murder, and doom. Oh, Jesus I do. I sell tragedy, vengeance, chaos, and fate. I sell the sufferings of the poor and the vanities of the rich. Children falling from windows, subway trains afire, rapists fleeing into the dark. I sell anger and redemption. I sell the muscled heroism of firemen and the wheezing greed of mob bosses. The stench of garbage, the rattle of gold. I sell black to white, white to black. To Democrats and Republicans and Libertarians and Muslims and transvestites and squatters on the Lower East Side. I sold John Gotti and O.J. Simpson and the bombers of the World Trade Center, and I'll sell whoever else comes along next. I sell falsehood and what passes for truth and every gradation in between. I sell the newborn and the dead. I sell the wretched, magnificent city of New York back to its people. I sell newspapers.

The first page bar is high. Make sure you sign up to play the long game for this singular element, because you'll feel the need to return to it over and over before you stamp FINAL on a draft.

- **SET-UP QUARTILE CRITERIA #5: THE PROTAGONIST IS INTRODUCED EARLY IN THE FIRST HALF OF THIS QUARTILE.** This is perhaps the highest priority of the set-up quartile. If there is no protagonist put in play in the first 20 pages or so, you should notice and seek to understand what may be overplayed or premature at this point.

The hero is frequently seen within the first scene, often doing something that will show us who they are in the context of this initial appearance. But it's perfectly fine to wait a scene or two, provided those preceding scenes contribute to an understanding of the protagonist or the story world to an extent that the story is better served by waiting a few pages to show us your hero.

In *The Martian*, the bestselling formerly self-published novel and ensuing published book-to-movie juggernaut, author Andy Weir opens with a log entry from his stranded hero-narrator. The perfectly rendered first line is: *"I'm pretty much screwed."* In less than a page, he establishes that he has been left behind, alone on Mars, when the crew had to suddenly evacuate to avoid certain destruction, believing that Mark Watney had already perished. It's a great hook. It's also the *concept* of the novel because it frames the whole story without telling the story. Notice, too, that's an example of a novel that opens after the First Plot Point (FPP) in a story-world chronological sense, but takes us back to show us how that dark moment transpired. By the second page, the narrative has already cut back to that moment, showing us how he survived (pure setup), and establishing how he has managed to stay alive against odds that are incalculable (also the heart of setting it all up). It leads to a forthcoming FPP transitional moment (again, which is the endgame of the set-up scenes), when the story shifts into a new context, from hopelessness to hope.

- **SET-UP QUARTILE CRITERIA #6: THE STORY WORLD IS PRESENTED AND EXPLORED IN AN INTRODUCTORY CONTEXT.** This is perhaps obvious, but if story world is a critical part of the reading experience (as it is in science fiction, fantasy, historical fiction, alternative history, some speculative fiction, or culture-specific novels like *The Help*, or even city-specific stories like the novels of Michael Connelly), then it becomes a major objective of the setup to make it vivid and contextually relevant.

It can be a mistake to devote a significant amount of focus on generalized description of the story world once you get past the FPP (which is the endpoint of the first quartile set-up context). That's what this Part 1 quartile is for, to put the dominoes in place, so that when the FPP tips the first one over to begin a chain reaction of consequence and further exposition, we are already present in a vicariously visceral way.

Again, Andy Weir's *The Martian* is a clinic on how to handle story world. In its case, quite literally.

- **SET-UP QUARTILE CRITERIA #7: WE SEE THE HERO BEING ENGAGED WITHIN A PRE-ARC FOCUS.** The reader sees who the hero is, warts and all, in a context that exists prior to the full launch of the story (at the FPP) that will consume her. For better or worse (often worse), the hero has values and beliefs and is immersed in consequences, already having been manifested. This situation—what the hero is doing or focusing on as the story at hand is launched—will either be put on hold, changed, or discarded in favor of the dramatic journey she is about to embark upon.

Back to *The Martian* for a moment. The context of Watney's survival efforts is that he really has no plan and no viable hope of rescue. He stays alive purely on the off chance that some shred of hope might somehow show itself. When the FPP arrives, the new context shifts toward the preparation for that specific rescue effort, which is something more urgent, with higher stakes than simply trying to make it to next week. Now he has real hope versus the context of simple survival in the Part 1 scenes.

A key job of these set-up scenes is to create a perception of the hero on the part of the reader. Unless your protagonist is an antihero, you want your reader to like this character, or at least understand him, because it will lead toward empathy. (If you can't empathize with a brave astronaut-scientist stranded alone on Mars, check your pulse.) This empathy is critical to the overall mission of the story because in about 50 to 80 more pages you're going to drop a bomb into your hero's life—perhaps a bomb of hope, albeit with significant obstacles in the way—and the entire point is to have your reader take the journey with them, rooting for specific outcomes along the way.

- **SET-UP QUARTILE CRITERIA #8: THE HERO IS SHOWN AT THE BEGINNING OF THEIR ULTIMATE CHARACTER ARC WITHIN THE STORY.** But not necessarily their experience, or launch within, the *dramatic* arc of the macro-story. Watney is a resourceful, hopeful, eminently likable hero (because he's a witty guy) from the very first page, and yet he must learn a few things about himself before the rescue effort will stand a chance. He has to achieve the impossible by facing the task of turning the impossible into the *possible* along the way.

  Here's a critical nuance: In genre fiction, the set-up quartile is the only place within the novel where scenes can play for the *sole* purpose of characterization. After the FPP, each scene will need to contribute to plot or transitional exposition, in *addition* to supporting or forwarding characterization. If there are inner demons, weaknesses, or traits that may be either strong or weak, they should show themselves in the setup so that later, as they become germane to the story, they will resonate as an extension of what has already been put into play.

- **SET-UP QUARTILE CRITERIA #9: A SENSE OF STAKES SHOULD EMERGE.** Because we meet the character in context to living a *pre-plot life* (which can manifest as a specific situation or condition), the reader gets a sense of what will be at stake—what the hero has to lose—as the story moves forward, into the new context of the hero engaging with a specific problem (something has gone wrong that demands a response). If family or reputation or employment or riches will become germane to the story's stakes, then it needs to be established here in the setup, in context to how it relates to and what it means to the hero.

  In *The Martian*, the stakes shift from surviving from day to day, to the long odds of success relative to a specific rescue strategy.

  This, too, is a critical nuance: Once the hammer hits at the FPP, the reader should be pre-positioned to *care* about how this impacts the hero you've introduced; in other words, what the hero is playing for and the consequences of failure. The story clicks into a higher gear at the FPP, so the place for backstory and ambiance—neither of which actually forwards the story—is present within the set-up block of scenes, but only to the extent that it contributes to reader engagement and dramatic clarity later.

- **SET-UP QUARTILE CRITERIA #10: ANTAGONISM AND THREAT (THE VIL-LAIN) IS CLOSER THAN THE HERO REALIZES.** But it isn't yet an *active* source of threat or antagonism. This is an issue of foreshadowing. Some sense of antagonism—often via proximity—can be shown in relation to the setting (she's right there in the office, seemingly harmless or inert at this point). Or relationally (friends, lovers, ex-lovers, foes, co-workers, the options are endless here), but in a less-than-fully threatening context, or even with no perceived threat at all. A storm approaches, but it isn't yet lethal or even detectible. A person close to the hero may turn out to be the villain, but neither the reader nor the protagonist is aware at this point, thus setting up a sense of emotionally resonant betrayal.

  In some stories—*The Martian* being yet again a great example—the antagonist is not a person but rather a situation, or a culture and its value system (as in The Hunger Games trilogy) or the environment itself. Mars is the villain. Mars is trying to kill Watney, each and every day. But that evolves after the FPP, because now there is a ticking clock that tilts the odds in favor of the planet killing him.

- **SET-UP QUARTILE CRITERIA #11: THE MECHANISMS OF THE APPROACH-ING FPP ARE PUT IN PLACE.** Films can do this with a seemingly mean-ingless visual reference (for example, we see a slight twitching in the face of someone everyone believes is harmless, but now, after seeing that little twitch, we suspect otherwise), but in novels we need to call out certain elements and essences that lead to the even-tual emergence (very soon, in fact) of change or threat or urgency. A pair of scissors on the corner of a desk needs to be visible to the reader (if not the hero) if, in fact, it is about to be plunged into the hero's throat by someone she thought she could trust. Other plot devices are more complex, requiring context and mechanizations that, while treated briskly, nonetheless justify the author's choices at the FPP turn and thereafter. Eye-roll-inducing moments can kill a story, so take care to seed that which will eventually bloom into something meaningful and relevant.

- **SET-UP QUARTILE CRITERIA #12: ESSENTIAL FORESHADOWING OF STORY ELEMENTS AND EVENTUAL REVELATIONS ARE PUT IN PLACE.** It isn't just the FPP that needs teeing up in a mechanical context. There may be elements farther down the story road that can and should be foreshadowed here in the setup. Remember this: *Nothing should appear out of the blue later in the story, especially if it is critical to the logic of the emerging moment.* Foreshadowing is a literary art because the reader may not notice a specific moment or nuance within the narrative that, in fact, portends something they *will* notice later on.

  The goal is to avoid any moment later in the story in which the reader can legitimately think, "Whoa, where the heck did that come from?" These points don't need to be sold and rationalized at the earliest points of foreshadowing, but a quick and subtle glimpse or reference adds a powerhouse punch to reveals that await later in the novel. (Read Gillian Flynn's *Gone Girl* to see this nuance handled artfully.)

- **SET-UP QUARTILE CRITERIA #13: THE FPP IS POSITIONED RIGHT BEFORE IT IS REVEALED.** Earlier it was suggested that each of the four parts can be thought of, and to some extent treated, as *novellas* in their own right. This applies to the Part 1 setup as validly as any of the other parts, and within this perspective, the FPP (see the next chapter for specific criteria) is the climactic moment of this 80-page (approximately) set-up novella. You wouldn't slam the reader with a climactic moment on page 410 that doesn't make sense after reading to this point in a full novel, so within this context, the same principle holds true in positioning your FPP.

Great Stories Don't Write Themselves

If the FPP is the Titanic hitting the iceberg, it works better when we learn that the ship's bridge officers have been notified of the presence of ice in the vicinity.

Then again, the FPP can be (if you knowingly decide on this, wherein we now depart the analogy comparison to a novella) a complete out-of-the-blue shocker, with absolutely no hint that something like that may befall the hero or the story world. Do what works for the story—but be aware that positioning is often part of pulling it off.

Obviously, a lot happens in the opening set-up block of scenes.

The presence of thirteen separate criteria within one quartile of a story supports the argument that this first quartile set-up block of scenes is the most important segment of your novel or screenplay. It's hard to nail them all if you are making up the story as you go along. The enlightened pantser fully understands that once the story has emerged, even if you've resolved it in the final pages of your draft, the first quartile requires another, more contextual evaluation and drafting pass. If you are planner, your ending will be clear before you begin to write (even if only as a placeholder, even if you think of a better ending as you go along), which means you can revisit your first quartile expositional plan with every new idea you inject into the story arc.

With the setup in place, we move on to the all-important FPP transitional moment, which is the payoff for all you have invested in the previous scenes.

I've said all along that none of these principles are formulaic and none of them are rules, per se. The same goes for these criteria. But some principles and their supporting criteria have weight that exceeds rules in any application. The FPP—which is, in this author's opinion, the most important *moment* in any story—just might rise to the level of a *rule*, given its function within a story that works. If you were going to christen something a *rule*, this is it.

Criteria for the First Plot Point

Fully Launching the Core Dramatic Arc

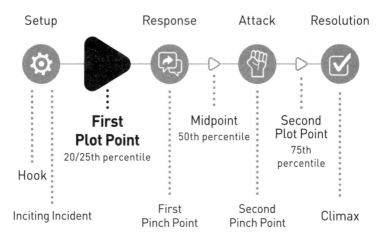

Setup   Response   Attack   Resolution

First Plot Point
20/25th percentile

Midpoint
50th percentile

Second Plot Point
75th percentile

Hook

Inciting Incident

First Pinch Point

Second Pinch Point

Climax

⚙️ Introduce hero; set-up, foreshadow stakes and forthcoming quest (arc); inciting incidents

💬 Hero reacts to the change resulting from First Plot Point; antagonist presence felt or observed

✊ Hero proactively reacts; villain ramps up, too. The story moves faster, goes deeper, but isn't resolved.

☑️ Hero steps up, steps in, confronts, resolves; ultimate confrontation; post-story state (consequences) are shown as final beat.

The essential First Plot Point (FPP) story beat, with its tight window of placement to achieve optimal efficacy, is arguably the most important narrative moment in your story. It defies pure pantsing—meaning, organic story drafters often need to retrofit this down the line, when the story arc and the ending have solidified—because it lights the fuse of the story's core dramatic arc after a setup in the chapters that preceded it. It is also something that must be at least accommodated, if not fully realized within a vision for the story, before the macro-flow (structure) of the story meets the criteria given for it.

The FPP is where the actual core story launches in a dramatic sense. If the story has been partially put into motion, it changes—it escalates—at the FPP. It is the point at which a more fully launched core plot arc becomes apparent. Because this is where the hero must drop everything and go into response mode. This shift is housed within a scene and may consist of several catalytic points within that scene. The character has been led to and positioned at this relative entry point via the set-up scenes and moves forth from that point (into the Part 2 scenes) with something specific to react to, and perhaps, something obvious to *do*. Like hide or run for their life. In most stories, this is where *something goes wrong*. If it has gone wrong earlier than the FPP (possible when a previous Part 1 inciting incident drops a bomb into the proposition), this is where the hero is summoned to the need to respond to it because of new information or proximity.

If you'd like visual proof, watch a movie preview. A movie trailer is easily seen as a condensation of the four contextual blocks (quartiles) of the story, though it will be cryptic regarding the actual ending. We see the hero, at home or at work, we sense their life or situation within the story world, we sense what will be at stake ... then it all changes (this is the FPP) ... something goes wrong, the unexpected happens ... the hero is pulled in ... it all gets worse and worse as the clock ticks, the villain gets closer and the stakes escalate ... and then the preview will stop short of showing how it ends, leaving you to buy a ticket to find out.

In a movie preview it'll play that way every time. Why? Because this is how commercial fiction—on screen or on the page—*works*.

A First Plot Point by any other name ... is still the First Plot Point.

Remember that different writing teachers—at least those who acknowledge this facet of structure; some don't, which doesn't remotely negate its omnipresent validity—refer to this story turn using a number of different terms: the doorway of no return, the point of no return, the launch of the hero's journey, the inciting incident.

Calling the FPP an inciting incident is a paradoxical choice. By nature, the FPP is *an* inciting incident, because it indeed incites the hero to respond and initiate a quest of some kind. But there can be one or more functional inciting incidents that appear within the set-up quartile prior to the actual FPP moment, which is why placement matters. Let's say a house burns down at the fifteenth percentile mark, which changes everything for the story, because the hero's husband was found dead inside. But then, at the twenty-third percentile, the hero is arrested for arson because an investigation showed that the hero's sister also was found inside the burned house, along with proof that she had been having an affair with the hero's husband. These facts give the newly arrested hero a motive, as well as a means. Now the hero's path is to prove herself innocent, an aspect of the story which wasn't in play at that fifteenth percentile inciting incident. It *is* put into play at the twenty-third percentile FPP moment of her arrest, thereby launching the core dramatic arc of the story.

The FPP is the moment when something goes wrong.

This is the overriding mission of this story point, infusing what follows with a context of a necessary response to it. Seven key criteria help us understand how to pull this off.

- **FPP CRITERIA #1: PRECISE RANGE OF LOCATION WITHIN THE WHOLE OF THE STORY.** The FPP optimally occurs as the transition between Parts 1 and 2, between the twentieth and twenty-fifth percentile relative to overall length. Earlier placement tends to compromise the opportunity for reader investment in the character, the clarity of the stakes and the means of setting up the transition itself, while a late FPP can result in reader impatience, leading to the dreaded verdicts, "It was a little slow," or worse, "I just couldn't get into it."

- **FPP CRITERIA #2: THE FPP SUMMONS THE HERO INTO ACTION.** Or at least, a response from the hero is necessary or unavoidable. The scenes prior to the FPP have tee'd up this moment. Whatever the hero was engaged with in Part 1 will be put aside or altered drastically when the sky falls at the FPP. It's a whole new story context now.

- **FPP CRITERIA #3: THE DRAMATIC ARC OF THE STORY FULLY LAUNCHES AT THE FPP.** Fiction is the story of something that has gone wrong, and this is where it fully enters the hero's journey. He must respond to what has gone wrong with an ultimate resolve. If the situational or threatening darkness has been visible earlier (like the burning house example), then the FPP is when the hero is called to respond to a deeper emerging threat from that situation.

- **FPP CRITERIA #4: THE VILLAIN MAY OR MAY NOT BE IDENTIFIABLE AS PART OF THE FPP EXPOSITION.** That is the author's call. Either way, the hero is about to have a major role going forward. Something has caused this need to respond, and part of that response is to find out who or what it is. The reveal of the actual villain is a powerful tool for endings, but great care needs to be taken with the diversion and sleight of hand that hides the true identity from both the hero and the reader.

- **FPP CRITERIA #5: THE FPP NEEDS TO CONNECT TO, ULTIMATELY, THE STATE OF THE ENDING OF THE RESOLUTION OF THE STORY.** This one can be massively subtle, or it can be on the nose. At the end of the story, there will be only one truth relative to what happened and why it happened. The characters and the reader may not fully understand this connection at the FPP. It may even require a bridge to make that connection, but the author needs to engineer it all.

- **FPP CRITERIA #6: THE AUTHOR NEEDS TO BE CLEAR ON THE CORE DRAMATIC STORY THAT WILL BECOME THE BACKBONE OF THE STRUCTURE.** Sometimes a story seems to have two levels. Often there is a love story intertwined with an exterior-dwelling dramatic arc. When this occurs, one of them—the author gets to choose—becomes the core structural spine of the story. It is that plotline from which the quartile contexts and the focus of the main transitional scenes is found, while the other story wraps around that spine like a snake around a branch.

While it may seem, for example, that the core dramatic spine of *The Hunger Games* is the raw grist for the structural contexts and milestones, that's actually not the case. The core structural spine is Katniss's perceived love affair with Peeta. This becomes evident from the Midpoint moment, and the fact that Katniss isn't thrown into the game itself (via that diabolical tube elevator) until the middle of the Part 2 quartile, after showing us in detail how the Tributes were trained. It is how Katniss leverages the perception of her relationship with Peeta that determines the amount of assistance she receives from the television audience, which is the key to survival in the arena.

- **FPP CRITERIA #7: AS A CHECKLIST, THE FPP MANIFESTS WITH STAKES HAVING ALREADY BEEN INTRODUCED AND/OR FORESHADOWED.** And in doing so, it gives the hero something specific to respond to, or pursue, or something new to fear or avoid, or an opportunity to investigate. The hero's life changes at the FPP, and while it may not be easy, the pursuit of a new path and the answers and/or salvation that awaits down that road is the primary focus of all that the hero does, decides, and acts upon from that point forward.

Deft handling of the FPP is a rite of initiation to the ranks of skilled practitioners of craft.

This is how it's done in the big leagues of writing fiction. If you doubt this, try to prove it wrong. Grab a bestseller in any genre, and you'll see this FPP principle manifesting within the broader context of the structural principles across the entire arc of the story. While there may be such examples out there, they are rare and often merely a subtle application of this principle, rather than a highly visible one. Like freefalling from a bridge without a parachute, hoping to be an exception to a natural law is a risky bet—and more so, it's a fool's bet for a beginner.

Seeing is believing. And believing is required before this becomes centered in the heart of your storytelling instincts. Internalizing the principle of the FPP can become, in fact, a turning point in the career of an author. Not knowing leaves it to chance or instinct to execute this properly, which is the reason many stories from newer writers don't work as well as they could or should. *Knowing* renders it an intention.

Here's an example from a recent bestseller.

Author Robert Dugoni, who wrote the foreword to this book, has written many bestsellers. *My Sister's Grave* wasn't his first *New York Times* bestselling novel, plus it was an Amazon and *Wall Street Journal* (both) no. 1 bestseller, as well, selling more than two million copies and still counting. It's a murder mystery, which can be the most challenging genre in which to find a perfectly executed FPP. Because sometimes the FPP is rooted in an external story turn and sometimes it can be found within a relational or internal landscape context (like in *The Hunger Games*). The key isn't that the reader recognizes the technical craft involved—they'll feel the effect of it either way—but that the author understands why this moment is so important to the story, as well as what is asked of it and why its placement matters.

My Sister's Grave is the story of an adult sister, Tracy, dealing with the murder of her younger sister twenty years prior to the story's chronological narrative setting (a key nuance, since there is significant narrative backstory from the time of the killing itself). She's a police detective on a violent crimes team, who changed her life's path in that direction because of the murder, and it has haunted her career and her relationships ever since. A suspect had been tracked down, arrested, and convicted, and he has been in prison for most of those years, in a rural Washington community with close ties and a good old boy sensibility among the officers and judges and patrons that are all still around, all of them wanting the past to remain the past.

The set-up quartile looks like this: We meet Tracy doing her job, where we get a feel for what she does, why, and the nature of the attitude and serious grit she brings to the job. We feel the weight of her ongoing grief, which is key to making this premise work. At the end of that scene, we see that hunters have found a dead body within her team's jurisdiction. Then we read a flashback of a scene with Tracy and her sister, twenty years ago, showing the fire and competitive nature of both women and the intensity of their deep relationship. This leads to the moment when Sarah, the younger sister, gets into a vehicle and waves goodbye. Tracy would never see her alive again.

That's a major inciting incident, but it happens on page 12, at the 3 percent mark. Far too early to be an FPP. Rather, given what you now know, it is easily recognized as a key moment, an inciting incident, in the setup of what will be the FPP dozens of pages later.

From there, the scenes tick off all of the requisite criteria for the set-up quartile. We meet other characters who will become germane to the unspooling of the story's core threat and dramatic question. We meet a man from her past, who arrives back in town and happens to still be attractive, and he's a lawyer. We see how they are drawn to each other. We also see how the forensic evidence from a newly discovered body leads to the conclusion that this is, in fact, Tracy's missing and presumed dead sister, Sarah. Another inciting incident that is not the FPP, because this is still setting up the moment in which Tracy rounds a corner to begin a focused quest in search of the truth. Which will be yet another inciting incident, but again, not the FPP.

As the focus narrows, Tracy begins to suspect that the man in prison for the killing may not have been given a fair trial. He may or may not be the actual killer. She and her new lawyer friend—sparks have ensued—start the process of petitioning for a new trial, which brings out the hidden fears of several of those other characters we have just met. We see that legal mechanism unfold, which is by real-world standards accurately portrayed (author Dugoni practiced law for 14 years) and vicariously fascinating. We see more flashbacks of the horror that unfolded in Tracy's life twenty years ago.

We aren't sure who the villain (the real killer) is at this point. It's the set-up quartile by design, and things are *not* as they seem.

In these scenes, we come to understand Tracy's dicey family situation, then and now, including her spotty relationship with her ex-husband and her father. We meet her old boss, who was and is the chief of the local police department, who helped put the accused in jail. All of which will become a factor in her journey, which is precisely why all of this matters to the setup.

Not a scene is wasted. None of it is peripheral, even if it doesn't manifest as relative until much later. All of it is *strategic*. Dugoni is unspooling the line, getting us to care about Tracy and suspect that something is rotten in rural Washington state.

The FPP shows up on page 97 (Kindle mobile edition), out of 402 pages total. That's just past the twenty-fourth percentile. Right in the criteria-defined sweet spot for the FPP.

Tracy has been sniffing around, turning over old rocks that the establishment wants left untouched. In the FPP scene, her old boss, the town sheriff, confronts her in a dark, isolated situation. He gets right to the point: Back off this nonsense about digging into your sister's death. It's over. The killer is in prison. Let the dead bury the dead. Leave it alone.

It ends with nothing short of a threat. Tracy has choice: Take the safe road and back off. Or dive in to the deep end, keep digging, and with her new lawyer friend's help, see what turns up, which may be a dangerous choice. It isn't over at all. In fact, it's just beginning.

That's the hallmark of the FPP. This is where the core dramatic arc actually begins, after a strategic setup in the first quartile block of scenes lead up to it.

Author Dugoni may or may not have thought of this as an FPP, at least within the context of criteria, or even a structural expectation. It was, in the core of his evolved dramatic instincts, the right time to up the drama and the stakes. His nose for the story led him to this place, this reveal, timed for this part of the story. For him it was a natural moment of choice. For a new writer, it would be much less likely to nail down this precisely (unless, of course, that new writer was aware of a criteria that defines that target landing spot). It's a story rhythm thing. This is how stories work. This is how a core dramatic arc collides with the hero of the story.

All of it hinging on the power, placement, and implications of a properly conceived and rendered FPP.

17 Criteria for the Part 2 Hero's Response

The Second Quartile of the Story

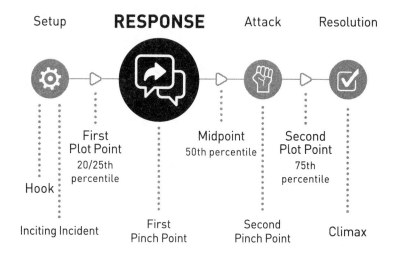

Setup   **RESPONSE**   Attack   Resolution

First
Plot Point
20/25th
percentile

Hook

Inciting Incident

First
Pinch Point

Midpoint
50th percentile

Second
Plot Point
75th
percentile

Second
Pinch Point

Climax

Introduce hero; set-up, foreshadow stakes and forthcoming quest (arc); inciting incidents

Hero reacts to the change resulting from First Plot Point; antagonist presence felt or observed

Hero proactively reacts; villain ramps up, too. The story moves faster, goes deeper, but isn't resolved.

Hero steps up, steps in, confronts, resolves; ultimate confrontation; post-story state (consequences) are shown as final beat.

Remember that story roller coaster we visualized earlier? In the analogous Part 1 story arc of that roller coaster ride, we observed a loaded car full of nervous riders death-gripping the railings as the cars rattled higher and higher toward that first ominous peak, where it seemed to pause for a moment, right before the nose dropped and the little train began to plunge into the insanely steep abyss of the ride itself. Obviously in this case, there is no turning back now.

The peak itself was the FPP that culminates that setup, where everything about the ride changes dramatically in the presence of an analogous plunge into a deadly threat from which there is no turning back (it certainly feels just like that when it's you in that front car). This is the beginning of the story journey, the true launch of the ride itself, even if—as it often does—it comes on the heels of a partial glimpse of what that dramatic journey might be.

Within the criteria shown below, notice that the context has shifted from Part 1's set-up mission to Part 2's hero's response context. Again, every scene in this new block shares the same contextual mission, but there is wide latitude here because, while it's all *response*, there are many possible dramatic options on the table. The exposition of the dramatic arc is now fully underway. The caution, which may be a temptation, is to avoid moving your hero into problem-solving mode or to expect much winning, because this is where things get worse and more complicated, as the villain becomes a more visible player within the narrative.

If the author is using the draft to continue to search for the story, this block of scenes becomes a target zone in which the nature of the hero's need, struggle, motivation, and ultimate goal begin to clarify, without much chance at confronting or in any way solving the problem at hand too soon, which would compromise the author's agenda to escalate the drama while increasing reader empathy, including fear of what lies ahead.

PART 2 CRITERIA APPLY TO THESE SCENES

As was the case in the Part 1 setup, there are multiple objectives to be served in this contextual quartile.

- **PART 2 HERO-RESPONSE CRITERIA #1: THE CONTEXT OF THIS QUARTILE (PART 2) SHIFTS FROM THE PART 1 SET-UP MODE INTO THE PART 2 *HERO INITIAL RESPONSE* MODE.** The hero is now shown embarking on, or having been thrown onto, a new path. The core dramatic arc of the story is now fully underway. The hero has something to elude, evade, escape, pursue, discover, or simply survive. The source of the threat and pressure, the extent of the stakes are now felt.

  If the airplane went down on a deserted island at the FPP, the first thing we see as the Part 2 quartile kicks in is the hero emerging from the wreckage, looking for other survivors and generally realizing that he has no food or water. Fear kicks in. And then, after a moment of calm reflection that proves to be a cruel illusion, he realizes the island is inhabited by venomous snakes and hostile natives. Despite his fatigue, this new sense of fear pushes him into hiding. The challenges and the danger begin to pile on, and it will all get worse before it gets better.

- **PART 2 HERO-RESPONSE CRITERIA #2: THERE IS URGENCY DRIVEN BY CONSEQUENTIAL STAKES.** Stakes have been shown or implied prior to the FPP (within that example from the previous paragraph, we will have learned back in the set-up quartile that our hero is a diabetic in need of daily insulin, and see how that initial withdrawal complicates this new predicament). At some point, though, as the Part 2 scenes paint a darker and darker picture, we realize the hero risks serious consequences if he doesn't take immediate action. Which is very often, at first, running or hiding from a threat. To do nothing is not acceptable. In another story (because there is nobody to reach out to on this deserted island) the hero may reach out to authorities or allies or warn others. Whatever she does, it relates to the proximity and nature of the threat that, via the FPP, has either befallen her or is at her heels. The stakes here, however, are likely to grow and evolve as more information enters the story.

- **PART 2 HERO-RESPONSE CRITERIA #3: THE HERO REMAINS LESS THAN FULLY INFORMED.** Successes are hard to come by. Risk and threat escalate and grow closer. Other than a growing threat and heavier stakes, the goal, nature, source, agenda, or scope of consequence of the threat isn't fully revealed to the hero or the reader at this point—because the variables and threats are likely to change again in the forthcoming Part 3 quartile. Nonetheless, the hero takes risks, suffers setbacks, and begins learning lessons in the aftermath of the antagonist's aggressive decisions, actions, and intentions. It is through the incremental discovery of the true nature of threat and consequences in this quartile that dramatic tension is unspooled for the reader.

- **PART 2 HERO-RESPONSE CRITERIA #4: NOTHING THE HERO DOES HERE SOLVES THE PROBLEM OR FULFILLS THE NEED.** Whatever she does or tries to do meets with only temporary safety or remedy, at best, or makes things worse despite intentions. The villain may gradually manifest within this block of scenes, and the obstacles before the hero become more cunning, more formidable, and more urgent.

- **PART 2 HERO-RESPONSE CRITERIA #5: THE HERO'S RESPONSE TENDS TO COMPLICATE THE PROBLEM, WHICH REVEALS ITSELF IN LAYERS GOING FORWARD.** In the first quartile, you established your hero's inner demons, faults, or weaknesses, and those become factors in this Part 2 journey through situations and options, leading toward even darker implications going forward. These are things the hero must unlearn before he can gain traction toward the ultimate goal.

  In our island crash example, the hero might fall from a tree and turn or break his ankle as he tries to climb to harvest coconuts. Things continue to go from bad to worse before they will turn a corner in the forthcoming Part 3 sequences.

- **PART 2 HERO-RESPONSE CRITERIA #6: ALL IS NOT AS IT SEEMS.** The cause-and-effect chain becomes intense, because the hero is digging a hole for herself. The villain becomes bolder, and yet may remain cloaked in stealth, perhaps right next to the hero all along at this point. Perhaps we see that someone else has survived the crash but isn't willing to share the resources he's already gathered under a shelter that is too small for two.

- **PART 2 HERO-RESPONSE CRITERIA #7: THE HERO REALIZES THAT A PLAN IS REQUIRED.** Many story models, such as The Hero's Journey, identify characters that are there to provide the hero with assistance: the mentor, ally, trickster, herald, shapeshifter, guardian, sidekick, wingman, and bestie. Even someone with an agenda who will help out for a price can assist the hero in overcoming the odds, as well as her own limitations to discover breakthrough information and receive advice that keeps her in the game (or perhaps sends her toward an abyss). Some of these seemingly peripheral characters may prove to be duplicitous or untrustworthy.

In the movie *Cast Away*, which somewhat aligns with the example we're working with here, Tom Hanks realizes he can't sit on his hands and simply wait to be rescued. He begins to calculate what it might take to build an ocean-worthy raft, taking stock of the slim pickings among the wreckage and available natural resources. (The Midpoint, then, would be when he casts off in that raft, which changes the story and turns him into a more proactive attacker of his problem in Part 3, which is discussed here very soon.)

- **PART 2 HERO-RESPONSE CRITERIA #8: THE READER EMPATHIZES WITH THE STATE OF THE HERO WITHIN THIS RESPONSE.** This critical criteria is often overlooked in favor of the forwarding of plot. The Part 2 situations the author creates are driven by scene as well as sequence micro-tension shown with the macro-tension of the bigger picture predicament.

Scene-specific micro-tension is something the enlightened author takes note of. I first heard it described as such in a Facebook video of agent and writing guru Donald Maass being interviewed in the hallway at a writers conference by Robert Dugoni (using a cell phone). That moment was an epiphany, one that I hope you'll open yourself to here. More on this when we get to the chapter on scenes; for now, know that this advanced nuance applies to Part 2.

- **PART 2 HERO-RESPONSE CRITERIA #9: FORESHADOWING AND MECHANICAL TEEING UP OF THE MIDPOINT STORY TURN.** The story will change at the Midpoint, due to new information that enters the picture. That exposition is set up within these Part 2 scenes. An entire chapter on the Midpoint is forthcoming, and it is important to round this corner smoothly and logically by teeing it up here. If the presence of someone else surviving the crash is the reveal that is the Midpoint beat, then we need to see signs that someone might be there within the Part 2 scenes leading up to it.

Here's a look at Part 2 within our bestselling case study.

In Dugoni's *My Sister's Grave*, the FPP showed the hero (detective Tracy Crosswhite) being advised by her old boss to back off any further investigation of the convicted and incarcerated supposed killer he helped put behind bars—advice which carries an implied threat. This becomes context for how Tracy moves forward in the Part 2 block of scenes, because that shadow of pressure and threat is imbued within every scene (it is the source of micro-tension). The stakes are higher, her motivation stronger. The story changes direction and urgency because of this warning, and she moves forward in the face of the implied threat and danger.

The reunion with her old boyfriend, the lawyer who just arrived in town, escalates when they join forces to dive deeper into this mystery (cementing a solid B-story with this love angle, which brings its own level of drama). Their initial goal is to have a new trial granted to the imprisoned and convicted accused. The boyfriend wants her to stay with him so he can help protect her, but Tracy is not a woman who needs protection. She's a force of nature on her own. They begin to go over the case, piece by piece, including flashbacks to the original trial. They visit witnesses with varying degrees of resistance and a nuanced sense of contradiction. Holes in the prosecution's case begin to clarify. Specific evidence found on the newly discovered body doesn't align with the evidence presented at trial, supporting Tracy's petition for a postconviction relief hearing. We begin to sense how some of the players wearing white hats twenty years ago may not have been as virtuous as they have pretended to be ever since.

Tracy and her boyfriend visit the convicted killer, Edmund House, in prison to get him on board with this objective. They confront him with the evidence used to convict him—blood, hair, and eyewitnesses that claim to have seen House and Sarah together that night—and he has a plausible explanation for all of it, claiming the evidence and witnesses were planted in the effort to frame him for the crime. (Notice that she is still pursuing a *response*—which is the overriding context of all of the Part 2 scenes—to her FPP call into action.) But the most intense scenes in this quartile are those that don't involve Tracy. They are the conversations between her old boss and others who might have been part of the frame job and its cover-up. They don't quite expose their culpability, but they do show us how Tracy is looking in all the wrong places where they are concerned, because they have much to lose if the killer is released and given a new hearing. This point of view back-and-forth can be a high degree of difficulty, but it is one of the best ways to escalate drama and evolve the plot in ways that the characters themselves don't fully control.

As all of this unfolds, Tracy's level of exposure to risk, because she is defying her boss, as well as the stakes of her mission (having that hearing granted), are pulled tighter and tighter, like a rope around the neck of a victim.

18 Criteria for the Mid-Block Pinch Points

Wherein the source of drama remains in play.

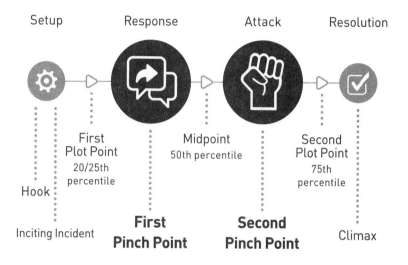

| Setup | Response | Attack | Resolution |

First Plot Point
20/25th percentile

Midpoint
50th percentile

Second Plot Point
75th percentile

Hook

Inciting Incident

First Pinch Point

Second Pinch Point

Climax

Introduce hero; set-up, foreshadow stakes and forthcoming quest (arc); inciting incidents

Hero reacts to the change resulting from First Plot Point; antagonist presence felt or observed

Hero proactively reacts; villain ramps up, too. The story moves faster, goes deeper, but isn't resolved.

Hero steps up, steps in, confronts, resolves; ultimate confrontation; post-story state (consequences) are shown as final beat.

You may have heard of a story moment called "a pinch point," especially if you've read the work of Syd Field. Because this often pops into a story organically, it is easily skipped in the conversation about technique and structure, but it is always good to keep this in mind, whether planning or pantsing the sequence of your unfolding dramatic arc.

There are two key pinch point moments called for with prescribed optimal placements. But like inciting incidents, there can be multiple occurrences of story points that inject the same type of effect on the story. The first of the two structural pinch points is optimally targeted for the middle of Part 2, and the second (with a slightly different nature, because the context is different since the reader will be quite familiar with the villain at this point) in the middle of Part 3. The page is wide open regarding how the author pulls this off.

A pinch point is simply the pointing of the story camera (direction of point of view) back toward whatever the antagonistic force might be. There needn't be an actionable purpose to this moment, though you certainly can show the villain in motion, using it to ratchet up the dramatic tension. Sometimes it's just someone talking about it (as in the second pinch point in Clint Eastwood's terrific film, *Million Dollar Baby*, where Eastwood literally narrates a description of the antagonistic force of the story to Hilary Swank as they ride in a car in the dead of night).

A very simple sample premise illustrates.

Let's say someone is being chased by a villain with a gun through a wooded area. It doesn't matter why in this example. At the FPP we saw when and why the hero had to run for her life. But for twenty pages or so that's all we've seen—her running, tripping, spraining her ankle. Barely dodging a snake. Showing that her phone is dead. A quick POV diversion to her boyfriend gazing at his watch, wondering why she is late. Tension is building. But at some point the reader needs to be reminded of the source of this tension—the guy chasing her with a gun—and that the stakes and motivation are nothing short of her survival.

We need to see that front and center within the narrative, at regular intervals.

Somewhere toward the middle of this series of Part 2 scenes, the story camera (point of view) switches to show the guy chasing her, gun in hand. And man, is he angry. He's tripping, too. In fact, there's blood on his face from running through low-hanging branches. But he's still there, still coming for her. The effect of this is to re-establish, reinforce, and escalate the dramatic tension in play. A story is always about the tension between hero and threat, and the pinch points remind us that the threat needs to be visible and palpable to the reader, if not the hero, as well.

A story about someone stranded on an island would, at the pinch points, remind us that the hero is alone and how dire this circumstance is. A story about a lover cheating on his partner would show him sneaking away on a false pretense, placing a call from his car as he drives away. A story about revolutionaries planning a computer hack to take down the largest evil corporation on the planet would be a scene that shows us how heinous the company actually is.

A pinch point in the third quartile will always show the hero aware of the nature and proximity of the threat, usually the identity of the villain himself. But the objective of the pinch point remains the same: to put the villain or source of threat directly in front of the reader in that moment, within the context of where that plot arc stands.

CRITERIA FOR THE USE OF PINCH POINTS

Even if the hero doesn't yet know for sure who the source of threat and antagonism is, the author absolutely does.

- **PINCH POINT CRITERIA #1: THE OPTIMAL LOCATION FOR A PINCH POINT IS NEAR THE MIDDLE OF THE PART 2 QUARTILE, AND AGAIN NEAR THE MIDDLE OF THE PART 3 QUARTILE.** There is a lot of leeway, however, with this placement. The mission of the scene is the higher priority. In general, though, authors need to remember the spirit and intention of the pinch point, which is to never allow the reader— and often the hero—to forget, or take for granted, the proximity and nature of what is threatening them, thus reinforcing their story goal.

    Optimal placement (literally the *middle*) is the thirty-seventh to thirty-eighth percentile of Part 2, and the sixty-second to sixty-third percentile of Part 3. But again, there is great flexibility in this particular regard.

- **PINCH POINT CRITERIA #2: SPECIFICITY DEPENDS ON WHICH OF THE TWO TARGET LOCATIONS IS AT HAND.** The villain may appear in a vague or stealthy form in the middle of Part 2—because the villain may or may not have been fully revealed at that point—and more vividly drawn in Part 3, where the villain is actively part of the narrative of those scenes.
- **PINCH POINT CRITERIA #3: THIS MOMENTARY FULL FOCUS ON THE VILLAIN,** or a sense of proximity to the hero, in either case can be little more than a quick peek or a full scene with its own exposition and micro-tension. The choice is the author's.

It is not critical that the pinch points *change* the story—though they can do just that if the author chooses to inject a twist at that point in the story. The main objective of a pinch point is to remind the reader, and possibly the hero as well, that a villain/antagonist continues to threaten and is nearby, if not out in the open. If the antagonist does not take human form (it may be nature, for instance, or a disease, or a threatening cultural paradigm, which was the case in *The Help*), the pinch point simply shows the antagonistic force in play.

The thing about villains ...

One of the most successful, and literary, pieces of fiction in modern times was Steven Spielberg's *Schindler's List*, based on the 1982 novel *Schindler's Ark* written by Thomas Keneally, as inspired by a true story. If you ask a sampling of folks who've seen the film or read the novel who (or what) the antagonist is, some would indeed say it was "the Nazis," referring to them as a collective whole. Certainly, the Nazis are the nastiest of villains in that and many films and novels, but Spielberg understood that it is scarier to create the face of evil within that larger whole. In other words, give us a character who is representative of the force or belief system that threatens the hero. *Schindler's* primary villain, who doesn't emerge until well into the second part, is Amon Goeth, based on and portrayed as the real-life Commandant of the takeover and purging of Poland, and a bit later as the senior officer running the concentration camp near Krakow. Much of the narrative focused on this villain, knowing that the audience would react more strongly to a singular villain than the whole of the Nazi entrenchment if left without a primary character.

A story works better when the antagonistic *force* has a face. Because emotional resonance is the objective, and nothing says fear and loathing better than a well-written villain. Both the author of the novel and the creators of the film understood this and leveraged it brilliantly.

An example of pinch points at work in a bestselling novel

Once you know what to look for, it's hard not to spot pinch points at work within a well-layered story. Almost always the villain will pop back into a story near those two prescribed optimal places. The threat and source of dramatic tension might pop up in numerous places within the narrative, as well, which doesn't diminish the power of properly placed baseline pinches. This is an organic principle, in the same context that someone swimming underwater must, at some point, surface for air if they are to survive.

Robert Dugoni's *My Sister's Grave* is 402 pages in length. That's easy math for framing the quartiles and the placement of milestone pinch points. Because his FPP is almost perfectly evident just prior to the twenty-fifth percentile, and the Midpoint moment nails the fiftieth percentile moment (as you'll see in the next chapter), we should find his first pinch point's optimal placement at or near page 150. (If that same FPP had appeared at the twentieth percentile, which is 20 pages earlier than the twenty-fifth percentile—both being within the optimal window of placement—that would slightly alter the math.) That said, I'm sure Dugoni didn't sit down to force this into alignment with those targets, but rather, they landed on the page according to the keen nature of his story instinct, which handles the placement of such things as a matter of optimal storytelling. As he states in the foreword of this book, Dugoni is a hybrid writer, one who understands and honors the shape and mission of structure.

On page 149—nearly dead center of the sweet spot for the first pinch point—the hero of the story (Detective Tracy Crosswhite) is made aware that her former boss is talking to her current department supervisor within a context that could threaten her job. That's key to the threat looming over her—there are people who want to block her path. The source of that threat, the sheriff of the municipality in which Tracy works, and her old boss at the time of the trial, is a primary candidate as the heavy at the core of the entire story (the reader isn't clear on this yet, which is one of the nuances of the pinch point, and it can go either way). This dark dynamic, including its meaning, is right there on page 149 for the purpose of furthering the story's level of dramatic tension and urgency, because we are reminded of what Tracy is up against. It's a perfectly executed and placed First Pinch Point.

In the third quartile, the Second Pinch Point is found on page 252. With an optimal target placement of page 250 (the center medial of Part 3), that's close enough to count as a bull's-eye. It arrives at the end of a scene depicting the concluding moments of a tense courtroom interrogation of a key witness by Tracy's attorney boyfriend. His questioning exposes untruths and gaps in the evidence used to convict her sister's killer, perhaps unfairly, and by implication point a finger at who is behind the deception. The reader is reminded of who the players are, who the villain may be (remember, this is a mystery, and it's still too early for the big reveal), and the lengths to which the villain will go to keep the truth, and the dark secrets that conceal it, buried.

Is this instinct, or is it the outcome of a writer choosing to design his story according to a principle? The truth is, it doesn't matter. As I stated earlier, the reader doesn't care about the author's process, or even which principles the author believes in or doesn't believe in. They only care about the efficacy of the story through the author's choices.

Instinct can take you there, when instinct has been honed by, and informed by, the core essences of the principles and criteria that will also take you there. When you allow yourself to be vulnerable to the highest truths about storytelling, it all becomes the same wonderful thing: great stories by authors who understand how they become great.

19 Criteria for the Midpoint

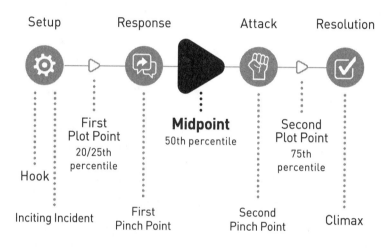

Setup	Response		Attack	Resolution

Midpoint
50th percentile

First Plot Point
20/25th percentile

Second Plot Point
75th percentile

Hook

Inciting Incident

First Pinch Point

Second Pinch Point

Climax

Introduce hero; set-up, foreshadow stakes and forthcoming quest (arc); inciting incidents

Hero reacts to the change resulting from First Plot Point; antagonist presence felt or observed

Hero proactively reacts; villain ramps up, too. The story moves faster, goes deeper, but isn't resolved.

Hero steps up, steps in, confronts, resolves; ultimate confrontation; post-story state (consequences) are shown as final beat.

Other than perhaps some authors at the very beginning of their journey (I've read their initial stories, so I know this to be truth), few argue that commercial fiction is not a process of an evolving narrative. A story is expected to twist and turn, exposing the realities in play bit by excruciating bit. This is true and becomes a criteria in virtually any genre, including literary fiction. Within the language of story structure, the dramatic through-line, or arc (the plot), has what amounts to a series of shifting contexts.

One of the most useful shifts, and a key essence of classic story structure, takes place in the very middle of your story.

CRITERIA FOR THE MIDPOINT SHIFT

Don't mistake the brevity of the criteria here (which are minimal when compared to, say, the FPP) as an indication of a lesser role of essential presence. Among the weight-bearing foundations of story, the Midpoint shift is the one around which everything pivots. When one refers to the most important moment in a story, the Midpoint can give the FPP a run for its money. That said, it's actually a moot argument, because both are essential to the story's efficacy.

- **MIDPOINT CRITERIA #1: LOCATION, LOCATION, LOCATION.** That says it all. After an effective FPP launch of the core dramatic arc, writers aim the story at the Midpoint—the target sweet spot used to shift the story into a higher gear on multiple fronts—which is the precise *middle* of the narrative, whether measured by pages or word count. The Midpoint will transform the Part 2 wandering hero into the Part 3 proactive hero, who is now ready to more fully and productively attack the problem. As you begin to notice and perhaps analyze published novels, you'll find that of all the key milestone moments in the structural paradigm, the Midpoint most reliably adheres to the optimal location that bears its name.
- **MIDPOINT CRITERIA #2: THE MIDPOINT IMPARTS NEW INFORMATION TO THE STORY.** The mode of delivery is often a single moment within a scene—very often the final line of a chapter or the last line of

dialogue—but it can also be delivered with a more layered exposition within a scene. This is something the reader is shown, but sometimes the author chooses to keep the hero in the dark, without the benefit of this information, for a while longer in order to elevate the level of tension (the threat may have been right next to the hero all along, in the guise of an ally, and now the reader sees this, but the hero doesn't).

When the reader knows something the hero doesn't, gripping tension is the result. It's not a criteria by any means, but it's an available strategy, especially in thrillers.

- **MIDPOINT CRITERIA #3: THIS NEW INFORMATION SHIFTS THE CONTEXT OF THE STORY.** Sometimes it discloses new information, which can shock as it shifts the story in a completely different direction. Or it can expand on or bring a new perspective to existing information, shifting the way the hero understands and reacts to it (see the case study below).

New information can arrive at the Midpoint when something is discovered, or it can be something that *happens* (in a mystery, someone else may be killed, with more clarity and implication this time), or *changes* naturally (snow melts to reveal something previously hidden). Or it can manifest through the *consequence* of an action (one character rats out another), taken either by characters or by an organization or institution not directly related to the story (like a bomb dropping in a foreign land, triggering a military response in the hero's home country). Or, in a love story, the smell of perfume on the collar of a spouse who has just returned from a business trip.

The reveal of new information or perspective at the Midpoint results in a shifted awareness within the hero, which influences what they believe and what they decide or do as a result. This awareness (or action taken from it) need not be immediate; it can be understood and responded to a bit later, even though the *reader* is now aware.

The net effect is a story that kicks into higher gear. The context is different now. It begins a convergence of the path of the hero and that of the villain, because the hero has (at the point of realization) more to go on.

I first encountered the principle of the Midpoint decades ago, in my reading of Syd Field's book, *Screenplay: The Foundations of Screenwriting* (highly recommend). I was also studying and analyzing storytelling in general, which is where I stumbled across it as real-world example of one of these principles within a story I'd already experienced.

The story was *Coma*, a 1977 novel by Robin Cook (a practicing surgeon who discovered the principles of story structure by analyzing two hundred bestsellers to learn what they had in common; this was before Syd Field summarized it for us all), and later, a major Hollywood film by Michael Crichton. The story unfolds in a hospital beset by a sudden rash of patients dying of complications during routine surgeries, the kind that don't normally end up in a morgue. The hero (played by Genevieve Bujold in the film) is one of the doctors on staff, who is heartbroken when one of her close friends dies from complications from an abortion procedure. Shortly thereafter a patient she had come to know and like dies during a routine knee operation after an athletic injury (played by Tom Selleck in the film; he made a great corpse). She suspects something is wrong and begins to look for clues in places she wouldn't normally be welcome to investigate. Her boss (played by Michael Douglas in the film) advises her along this path, promising his full support if she can come up with something actionable. Meanwhile, patients continue to die at an alarming rate.

The death of her friend was a mid-Part 1 inciting incident that served to set up the forthcoming FPP. The death of the Tom Selleck character *was* that FPP, because it thrust the hero down a path of no return as she set out to learn the truth. The First Pinch Point happens in the middle of Part 2 (all of these spot-on in alignment with the principles of mission-driven writing), when she has a near-miss accident that she suspects was not an accident at all.

Now for the Midpoint (spoilers ahead) ...

... which shows that none of this is the product of a streak of bad luck for her, or random choices the author made for her. She discovers that this is a dark conspiracy, in which the newly dead patients have

Great Stories Don't Write Themselves

their organs harvested and sold on the black market, with the surgeons involved taking a healthy cut. The hero shares her findings with her supportive boss (Douglas), who is appropriately concerned. But—I'm guessing you're way ahead of me here—it is revealed at what turns out to be the Midpoint that *he has been in on it all along.* He is a key part of the conspiracy and the cover-up. He's been feeding her proximity to the truth to the bad guys, who are now about to eliminate her upon his instruction.

It's an emotional blow to the reader and the film audience, but not to the hero herself. At least not yet. Because the Midpoint reveals this pertinent information *only* to the audience, leading us to escalate our empathy right along with the dramatic tension it creates.

That's a classic Midpoint. After understanding what I'd read in the novel and seen in the film, I couldn't ignore it or unsee it going forward in the novels I read and the movies I watched. And in turn, it quickly became part of not only my process, but my core instinct, which always appreciates a little real-world validation before giving up its claims to genius or the communing with muses.

Here's one more proving example, quickly rendered.

The Midpoint of *My Sister's Grave* occurs at the bottom of page 200, when a key witness warns Tracy that if she keeps pressing forward on her current path she will find herself in great danger. Which means the truth, and the perpetrators of that threat, are closer to her than she'd suspected, and perhaps come from precisely who she suspected. Where she had been fueled by suspicion, now she moves forward empowered by truth. It's an almost dead-on perfect landing at the target fiftieth percentile, based on 402 total pages. (For you math geeks, that's the 49.75th-and-change percentage mark.)

The Midpoint: the same, but different.

Notice, too, that the Midpoint shift seems to mirror the exact same criteria as those that, other than location, apply to the two major plot points and the pinch points. This is one of those truths that may only be half true, half of the time. Yes, the Midpoint can do the same things as the FPP (via changing the course of the story), and a pinch point (pointing out the source of threat and antagonism). But the Midpoint isn't constrained to those narrower lanes. The Midpoint can be *any* type of information that changes the story—either by moving the existing core story forward or changing it completely. With historical novels and time-travel stories, for example, the Midpoint can put us in a different decade or century. It can take characters out of play (however you want to define what that implies), or change the rules of the game (a human is revealed to actually be something other than human), or change the characters' uniforms in the middle of the game. Just like that boss in the *Coma* example we saw earlier.

Within the lexicon of learning and teaching how to plot a novel, the Midpoint has taken on a weightier and growing respect as a story beat worth understanding. It is the classic *plot twist*, whereas the FPP could be argued to be more plot inception than twist. The logic is solid—if you work from a completed version of a premise that meets all eight of the criteria shown earlier (in Chapter 8), it is an organic jump to conjure a means of changing the hero's path and awareness using a dramatic proposition. And from there, plotting how the story gets there and where it goes from there. This would seem to be more comfortable for story planners than pantsers, but the application of a context-shifting Midpoint is an essential story beat, regardless of process.

Notice, though, how you can't really get there until you have a premise to frame the entire proposition. That's a full-circle realization—one that I hope has sunk in. Premise, and the criteria for it, is the pot of gold from which all story blessings flow. The Midpoint, when you get it right, is where the reader will look up and say to anyone nearby, "Wow, I did *not* see that coming."

When that happens, you've got them right where you want them. Perhaps even better, you've got your story right where you need it.

20 Criteria for the Part 3 Hero's Attack

....

The Third Quartile of the Story

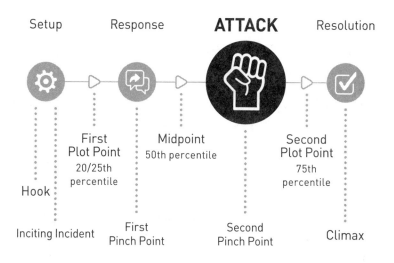

Setup   Response   **ATTACK**   Resolution

First
Plot Point
20/25th
percentile

Midpoint
50th percentile

Second
Plot Point
75th
percentile

Hook

Inciting Incident

First
Pinch Point

Second
Pinch Point

Climax

Introduce hero; set-up, foreshadow stakes and forthcoming quest (arc); inciting incidents

Hero reacts to the change resulting from First Plot Point; antagonist presence felt or observed

Hero proactively reacts; villain ramps up, too. The story moves faster, goes deeper, but isn't resolved.

Hero steps up, steps in, confronts, resolves; ultimate confrontation; post-story state (consequences) are shown as final beat.

It's fair to say that up to the Midpoint shift in the story, the term "hero," as applied to your protagonist, may be less than obvious or clear. He's been wandering, stumbling, getting socked in the face (literally or metaphorically) for the last 200 pages or so. *Helpless* or *victim* are better adjectives here. That's because back in Part 1, the protagonist—not yet having earned the nametag of *hero*—wasn't yet fully engaged, if at all, with the macro-story's core dramatic question and its inherent need and threat. Your protagonist was an innocent relative to the forthcoming dramatic tension, a metaphoric orphan from what lies ahead. But because of the FPP, he is an innocent or an orphan no longer. He is in the thick of it, getting pummeled as things seem to get worse and worse in the second quartile block of scenes, where contextually she is wandering through options, hazards, and choices.

After the FPP launches the hero into that core dramatic macro-arc (thus transitioning the story from Part 1 into the Part 2 scenes), beginning with a block of scenes that show the experience of the protagonist's response to the call to action, we aren't yet seeing what you would normally describe as overtly *heroic* decisions and actions. If for no other reason than the protagonist under fire and pressure doesn't yet possess all of the information necessary to formulate a heroic response.

It's high time we get the hero into the game in a more meaningful way. That's what the criteria for the Part 3 block of scenes do for the story.

As we learned in the last chapter, the Midpoint launches the players and the reader into the new context for the Part 3 quartile, which is a more proactive attack on the problem at hand. It is here in the third quartile, with its new *warrior* character context, that the *hero* begins to earn the right to put that label on her name tag.

The facilitation of a shift into warrior mode

Nothing about either the dramatic or character arcs should be random or simply inevitable. Which means something needs to emerge as a catalytic force—something that when perceived, or thrust upon the hero, shifts him into a higher, more proactively productive gear. It's like a sick person is suddenly on the mend. A fighter without a weapon finally finds one. A person without a friend encounters an ally. You could say that until the Midpoint, the story was happening *to the hero*, and now, beginning with the first scenes in Part 3, the *hero is happening to the story*.

In Part 3, the hero becomes a *warrior*, if you will. It may not click at first, and certainly, the story has more surprises to offer, but now the readers have even more exciting things to root for, manifesting through decisions and actions and opportunities, because there is hope and strategy for an outcome that allows our hero to resolve the problem and fulfill the quest. With enough courage and cleverness, a new road to success awaits, even as the villain is upping her own game in the meantime.

But let's not get ahead of ourselves. An upped game from both sides is the stuff of Part 4. Let's linger here in Part 3 to make sure the groundwork we are laying delivers a vicarious experience saturated with emotional resonance.

CRITERIA FOR THE PART 3 ATTACK (WARRIOR) QUARTILE

Get ready for your weary protagonist to get her hero on.

- **PART 3 CRITERIA #1: THE HERO'S PART 3 DECISIONS AND ACTIONS LEAN INTO THE PROACTIVE**, (rather the *reactive* context of Part 2), leveraging new information delivered at the Midpoint. This shifts the context of the entire second half of the story. Because of new information put into play at the Midpoint, the path ahead is now clarified and more strategic. The hero moves forward in accordance with that higher understanding. The pace quickens. The need for action may be more urgent now because the threat has escalated and may be closer at hand. Whereas the context in Part 2 was responding to what happens, the Part 3 scenes show a context of attacking the problem.

But, as they say, it ain't over yet. Because the villain may be aware that the hero is now more woke and in response ups her own aggressive effort to block the hero's path. Or not, the hero may simply up the ante, by virtue of showing up differently. In either case, confrontation becomes inevitable.

- **PART 3 CRITERIA #2: IN PART 3 THE HERO BUILDS ON PRIOR DEFEATS, FEARS, AND LESSONS LEARNED.** This combines with the new Midpoint information to inform the hero's decisions and actions going forward. If nothing else, the hero may have learned things about the antagonist or villain, the situation, the story world, or about themselves (inner demons surfacing under pressure) in the Part 2 scenes that came before. Part 3 is where she applies that learning, and the new information, to show up with greater courage, keener strategy, a bold opportunity-seizing aggression, and the general proactivity that redefines the hero's journey and quest. In historic battle stories, this is where the hero attacks the castle of the villain. If Part 2 was imbued with a sense of hopelessness, Part 3 is where the reader begins to sense that maybe there is a pathway toward success, after all, along with a sense that there is a willingness to pay the price to get there.

- **PART 3 CRITERIA #3:** In the midst of hope and higher levels of learning and efficacy, the Part 3 pathway becomes steeper and the threat darker and more urgent—because the villain isn't backing off. An easy mistake here is to show your hero coming out swinging and succeeding early in Part 3, but the rounding of the corner needs to be wider and more fraught with setbacks than these criteria might imply.

Both Parts 2 and 3 are designed to show the hero plodding treacherous, even torturous ground, the difference being a more hapless response (Part 2) versus newfound proactivity (in Part 3) that is more courageous and strategic, based on a greater awareness of the problem and the nature of the villain. It's like a team that is far behind at halftime, but they come out really strong afterward, and even though they're doing well, they're still chasing the win.

This new knowledge eventually steers the hero toward hope rather than fueling immediate success, but as the author of this sequence you need to show your hero *earning* whatever success comes as a result.

- **PART 3 CRITERIA #4: DRAMA, STAKES, AND PACE ESCALATE WITHIN THE PART 3 BLOCK OF SCENES.** This is the consequence of the preceding criteria. Within the eight to twelve scenes in Part 3 (a number which varies greatly, according to scene and macro-story length), you may have as many as three different dramatic sequences that take the story deeper into the dramatic proposition. These sequences should include at least as many hero-driven attempts to further her goals as there are villain-driven strategies.

- **PART 3 CRITERIA #5: PART 3 INCLUDES WHATEVER MECHANICAL, CONTEXTUAL, AND SITUATIONAL SET-UP** sequences are required to put the forthcoming Second Plot Point (SPP)—which is the turning point between Parts 3 and 4, where context will shift yet again—into play. Any necessary foreshadowing that will inform Part 4 beyond the SPP should also be woven into these Part 3 scenes. If the walls of the villain's fortress have a weakness, we should have seen that foreshadowed earlier, before the charge commences.

- **PART 3 CRITERIA #6: IT'S TIME TO UNLEASH YOUR MAIN CHARACTER'S INNER HERO.** Not everything your hero decides and does in Part 3 will work, or at least be fully successful. Your villain isn't giving it up easily. But, your mission here is to allow us to experience the inner heroic essence of your hero through those decisions and actions. There is an art to this; it isn't an on-the-nose proposition. The Midpoint shifts may not have been good news; they may add to the threat and pressure. Either way, though, your hero now has something to leverage or use that puts him back into the game in a bigger, more urgent, more meaningful way than before.

- **PART 3 CRITERIA #7: THE FINAL PART 3 STORY BEAT (SCENE) IS OFTEN A LULL.** This is an all-seems-lost context, even though the hero has emerged as courageous and heroic. Sometimes things just don't work out, and it appears, for a moment, that this is the case for our hero. It's critical that the villain ups the ante as well, and the net result of that might find your hero in a corner. She will come out fighting, of course, but that's what Part 4 is all about. The author is always pulling the strings of the reader's emotional engagement, and when you end Part 3 with something dire, that gives you even more room for your hero to rise to the occasion later, when the final quartile brings it all to a resolution.

A fresh case study to witness Part 3's context at work

Let's take a look at *The Girl on the Train* (again, spoilers follow), a massively character-driven psychological thriller with three different unreliable first-person narrators that keep the reader on her toes and often in the dark. This 2015 novel was a #1 bestseller by British author Paula Hawkins.

There's the setup. We meet protagonist (Hero? We're not quite sure for the duration of the story) Rachel Watson (played by Emily Blunt in the film) in her bleak post-divorce life, now an unemployed alcoholic who has burned all her bridges and has little by way of hopes or dreams. To give the illusion of having a job to which she commutes, she boards the same local train each morning, sitting in the same seat to gaze out the same window every time, marveling as the real world whisks by, vicariously gazing at beautiful and perfect lives unfolding within all these beautiful and perfect houses. One of them was hers before she blew up her life and got divorced.

And so, she drinks every day, to excess, as her life slips even further into darkness.

Thus begins a very intimate narrative full of flashbacks and expositional reverie from all three of the main players, which include Rachel, her husband's new wife, and the babysitter they employ. Other characters, who become critical to the convoluted plot, show up in these little memoirs which add up to a layered murder mystery. This deception goes on for six months, riding the train every morning, drinking in town all day, then riding the train back to her lowly abode near her old life—and nobody is the wiser. Because nobody is paying any attention to Rachel Watson.

One day Rachel sees something disturbing from her seat on the train (a key inciting incident that looks and smells like a FPP, but isn't, if nothing else than because it's too early within the exposition). On the balcony of the house three doors down from where she used to live, she notices Megan, the babysitter employed by her husband and his new wife, Anna—Megan is married, by the way, and Anna is pregnant—canoodling on the balcony of her house with a man that Rachel suspects is not her husband. She isn't sure who it is. A few days later, Megan goes missing. Rachel goes to the police to report what she saw but is turned away as a crackpot. After making waves in other places, the FPP arrives (dead on at the twenty-first percentile, on page 67 of 326 total pages) when an old friend calls to tell Rachel that the police are at her house, looking for her. Suddenly she is a person of interest in the disappearance of Megan (which layers on the threat and tension for her), because she is the only witness who came forward to say she'd noticed something not right in Megan's life.

At the Midpoint (on page 158; if you do the math, just prior to the optimal fiftieth percentile target), Megan's body is found. The story-altering news is that she was pregnant when she was killed. That goes to motive, and it connects to virtually anyone on that list of players. The police come for Rachel, suddenly very interested in what she has to say. Her ex-husband; his new wife, Anna; Megan's rough-around-the-edges husband; and Megan's shrink (as well as two different strangers Rachel meets on the train) are all in play as possibly threatening, complicit villains. But the spotlight is on Rachel, and only she can get herself out from under the glare of suspicion.

This is all context for how the Part 3 quartile plays out. It's a new context of the hero attacking the problem, fueled by new knowledge that narrows her vision toward the truth. Rachel is not going down without a fight, but now she is fighting for truth and justice for the murder of Megan and her unborn baby. It's a fight not only for justice, but for her own resurrection of a person of worth and purpose. Her proactivity takes the form of cultivating relationships with Megan's husband, who is angry to the point of violence, with the victim's shrink, who had an affair with Megan, and with the police who have not quite cleared her and aren't patient with her involvement. Gradually the shadows of the truth become evident, especially in the minds of astute readers of mysteries and psychological thrillers, among which *The Girl on the Train* is one of the best.

Part 3 ends at the SPP (on page 246 at the seventy-sixth percentile mark). Notice that all of these key transitional milestones appear as if Paula Hawkins herself had invented this structural paradigm; she didn't. She just applied it to her story and tapped into its inherent dramatic potential. Perhaps she did so instinctually, perhaps during a revision, or perhaps it was something she learned to do.

That SPP was forensic verification that Megan's widowed husband was not the father of the child that died with her, which is a game-changer (the consistent hallmark of both plot points). This ignites a fuse that burns a path to the feet of the real father, who, amidst a continuing question as to who might have killed Megan, is suddenly an injured animal in the headlights coming his way, with Rachel (this is a metaphoric teeing up of the resolution) behind the wheel.

Killer stuff. And an example of how once you are aware of the principles of these criteria-driven story elements, the best way to learn how to use them is to verify and witness their magic in the bestselling work that owes its success to the author's abilities to wield their power—power that is ultimately available to all who seek to write stories that work, simply by leveraging the criteria that apply.

21 Criteria for the Second Plot Point

Transitioning from Part 3 to Part 4

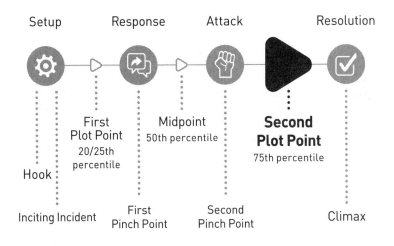

| Setup | Response | Attack | Resolution |

Hook

Inciting Incident

First Plot Point
20/25th percentile

First Pinch Point

Midpoint
50th percentile

Second Pinch Point

Second Plot Point
75th percentile

Climax

Introduce hero; set-up, foreshadow stakes and forthcoming quest (arc); inciting incidents

Hero reacts to the change resulting from First Plot Point; antagonist presence felt or observed

Hero proactively reacts; villain ramps up, too. The story moves faster, goes deeper, but isn't resolved.

Hero steps up, steps in, confronts, resolves; ultimate confrontation; post-story state (consequences) are shown as final beat.

While not impossible, it's very difficult to render an effective Second Plot Point if the actual climax of the story—the moment of resolution—isn't completely clear in the mind of the author. That is a paradoxical truth, because sometimes it's nearly impossible to know the precise machinations of the ending—as opposed to a general intention for an ending, which is much easier to envision at the premise level, where it belongs, if nothing else, as a placeholder—until you get there in the manuscript.

Until you know, writing toward a placeholder idea for how the story resolves is an empowering strategy to employ. But most likely, when you get to this SPP moment, you will have landed on a significantly solid plan for how it all ends.

Earlier I suggested that many authors—most, in fact—whether they consider themselves planners or pantsers, end up applying at least a little of the other process to get to that point. The fourth quartile resolution sequence of the story is when that duality of process is most likely to happen. There are fewer criteria to apply in this block of scenes than any of the others because the story's own unique path toward the climax and the nature of what the hero has experienced and learned becomes the applicable context for that ending. The SPP delivers new information, or a new perspective that arises from that story point, that will shift the story into this new context.

It's like rounding third base. There is very little advice you can give the base runner who is turning that corner at full speed and heading for home, other than waving him on and don't forget to slide if you must. The hope is that, by this point, you'll have sufficient context and raw grist to find an ingenious way of turning the story toward its ultimate conclusion with a killer SPP.

CRITERIA FOR THE SECOND PLOT POINT

The contextual application of the SPP is different than that of the FPP or the Midpoint. All three, as a functional mission statement, change the story. The FPP actually launches the dramatic arc. The Midpoint shifts the nature of the hero's experience from responder to warrior. And the SPP uses all that has happened thus far to inject yet another new piece of expositional information in a way that doesn't so much change it materially, but focuses it on what will become converging paths of the hero's quest and the antagonist's agenda, with whatever new information serves that intention. Often this is some kind of final barrier dissolving or a teeing-up mechanism working its magic, and the result is an open path for the hero to make the ending happen. Remember in *Butch Cassidy and the Sundance Kid*, when the posse chasing them seems to turn tail and give up the chase? That was the SPP of that story. It occurs on page 134 of the 186-page script, which is the seventy-second percentile (a bit early, but the SPP nonetheless). Butch himself virtually announces this story shift when, staring at the retreating Corregidors, he says, "Isn't that a beautiful sight? We're back in business, boys and girls, just like old days." Which begins a sequence of bold new bank robberies that sets up the ending confrontation to come.

- **SECOND PLOT POINT CRITERIA #1: THE OPTIMAL PLACEMENT OF THE SPP** is the seventy-fifth percentile mark, give or take. Many stories cheat that pivot point on both sides, but usually by only a percentage point or two.
- **SECOND PLOT POINT CRITERIA #2: THE MISSION OF THE SPP IS TO YET AGAIN SHIFT THE CONTEXT OF THE STORY,** from the hero-attack mode of the Part 3 scenes to a Part 4 story-resolution context. New or shifted information informs the Part 4 scenes. The new information given at the SPP is something that may send either or both sides hurdling toward an inevitable endgame.
- **SECOND PLOT POINT CRITERIA #3: THE SECOND PLOT POINT IS THE LAST POINT AT WHICH MAJOR NEW STORY INFORMATION APPEARS** (*other than* the moment of a surprise twist at the ending, which should, in retrospect, have had some nuance of foreshadowing or teeing up in play, something that legitimizes it when put into the story). Once again, the players will react from within the context of this new information and from within the context of who we know them to be (you can't get away with suddenly imbuing either the hero or villain with new capabilities or powers at this point simply

to facilitate an ending), to whatever extent they are aware of it. Full awareness of all variables of the framework for the end, however, is not a requirement. A character can react from surprise as much as the reader can. The author can play this however he chooses to either inform or deceive the characters.

- **SECOND PLOT POINT CRITERIA #4: THE PART 3-ENDING LULL IS LEFT BEHIND.** The means of *emerging from the lull* often becomes the raw grist, as well as the mission, of the SPP. Whatever happened at the end of Part 3 that imparts a sense of hopelessness, just prior to the SPP itself—often an effective manipulation of the reader's emotions—should be logically resolved, usually through new information or better choices for the hero, which are usually informed by that new information. This need to resolve a lull creates context for the specific nature of the SPP in the moment and the method of its revelation. The SSP is, in fact, what re-energizes the hero's quest after what may seem to have been an all-is-lost lull.

In a thriller—even a character-driven one like *Butch Cassidy and the Sundance Kid*—the SPP is often the moment at which the final confrontation sequence becomes inevitable.

Or, as was the case in *The Silence of the Lambs*, which has an SPP showing Hannibal Lector's bloody escape back into the real world, where he tauntingly reconnects with Clarice Starling for a final game of cat and mouse.

Notice how, in both stories, those SPPs change the story context without major alterations or additions such as new characters or new story world rules. It's the same story, only now it is evolving—via new or expanded information and a new perspective—into a focus that will lead to resolution.

In Robert Dugoni's *My Sister's Grave*, we see a classic lull in the scene that immediately precedes the SPP. Two of the suspected villains are commiserating about the most recent turn of events, in which it appears that the person they had framed and thus helped convict of the murder of Tracy Crosswhite's sister is about to be released. Tracy and her lawyer have been successful in bringing the case back to court to appeal for a new trial, which may or may not happen, even after the prisoner's release by order of a local judge. Tracy seems outnumbered and outgunned here, hence, the lull.

The SPP in that novel is itself a reference, in the next scene, made during an introspective reverie that Tracy is having on the stormy night of the judge's decision. It seems that despite everyone assuming it would take a few days for the prisoner to be released, the judge has already ruled on it. The convicted killer is suddenly, unexpectedly back out on the street, with significant implications as to the dark consequences that might ensue, including—according to the speculation of those two other suspects in the prior lull scene—that he won't be brought to trial a second time. Those dark consequences are the stuff of the Part 4 resolution quartile, creating a convergence of paths toward an ultimate confrontation that will resolve the entire story.

Surprise and high drama await. Or as I like to say, "hijinks ensue." But make no mistake, this SPP or another version of it (because within ten novels you may find ten flavors of second plot point) leads to the altered context of the remaining story. It needs to trigger a new situation before that fuse, leading to a convergence of several duplicitous paths, can be lit.

22 Criteria for the Part 4 Resolution

The Fourth Quartile of the Story

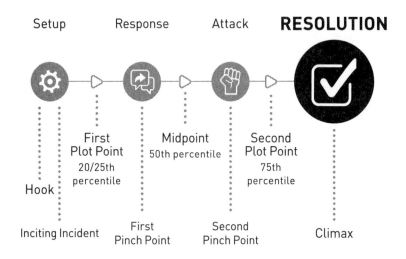

Setup   Response   Attack   **RESOLUTION**

Hook

First Plot Point
20/25th percentile

Inciting Incident

First Pinch Point

Midpoint
50th percentile

Second Pinch Point

Second Plot Point
75th percentile

Climax

Introduce hero; set-up, foreshadow stakes and forthcoming quest (arc); inciting incidents

Hero reacts to the change resulting from First Plot Point; antagonist presence felt or observed

Hero proactively reacts; villain ramps up, too. The story moves faster, goes deeper, but isn't resolved.

Hero steps up, steps in, confronts, resolves; ultimate confrontation; post-story state (consequences) are shown as final beat.

Writing a novel or a screenplay is nothing if not a long-distance race. If you've done it right, you've varied your pace across the course of the run, swim, or in our case, the unspooling of a novel. You've run the race from a strategy, all of it leading to an endgame. As with a long-distance run, when you see the finish line there is only one strategy that remains: you go all out. You leave it all on the road.

Nobody ever won a distance race by *just running.*

The need for a strategy applies to the homestretch as much as anywhere else, even if pantsing is your chosen process. Because you need to know precisely when to hit the gas. The essence of successful pantsing is, in fact, the discovery of a solid premise and the arc that fleshes it out—the earlier the better—and then pouring it into the framework of structure. There should be enough left in the tank for a full-out acceleration that is sustainable until you break the tape, which could include the sudden intervention of the unexpected. You have been playing your reader the entire time, and now it's time to make the finish as big for them as it will be for you.

The Part 4 Quartile ... let us count the ways.

There are infinite ways to build an effective Part 4, to the extent that it defies a universal form.

There is, however, a universal context in play: Each scene in the Part 4 quartile exists to lead into, to tee up, the climactic scenes and any resolution that comes after them, perhaps in an epilogue-like closing scene. And while that may feel a bit like your coach leaving the stadium before you run through the gate for that final marathon lap, it's actually your race to lose. Only you know what you have put into play. No matter what your process, you have implemented certain arcs and variables and questions that need to be answered, and in the mind of a professional writer there was never any intention of leaving them unresolved.

The reader gets one ending. But often the author may have considered several alternate ending sequences, some of them perhaps quite viable. The way your novel spirals and converges and then collides with the climatic moment is a choice as much as it is a design. It is not something that is framed by specific criteria. (There are a few criteria, but they relate to reader perception rather than specific nuances of scenes.)

The goal isn't to land on "an" ending, but to determine the *best possible* ending for the story you have built to that point.

THE CRITERIA FOR THE PART 4 RESOLUTION SCENES

While not a criteria, per se, as the author *you* get to decide if you offer up a happy ending, or not. (Unless you are writing a classic romance for a romance label, in which case you are obliged to give your reader a Happily Ever After, or HEA.) You get to decide if the ending will be tidy or messy. If there will be clear and total resolution or a partial answer that leaves other elements hanging. You get to decide if your ending leaves room for a sequel (maybe the novel didn't begin as a series, but now you see potential in bringing back these characters or this story world for another go around) and how to leave that door tantalizingly open.

That's why structure is *not* formula. Because *you* get to decide how the story plays.

- **PART 4 RESOLUTION CRITERIA #1: THESE SCENES ALL CONTRIBUTE TO SOME FORM OR LEVEL OF STORY RESOLUTION,** including the plot movement and character machinations required for it to play clearly and dramatically. You aren't building the plot here as much as you are resolving it. After the SPP, with a surprise ending twist notwithstanding, you really can't inject new information into the story. The characters must make the best of what is on the table.
- **PART 4 RESOLUTION CRITERIA #2: THE BEST ENDINGS OFFER SOME SORT OF SURPRISE TWIST.** Even if the ending is inevitable (also your call), your reader will appreciate the unexpected in the path leading to that point. Most of the time this requires some form of foreshadowing earlier in the story, at any appropriate point within any of the three preceding story blocks (of the four contextual parts).

    Remember *The Sixth Sense*? Bruce Willis discovers (warning, spoiler alert), right at the finish line, that he has, in fact, been a dead guy all along, investigating his own paranormal phenomena. While

Robert McKee says this is one of the biggest sellouts of any ending in Hollywood, viewers were nonetheless knocked out of their chairs, lending iconic status to this story primarily because of the ending.

- **PART 4 RESOLUTION CRITERIA #3: THE KEY TO AN EFFECTIVE ENDING IS EMOTIONAL RESONANCE.** Leave your readers with an emotional response that fulfills their hopes for the character, or on the flip side (again, your call), realizes their darkest (or worse) fears in that regard. Pay off what you've asked them to root for or against. It doesn't need to be immediately clear—endings that send people into chat rooms to debate the ending have their own sort of power—but it does need to cause the reader to have a reaction.

- **PART 4 RESOLUTION CRITERIA #4: THE FINAL MACHINATIONS THAT SET UP THE ENDING CAN BE EXTREME.** Because your hero or the villain might be desperate, and desperation leads to drastic measures, the ending doesn't have to be logical or safe, though it does need to make sense in the story world you have created. The less obvious it is, the better, provided you don't cross the line to suggest something absurd. This is a risk area for authors, because an author's stretch of reason can be a reader's absurdity.

- **PART 4 RESOLUTION CRITERIA #5: THE GROWTH-END (OUTCOME) OF THE HERO'S CHARACTER ARC** manifests within the decisions and actions taken that facilitate the ending. Lessons learned and applied here connect to things that have transpired earlier in the story.

- **PART 4 RESOLUTION CRITERIA #6: THE HERO NEEDS TO BE A PRIMARY CATALYST—IF NOT *THE* PRIMARY CATALYST—IN THE RESOLUTION OF THE STORY.** The hero can't be rescued and shouldn't be allowed to simply observe the story's ending at someone else's hands. There are two exceptions to this criterion: The hero should not simply observe the story's ending unless he is responsible for putting all of the elements in place that will lead to such an outcome. Or unless the hero is dead—this part isn't known as the martyr quartile for nothing—which is fine, providing that it was the hero who put all the pieces of the resolution into play before dying.

One story I was hired to evaluate and coach showed a proactive hero putting all the pieces of a major confrontation into play but was arrested before the final confrontation went down. He was sitting in a jail cell as his minions executed his plan. All the emotional weight of the story was on that character's shoulders, and he was wearing an orange jumpsuit when he needed to be out there leading the charge. Don't make this mistake in your stories.

- **PART 4 RESOLUTION CRITERIA #7: THE MORE COURAGE AND WIT SUMMONED BY THE HERO** in the process of facilitating the ending, the better.

- **PART 4 RESOLUTION CRITERIA #8: AT ALL COSTS, AVOID A DEUS-EX-MACHINA** element in the lead-up to, and the execution of, the story's resolution. *Deus ex machina* means "God in the machine," referring to acts of God or unlikely coincidences playing into the hero's intentions in an unplanned or unforeseeable way. No convenient coincidences (deus ex machina) allowed.

- **PART 4 RESOLUTION CRITERIA #9: PLAY INTO THE *SURVIVOR* CODE** (from the reality television series) with your ending: The hero *outwits, outlasts, and outplays* her opponent (the antagonist), rather than simply meeting the opposition in an alley and beating him senseless.

- **PART 4 RESOLUTION CRITERIA #10: AVOID SERMONS AND SUMMARIES TELLING THE READER WHAT IT ALL MEANS.** Don't wax wordy the inner thoughts of your hero as he basks in the dust of what has happened, and don't provide a narrative manifesto that suggests deeper interpretation. Rather, *show* the state of your post-climax story world, via action and interaction, within a concluding scene that depicts the consequences of what was chosen and has just occurred. Allow the readers to define, for themselves, what it all means and implies, both in terms of the story and how it might relate to their reality.

- **PART 4 RESOLUTION CRITERIA #11: EVEN IF ONLY THROUGH A QUICK MENTION, SHOW YOUR PROTAGONIST IN AN AFTER-STORY STATE.** This is part of the job of that final, post-climactic scene. Back at the beginning of the story, you plucked your hero out of her life, interrupting it with a sudden need to put it all on hold and pursue an urgent need or goal, and now that goal has been met, or at least the situation has been resolved. The hero now returns to *normal*, which will likely be different than before, if nothing else than because the hero is different than before. Even if the hero goes back to the same daily routine and environment (on to the next case for a cop or agent), there should be some sense of change, of being affected or regretful or satisfied.

- **PART 4 RESOLUTION CRITERIA #12: AVOID THE CLASSIC ROOKIE PANTSER TRAP RELATIVE TO ENDINGS.** Which is, you've organically written yourself into a corner, and when you reach the endgame you have ... nothing. At least, nothing that meets these criteria. To avoid this, observe the next point.
- **BONUS BEST PRACTICE RESOLUTION CRITERIA: KNOW, OR AT LEAST COMMIT TO, THE ENDING OF THE STORY AS EARLY IN THE PROCESS AS POSSIBLE.** Prior to writing the draft, in fact. Which means, the ending is a key part of finishing your premise and your story plan, however you've gone about finding it. If you believe you *just can't write this way*—it's a choice and preference, rather than an issue of capability—make sure you have your story radar on alert during the drafting process, looking for an ending even when you are still hundreds of pages from reaching that point. Unless your story is, in fact, a journey toward the unknown (perhaps within a saga), you'll be frustrated arriving somewhere that hasn't been foreshadowed or imbued with dreams and goals on the part of the protagonist.

Resolution results from a chain of events.

Endings can be challenging to pull off, especially when your qualitative bar is high. It may seem paradoxical to suggest that the means of resolving a story is one of the most essential elements of story *planning*, while in the same breath acknowledge that it may be the most challenging phase of the story to envision. Within this paradox, the pantsing organic story developer may have what feels like an advantage, because the path toward that resolution is more specific and precise than a series of yellow stickies on a wall. It is a manuscript full of scenes that have led to this point. This is where instinct has its greatest role. You may find yourself needing to know it when you see it. The more you understand about story *physics*—the dramatic forces that elicit an emotional response within the reader—the better your odds.

Either way, the truth is inevitable: Endings are hard.

They are also critically important to the overall impact and success of the story.

Rare is the freshman law student who knows with certainty what kind of lawyer he will end up choosing to become, or what niche in the business world he will occupy. And yet, an *intention* has value—visualizing a solid ending as early as possible, and then using it as context as you write or plan toward it, setting things up for it as you progress—because it points destiny in a certain direction. So many things can come into play that influence what the endgame will look like. And sometimes, when the vision for an ending arrives when you are too far down the road, it can compromise all that you've done until that point.

Preparation has never been a bad investment, in life or in storytelling. Changing lanes is always an option, even when it forces you to backtrack to get turned in the right direction. But changing lanes on impulse, without looking in the mirror, can send you off a cliff.

And so it goes within story development, either planned or pantsed.

Case study: The Legendary Ending of *Night Fall* by Nelson DeMille

Here's a dirty little secret about the publishing business. Sometimes famous authors can get away with things the rest of us can't.

Nelson DeMille, for example (one of my personal writing heroes, despite what you are about to read), is one of the most popular commercial authors of the past few decades. Top ten, by any metric. In fact, his novel *Night Fall* was the book that nudged Dan Brown's *The Da Vinci Code* out of the No. 1 spot when it debuted on *The New York Times* bestseller list in December of 2004. Brown had owned that ranking for more than two years. *Night Fall* remained in the top spot for eleven weeks, when *The Da Vinci Code* won it back. It must have been a pretty amazing read to accomplish that, right? And it was, *if* the writing of Nelson DeMille and the integrity and humor of his iconic hero, John Corey, is your cup of tea. And *if* an alternative history of one of the greatest modern airline disasters is your cup of literature. Personally, I love that stuff. Alternative history is as conceptual as it gets.

However, as good as *Night Fall* was at delivering a narrative hero's quest slathered with thick layers of reader empathy, my theory is that DeMille got to the ending and wasn't sure where to go next, because the ending he chose violates a universal criteria (some readers and even a few professional reviewers loved it, which just goes to show that there are really no rules, after all). Which is a classic panster's paradox.

Here's how I see it: DeMille is an instinct-driven, research-reliant pantser which means he neither proves nor disproves pantsing as the preferred method for anyone else, just for his own work, which is the choice we all entertain. What he ended up doing is perhaps the most heinous, convenient, and against-all-odds contrivance of any bestselling novel in modern history. One that redefines the word *coincidence*. The entire Part 4 quartile of the novel was the arrangement of dominoes and choices that would lead the hero to a final, climactic moment, which splashes onto the page with a thud that resonated around the entire publishing world.

Night Fall was a speculative history based on the real-life conspiracy theory that TWA Flight 800, which exploded shortly after takeoff from JFK bound for Paris on July 17, 1996, killing all 230 souls on board, was actually shot out of the sky by a missile launched from a ship. Supposedly there were witnesses on the nearest shoreline who swear they saw tracers from the missiles heading skyward moments before the 747 exploded into a fireball that slowly sank toward the pitch-dark sea.

DeMille took that much, stirred in the loudest conspiracy theories, and he was off to the keyboard. All of the players in his novel, including the beloved hero from previous DeMille novels (Corey), find themselves part of the secrecy-riddled aftermath of the investigations that followed. The official report from the National Transportation Safety Board that investigated the incident and was endorsed by the FBI and the CIA, state the accident was the result of an electrical malfunction that sparked near the fuel lines, igniting a catastrophic chain of events.

Corey, of course, ever the rebellious hero (that's why readers love him), dives into the collision of self-interests and agendas against the wishes of his Federal Anti-Terrorist Task Force bosses, as well as those of the military and a plethora of various agencies, including the ones that investigated the accident. Of course, hijinks ensue, people are killed, evidence disappears, stories change, and generally it all descends into the cluster of chaos we've come to expect when final federal verdicts collide with popular mythologies and hypotheticals. (Personally, I'm not sure the story would have worked, even with DeMille's name on it, or at least as well as it did, had the core inciting incidents and story focus not been a real-life tragedy, after which some of the conspiracy theories that populate the narrative became quite loud.)

In the Part 4 quartile of DeMille's fiction, the hero has managed to get enough people on the same page relative to the story, and has gone to great lengths to arrange a gathering of all relevant players on a specific day, in a specific place, with irrefutable evidence in hand. The truth was about to be revealed to all.

That day was September 11, 2001. That place was the North Tower of the World Trade Center in New York City. The meeting was scheduled for 9:00 a.m.

Of course, the hero was stuck in traffic and called ahead to say he'd be late. About twenty minutes late, in fact. Late enough, as it turns out, to survive the day, but with nothing to show for his investigative work relative to TWA Flight 800, and no one left to back the truth.

In DeMille's resolution, the evidence, the proof of the conspiracy, including the identities of the guilty, as well as all the people who had the means and credibility to do something about it, all perished that day, shortly after 9:00 A.M. when terrorists flew two American Airlines Boeing jets into the towers of the World Trade Center, one after the other.

You know the rest of *that* story.

That's a deus ex machina on steroids.

Don't try this at home. Don't try it all, wherever you are. Because unless your name is Nelson DeMille or someone at that level, it will get you rejected at best, or laughed off the internet in the form of reviews of your self-published novel on Amazon. Rolling the dice in the pursuit of an exception is the worst odds bet you can make in a field so rigidly lined with lanes and predictable in its tastes.

As Pablo Picasso advises—stated earlier, but repeated and paraphrased again here, for relevance sake—*Learn the principles like a professional, so you can break them like an artist.*

DeMille rolled the dice and won, perhaps because of what Picasso advised, more likely because of his stature in the business. Whether he was artful or lucky, or if he got there because he was simply stuck, is another mystery that will never be fully revealed.

The Resolution of *My Sister's Grave*

Robert Dugoni's Part 4 quartile is a narrative mosaic brought into a final, emotionally resonant resolution for the reader. He switches between various points of view of the players, including some that don't survive the night, to show us a dark truth that is truly unexpected. I won't spoil it here. If you want to see all of this put to work within a novel that deserves the critical praise and commercial success it has garnered, my recommendation is that you read *My Sister's Grave* and observe and marvel at the principles and their contexts and transitions and forces at play. Read it as an analytic learning exercise, using the criteria you now possess as juxtaposition, with the assurance that you'll nonetheless experience the ride mystery readers come for.

That's the best way to become a criteria-driven novelist.

Or screenwriter, or short story writer, or any other writer that you might seek to become. You need to *know* certain principles and criteria in any field that requires the rendering of words to a blank screen or piece of paper. If you've read this far, you are deep into that learning.

Once you know it, you can't un-see it when you encounter it in the novels you read. Because in work that succeeds, it's always *there* in some artful form.

PART
IV

The Sum of the Parts

23 Criteria for Effective Scenes

Where planning and theory collide with reality

Once a story premise has been finalized and committed to, the writing of scenes becomes our purpose and our daily bread. Scenes that deliver the most visceral, immersive, emotionally resonant reading experience possible, given the parameters of the scene and its mission. Once we get beyond premise, scenes become our highest art and most essential core competency.

More so, even, than the prose that goes into them. Less than stellar scenes can sink a promising premise. This is where the gap between polished professional and aspiring newbie is most often found, and glaringly obvious.

The mission of a given scene is found in an understanding of how our scenes *exist in service to a higher purpose* than themselves. They serve a higher master, which is the macro-arc of the story in context to which block of the story it exists within. The enlightened author realizes that scenes do *not* stand alone as remote islands of literary art or backstory or life experience that isn't relevant to the *plot*. Too often, especially with newer writers, this mistake is omnipresent.

Everything we've covered thus far focuses on the macro-story. From premise to structure to the hero's quest. It's been a big-picture workshop thus far. But for all of that essential complexity, sooner or later we need to put butt in chair and write the story. We do that by writing *scenes*.

It's easy to mess this up. To believe you've got it right, when in fact your process may have led you to a mistake that plays like a wrong note in an a cappella solo. If you're Adele, you can get away with it. If you're in the corner karaoke bar, no one will care. But if you're a new writer trying to break in to the writing business, you can't. Even one mistake like this within a story, one wrong note, can take your name off the board.

Pantsers, pay special attention to what's next, because this one is for you. The mistake you are about to witness here was totally preventable through knowledge and a criteria-driven, structurally integrated approach to the story.

This is an all-too-common stumble.

I recently read a draft from a writer who, in contacting me for coaching, proclaimed herself to be a pantser. Somewhere in the Part 2 quartile, after introducing readers to a municipal judge (the protagonist) in Part 1, we come across an 18-page scene depicting a particular trial over which this judge was presiding. Structure gives us the target context for the scenes within this quartile, including the use of a Pinch Point near the middle of it to remind us of what threatens the hero. All this after the hero has been launched down a specific path at the FPP.

The plot has been initiated. Hence, this 18-page scene needed to forward that plot. Unfortunately, in this story it didn't.

The writer knew nothing about any of this. She was new, and she was pantsing. Not sure if that is a cause-and-effect truth, but it needs to be noted. The 18-page clunker of a scene that I am about to describe is where the story paid the price for her ... I hate to call it this, so take this literally instead of critically... ignorance.

From the first line of the scene the reader assumes this scene will relate to the story in some way. That it is, in fact, essential to the newly-ignited macro-arc that is the hero's quest in this story.

That's what readers expect—it's always what they expect, because they don't expect the author to make a mistake—because that's how it's done.

The scene takes us into the courtroom for a civil lawsuit dealing with damages for a traffic dispute. We meet the defendant and his lawyer. (We've already met the judge, who is the novel's protagonist; the author did that much correctly back in Part 1.) We meet the prosecuting attorney and her client, who weren't in Part 1, nor do they appear in the story after this scene. We are whisked through the backstories of each, at a depth worthy of a main character, which demands relevance. We see, in a flashback, the mechanics of the accident itself, which also demands relevance. We listen in on opening arguments, detailed to an extent that they feel like a transcript from the trial itself. We see the judge admonish the lawyers and generally administer the procedures and precedents that are the raw grist of a trail.

Eighteen pages of this, all in one scene. And then it ends. The judge rules. One winner, one loser.

From there, beginning with the ensuing scene, *nothing* more was heard from or about those characters (other than the judge, of course) or the trial itself. The accident had absolutely nothing to do with the core story being told. Nothing about it, other than the hero's profession, relates in the slightest way. Not to the core dramatic arc too lightly hinted at with a FPP, not to character arc, not to anything that is germane to the narrative to come. It plays like Harper Lee showing an 18-page detailed scene of Atticus Finch going to the dentist as a kid in the middle of *To Kill a Mockingbird*.

The scene *didn't matter.* It had no mission that met the criteria for scene writing. It was a waste of 18 pages, a waste of the reader's time (because the reader would naturally assume he was consuming this for a *reason*), and when viewed from an informed criteria-driven perspective, easily seen (and avoided) as a violation of the principles and criteria of effective scene writing.

The writer couldn't understand my pushback. How could she without an awareness of the principles and criteria that expose this scene as a bad call? She defended it as a means of characterizing the protagonist, the judge. To show us who she is by experiencing what she does. (You'll recall earlier that one of the criteria states that no scene after the Part 1 block can be there exclusively to show characterization; from the FPP forward, points of characterization occur in context to the forwarding of the core dramatic arc, which is the *plot*.)

The scene was decently written, and she loved it. She went forward with it in place, my coaching disregarded and her opportunity to learn from her investment blown. My guess is—because I've been looking for it as a self-published work ever since—it never made it into the market. There were other issues, too, all of them explained simply by the truth that this writer didn't know what she didn't know, and wasn't ready to learn it. She refused to kill her darling (to quote a common writing meme). After enough rejection and pain and explanatory feedback, she might finally get it. I hope so. Not everyone does get it, though, and thus we understand how and why the ditch at the side of the road is full of the bodies of broken writing dreams.

Don't let this be you.

You need to make these criteria—for scenes, as well as the rest of the parts and elements discussed here—part of *your* base of knowledge. Because these aren't tips, they are essential knowledge, in the form of explanations of what works and what probably won't.

But even when you know the mission of a scene—moving the story forward, rather than descriptively treading water or relying on backstory—there are other criteria that can help you elevate your scenes, and thus contribute to an even higher level of storytelling.

CRITERIA FOR WRITING SCENES THAT WORK

We know now that every scene needs to add something new to the unspooling context of the dramatic narrative. That's the mission. We can get inside this mission—for some, this may be the final parting of the clouds—by viewing it from a different perspective, which is to state an outcome that you want to *avoid* at all costs:

When a scene is either skimable or skipable by the reader, because there is nothing there that is essential, you have fallen short of successfully completing the mission.

Sounds easy, right? Just stick to scenes that evolve the plot, while demonstrating the character and setting to which we were introduced in the Part 1 quartile, which is, for the most part, the only place where character and setting become the primary mission of a scene.

But, as you are about to discover, this is neither one-dimensional nor simple.

Specific criteria will help us get there.

There are four (out of the ten criteria offered here) that are especially and massively consequential, either as empowering techniques when you use them or potential devastation when you don't. I'll mark those with an asterisk. Consider this an awakening.

- ***SCENE CRITERIA #1: YOUR SCENES ARE FOCUSED, CONTEXT-DRIVEN DELIVERY VEHICLES FOR STORY EXPOSITION.** Each scene, with no exceptions, drives the story forward, deeper into the unspooling exposition (Part 1 scenes have a unique context, with a mission to contribute to the *setup* of the story, rather than the exposition of it). Like cars in a train, each car contains *cargo*. It isn't just an empty car in which the hero is hitching a ride to the next story point without learning anything about the journey. It *is*, in either a major or more subtle way, a story twist in and of itself. Each scene, while created in context to what has been imparted to the story prior to it, changes or evolves or clarifies the landscape of the story by moving it forward.

  Revelation or clarification both escalate the level of *drama* in play.

- **SCENE CRITERIA #2: THERE ARE DIFFERENT KINDS OF SCENES, SO ENSURE THAT THE RIGHT KIND OF SCENE IS APPLIED TO THE RIGHT STORY MOMENT.**

  As the scenes continue, the story grows and evolves by virtue of the scenes that, bit by bit, contribute to the evolving exposition. Some of those changes can be major (plot twists and structural transitions), while some are more nuanced (like the hero realizing that what she must do next is something she fears or isn't prepared for, which heightens the inherent drama of that following scene). And some exist simply as transitional tools (which become that scene's mission), acting as connective tissue from one time or place or point of view to another.

  Opening scenes, transitional scenes, Part 1 scenes, tee-up scenes, connective tissue scenes, climactic scenes, the ending epilogue-like scene ... all of these have unique tonality and objectives, which you should seek to understand and master.

- ***SCENE CRITERIA #3: THE CONTEXT OF A GIVEN SCENE ALIGNS WITH AND CONTRIBUTES TO THE CONTEXT OF THE QUARTILE** within which it appears. Reference the structural diagrams provided in previous chapters and follow along here. All of the Part 1 scenes have a contextual mission to contribute to story *setup*. All of the Part 2 scenes connect to how the hero is *responding* to the new (at the FPP) call to action. All of the Part 3 scenes contribute toward a shift into a more proactive *attack* mode for the hero. And all of the Part 4 scenes become part of the way the converging paths of the hero and the antagonistic force (the villain) converge via strategy, deception, courage and heroism, or inevitability (never by coincidence or deus ex machina), and leading to *resolution*.

- **SCENE CRITERIA #4: THAT CARGO—THE BIT OF INFORMATION THAT SERVES TO EVOLVE THE STORY—FORWARDS THE CORE *DRAMATIC* STORY.** In other words, the *plot*. If a scene doesn't forward the plot, either through new information or clarification or reorientation, then it is a scene that readers might quickly sense to be skimable (because it actually *is* skimable). If you keep doing this in your novel, it will soon be skipable, as well.

  It is fine to pepper the narrative with scenes that focus on launching (in Part 1) and contributing to a subplot, but it is just as important that in the second half of the story the subplot scenes begin to inform at least some nuance of the core dramatic plot.

  In *My Sister's Grave* there were set-up scenes with only this love story subplot front and center. But the story shows these two characters end up in a relationship that is part of the macro-story plot, and thus those scenes become a means to advance the subplot as well.

- **SCENE CRITERIA #5: EACH SCENE REINFORCES OR ALIGNS WITH CHARACTER AND SETTING AND THEME.** Which is to say, after the exception of early Part 1 scenes, character and plot are not fodder for the primary establishment of setting and theme, but rather, infusing them into the dramatic purpose of the scene. Each scene is obliged to unfold in context to the characterizations and settings already put forth. Those become context for the story, which is different than *content*. After the earliest scenes in Part 1, each scene is tasked with the delivery or clarification of new *content*, within a pre-existing *context*.

You won't see a scene in the middle of a Jack Reacher novel (an action thriller featuring a recurring hero) in which he realizes his father has influenced the way he sees the world. That's either an early Part 1 scene, or more likely, a tangential reference within a scene that does, in fact, exist to drive us further along the dramatic arc.

- **SCENE CRITERIA #6: SOME SCENES TRANSITION EITHER TIME OR LOCATION OR PRIMARY POINT-OF-VIEW PLAYERS.** Best practices tell us to either skip a line of white space to indicate the transition, or jump to a new chapter heading for any of these shifts in context. Avoid using a graphic mark—such as a hashtag—to indicate any of these transitional pauses. The exception is when white space exists at the very bottom of a page or at the very top of one, in which case the insertion of a graphic symbol clarifies what is happening. Leave this choice to your publisher, or to the page-design phase of your self-publishing process. Less is more, which means white space says it more clearly.

- ***SCENE CRITERIA #7: STRIVE TO ENTER YOUR SCENES AT THE LAST POSSIBLE NARRATIVE MOMENT,** within an artful approach to setting up and framing the moment the new information (the mission of the scene) is delivered. Tee-up chitchat and mechanics are implied or minimized. Get to the point of the scene quickly, yet dramatically.

This is a massively effective best practice, possible only when the author knows where the scene is headed. Often the ramp-up to the key moment within a scene is implied. If the couple is about to get into an argument in a movie theater, we don't need to see them arriving and parking the car, buying their tickets, and standing in line for popcorn, and we don't need to hear the chitchat they have with the guy standing behind them. Nor do we need a detailed description of various outfits worn by patrons of that theater, unless any portion of it becomes germane to the story.

This criterion can't be fully met unless and until the author knows how the scene fits into the macro-story, and thus, can define a succinct narrative mission for the scene. Pantsers sometimes write scenes that are seeking to establish a purpose but take pages of meandering to find their mission. That's a rewrite waiting to happen.

This is a skill demonstrated fluidly by experienced authors. Begin to notice how it's done. Overwrought scene setups expose an author as a rookie, which is a moss-gathering rock as the story progresses, eventually tanking the whole thing.

- ***SCENE CRITERIA #8: EACH KEY SCENE PLAYS WITHIN A CONTEXT OF MICRO-TENSION.** This is another advanced understanding that is a best practice among proven pros. Within each key scene there should be someone at risk, something at risk (stakes), and something to root for. All of this will relate to the outcome of the scene that hangs in the balance. There is an organically logical resolution to the scene as it closes with a transition moment that drives the reader forward into the following scene. This criteria basically asks you to unspool each individual scene as a sort of one-act play. Certain quick transitions and connective narrative tissue are less dependent on this technique, but micro-tension is the hallmark of an author who knows how it's done.

- **SCENE CRITERIA #9: EVERY SCENE REPRESENTS A UNIQUE POINT OF VIEW** through which we experience the scene. If the scene changes point of view or changes its expositional mission focus, it should play within its own scene. Changing point of view within a scene is a rookie flag, as is having two or more primary narrative missions (specific pieces of narrative that become the purpose and contribution of the scene on the whole) revealed in a single scene.

One mission or purpose, one delivered story factoid or change, one point of view … one scene. That's the guiding criteria on this point.

- **SCENE CRITERIA #10: END YOUR SCENES, AND YOUR NOVEL, WITH HIGH ART.** If you are writing a series, or plan a sequel, know that the first book in the series needs to stand alone. You can't just end the first story (or any titles in the series) with a cliff-hanger without resolution, *unless* that cliff-hanger is part of a bridging strategy, connecting the prior book to the subsequent one following a full resolution of the book in hand. This is a scene-related issue, because the concluding scenes of a novel are where the novel needs to end gracefully, rather than with a "to be continued" context.

Often the most powerful transition moment is unleashed in the final words of a scene, making it impossible to stop reading at that point. This is especially true with the major milestone transitional scenes listed above. In Parts 2, 3, and 4 especially, notice how experienced authors leverage the very end of their scenes to thrust the reader forward into the scene that follows.

Here's an example of leaving the impact moment of a scene until the very last line of its narrative or dialogue.

Deep in the Part 4 quartile of Dugoni's *My Sister's Grave*, the moment of convergence of the hero's and the villain's paths is at hand. They are about to collide, in this case, which will lead straight into a context of confrontation and resolution. This is no accident, because it is precisely the criteria for the Part 4 scenes as they arrange and align themselves to get this job done.

The last line of the scene is the moment it achieves its mission. Which is to bring the hero (Tracy Crosswhite) to an unavoidable moment of discovering the identity of the person she's been seeking, which is her core dramatic quest in this story, and thus, the *through-line* of the story. And it does so with an amazing mid-Part 4-quartile surprise ... delivered with the scene's final line. The scene plays for about two pages, which begin (per criteria) right where the preceding scene left off, cutting into this specific scene literally at the last possible moment to tee up the projectile ending, which is the mission of the scene.

> Tracy sprang to her feet but was unable to turn before she felt the dull impact against the back of her head. Her legs buckled and the gun slipped from her hand. She felt arms around her waist, catching her, keeping her upright. Breath blew warmly against her ear.
>
> "You smell just like her."

That's the end of a chapter, and you can't stop here, you have to keep reading.

Notice the exquisite slow-motion moments of this attack as the precise moment of converging paths approaches (the paragraphs just prior to this excerpt do this brilliantly). The entire scene is high drama. Notice how the last line not only shocks, but the effect is heighted by the use of a crisp, short, single-sentence paragraph to deliver it on its own, without attribution. The reader may not be sure who has just done this to Tracy, but they absolutely know who "her" refers to in this moment of truth, and it's not Tracy at all. It's her younger sister, murdered at the hands of *this* guy twenty years ago. And now we understand that he's about to kill Tracy, too.

It's the most emotionally resonant moment in the entire novel, which is full of them. And it absolutely demands the reader to keep going, into the following chapter. Even then, the line reveals a shadow of identity in a way that sends shivers down the reader's spine.

The criteria-driven author pays close attention to how elite professionals do things. When you juxtapose those observations against an awareness of the criteria that explain why it works within a given story beat, you begin to learn. To believe. And with enough of both, to evolve.

24 Criteria for Professional Narrative Prose

....
Because your voice matters.

You may have noticed that this topic—the writing, or narrative prose itself, including dialogue—appears as the final entry in this roster of element-specific criteria for the mission-driven author. And it didn't get a lot of airtime until now. It would be a mistake to assume that this is because the author undervalues the contribution or necessity of compelling narrative and dialogue, or even stellar prose. Not true at all. A certain level of prose-writing skill is a prerequisite to publishing fiction, via any channel. That said, this topic is a can of worms, one that may or may not be a difference maker for you. And like the appeal of the premise itself, this is sensitive territory, which means friends and even professionals, within their feedback, will usually comment on fine writing, but they may not be as forthcoming when the writing is part of the problem.

It's here at the end because, unless and until the story works, the writing doesn't matter. Just as true is this: Until the *writing* works, the best story premise and its expositional and structural execution will have to wait until it does.

First off, who is to say what constitutes *compelling* writing? Or even adequate or stellar prose?

Well, reviewers and readers, to name two. Agents and editors, too, because they'll reject you the moment they sense narrative skills that aren't at a professional level. (This isn't at issue with a screenplay; the minimum criteria there is that the writing is clear and uncluttered, which is part of the criteria for novels, as well.)

That bar is as high as the story bar.

It's accurate, but unprovable, to say that more writers compose prose at a professional level than there are writers who bring forth brilliantly original story ideas and can execute them optimally and deliciously across unspooling dramatic and character arcs. The necessity of doing the work at *both* of those high levels in both of these core competencies is the truly challenging and rare reality.

Remember, roughly half of all rejection stems from the stories themselves, no matter how well written: stories that don't compel or appeal, at least to the degree required to set them apart and be put onto the market successfully. The other half of the collective body of rejection is explained by *execution*, a huge portion of which includes writing that isn't *there* yet.

Your prose may not *make you* on that journey, but it can certainly break you.

If you are writing literary fiction, your prose skills reside at a somewhat higher level on the hierarchy of what might get you published and read. And certainly, your lit professor had no problem telling you what she thought about your writing. But sentences aren't the only assessable thing in a literary novel that matters, and when it comes to literary style and story sensibilities, more isn't necessarily better in this genre, either.

You don't have to be the next John Irving to get your mystery or romance novel out there. But you *do* have to write well enough to compete. It isn't that the bar is lower for this core competency compared to the others (conceptualization, character, theme, structure, and scene building), it's just that more of the writers in the room have this base covered than they do the others.

And even then, poorly written manuscripts, in terms of the prose itself, flood the commercial marketplace both online and within brick-and-mortar stores. The criteria-driven novelist understands that he can never relax on this front.

In commercial fiction particularly, the prose skills of the author can be comparatively likened to the intimacy skills of a newlywed.

(Not the analogy you were expecting, I'm sure, but stick with me here; this is a PG-13 simile, so if that much might offend, feel free to skip to the next paragraph). The conventional wisdom within this parallel context is this: When things are going well in bed, when both parties have no complaints, then, at least after the honeymoon, this particular acumen occupies about 10 percent of the mind share, as well as the focus, blame, or credit, within the collective whole of the various issues that constitute and challenge a primary relationship. Success there fuels the odds of success on other fronts within the relationship.

But when things *aren't* going well in the bedroom, when one or both are doing it wrong or even just not well enough or often enough (or even too often), in a way that isn't compatible with the standards of their partner, it suddenly looms as 80 percent or more of the core essence of the relationship. It becomes the focus of discussion (or not, which is another issue altogether), diagnosis, and ongoing improvement, and perhaps the blame when it all falls apart. Because without healthy and clear communication, the rest really doesn't have much of a chance.

Just like our prose with the telling of our stories.

It's the same dichotomy. The standard boils down to this: If the reader notices the writing, even when the writer is shooting for eloquence, then the story is at risk. Readers are used to experiencing prose told at a professional level, which is not to be confused with Nobel laureate-level writing, which is a different thing altogether. Shooting for eloquence can be a deal killer, because one reader's poetry is another's purple mess. If the reader notices the prose because the writing is deficient or sophomoric, or it simply lacks a certain professional veneer or academic verisimilitude (I thought this might be a good time, ironically, to whip out that particular $5 word), that compromises the reading experience. It can even kill it altogether.

With prose, two standards apply:

1. Less is more, which goes for attempts at sophistication as well as irony, humor, or street cred. And …

2. ... where dialogue is concerned, proper handling of punctuation and attribution (common pitfalls for newer writers) is essential, as well as an ear for the difference between how expositional sentences play in real life versus on paper.

Perhaps ironically, it is the effort to make dialogue read as *grammatically* proper, rather than the more casual cadence and omissions of real-life conversations, that imbues troubled dialogue with issues. If your dialogue is too on the nose, it if is too reliant on or void of social reference, if it plays like lines from a seventh-grade stage play, your reader will notice. And not in a good way. (More on this in the Criteria menu that follows.)

In my opinion as a story coach, this is the most common unmasking of a new writer versus the tonal dialogue ear of a seasoned professional novelist. And it's not something easily taught or learned with a single how-to lecture. To make matters more complicated, the writer might actually talk that way in real life. (Example: The villain, when staring down the barrel of the gun held by the police officer arresting him, utters the expletive, "Golly Gee, officer, this just isn't my lucky day!" This actually appeared in a project recently sent to me. It's the kind of thing that will get you rejected the moment an agent, editor, or reader comes across it.)

The key to learning how to write great dialogue is to study esteemed authors in the genre of your choice and to compare it to your own work. Then you can juxtapose your choices against what you are hearing people speak in real life, including critically assessing how it would sound out of the mouth of a famous actor portraying your character on screen. (Detective, crime, and thriller authors are usually really good at this, to the point where their snark becomes an art form of its own.) If you can picture Al Pacino saying, "Golly gee, officer..." without a trace of irony—it's easy to hear him say it as a smart-mouthed cynic—and if it doesn't send up a whipping-in-the-wind red flag for you, then keep studying. Your *ear for dialogue* isn't there yet.

I offer that with all sincerity.

Cast your story with actors who fit your vision of the character, and then imagine them saying the lines you have written for your characters. If the fit seems unnatural, and if you've hypothetically cast it well, something may be amiss. And it might just be your *ear* for dialogue. Which if it is, you'll at least know where to focus your learning curve.

Nobody said this would be easy, even for the criteria-driven author. Make it your mission to play the long game and acquire the ear and the instinct that will define your writing career.

CRITERIA FOR ELEVATING YOUR NARRATIVE PROSE AND DIALOGUE.

Work these into your long-range strategy to become a better writer.

- **WRITING VOICE CRITERIA #1: BE JUDICIOUS AND MINIMAL WITH YOUR USE OF ADJECTIVES AND ADVERBS AND DESCRIPTIVE PHRASEOLOGY.** More than a few famous novelists have published their own personal list of "writing rules," and avoiding descriptors is usually on it. This doesn't have to be an absolute, even when it's on such a list, but take note every time you apply an adjective or adverb in your prose. It's a bit like swearing in front of your parents … you need to consider your audience carefully before taking a risk.

- **WRITING VOICE CRITERIA #2: LESS IS MORE RELATIVE TO REPEATING PHRASES, SPECIFIC WORDS, OR SYNTAX.** Again, this is a common misstep from new writers, so even if you're new, try to notice when you fall into specific habits and defaults with your language. We all do it (notice how often I repeat the phrase "That said …" in this book). It's fine to create your own style—Nelson DeMille, for example, always manages to fit the word *apropos* into his narrative at least a few times in every book he writes—just don't let it become a distraction instead of the distinction you intend.

  The rule of thumb for prose is this: If the reader notices—and this includes your efforts to sound like you just graduated with a poetry degree—you're in risky territory. Your prose is like a scent

… the best and safest choice is to splash something clear and clean onto your pages.

- **WRITING VOICE CRITERIA #3: SPREAD YOUR PEARLS SPARINGLY.** Every once in a while it may serve you to craft a sentence, or a fragment of one, or a transition, that glows in the dark. Something the reader might underline or note. Or at least notice and remember. Something that encapsulates an entire lecture full of wisdom. This is perhaps more apropos (thank you, Mr. DeMille) to nonfiction, but it can make your novel sparkle in the right places, as well. There is a tool chest for this that includes irony, alliteration, sarcasm, the rare $5 word, a shadow of a well-known meme or cliché or quote, etc. But like adjectives, too much too often is risky. Step to the front of the room with caution in this regard, but be bold in trying a few swings for the fences.

- **WRITING VOICE CRITERIA #4: OBEY THE BEST PRACTICES STANDARDS FOR PUNCTUATING DIALOGUE.** These little marks are not negotiable. Getting sloppy here can get you rejected, even at the first moment the agent or editor notices. Because they scream *rookie*. An author who doesn't know how to punctuate dialogue is like a doctor who doesn't know how to give a shot. Google *how to punctuate dialogue*, you'll find more information than you'll ever be able to digest. One or two sources will probably give you the standards you need. Bottom line: Sentence-ending dialogue punctuation, like periods and commas and question marks and exclamation marks, always go *inside* the quotation marks, not after.

There are many other specific *rules*—that's exactly the right word here—that apply to dialogue. Google that, too, and begin to notice how the pros do it.

Attribution is another place where your lack of experience will be exposed.

- The *placement* of attribution, including single-sentence versus multi-sentence dialogue turns (attributing earlier within is always better than later).

- The *frequency* of doing so (you don't have to attribute every exchanged volley in a dialogue conversation).
- The goal is to prevent the reader from getting confused over who is speaking and who isn't.
- The use of paragraphing (every time you change speakers you start a new paragraph.
- Never have two spoken volleys from different characters in a single paragraph).
- Avoid changing paragraphs within the monologue of a single speaker.
- Avoid the use of adjectives to convey tonality ("she said" is always better than "she bellowed") ...

All of these little hurdles can have a high degree of difficulty, one that can make you feel naked on a stage full of sharply dressed professionals as it exposes your lack of skill here. Get this right, or it will get you rejected.

- **WRITING VOICE CRITERIA #5: OTHER LITTLE GRAMMATICAL NITS ARE IMPORTANT, TOO**, but not quite as deadly as the dialogue mangle. The use of the em dash, for example, rather than an improper hyphen or an en dash. Again, find a source of academic propriety on this issue (it could be its own chapter here, but is a little off-topic) to get it right.

And finally—this being a personal nit as an editor—is the aforementioned dreaded semicolon. If you're writing a white paper on the use of petroleum resources within an industrial society, then by all means, semicolon yourself into blissful academic oblivion. But in fiction, a semicolon plays like a Southern gentleman proudly sounding off his lyric twang while trying to recite Shakespeare. People don't think or speak in semicolons, which is why you shouldn't narrate your novel using them, either. Yes, I've used them in this book, but I've used them sparingly. This is nonfiction, after all. When I'm editing fiction, I slash out every semicolon that I come across. It's a transitional pause, better served with a comma or through the advent of a brand-new sentence. Or even an ellipsis … which is its own kind of spacing nightmare if misused.

- **WRITING VOICE CRITERIA #6: NARRATIVE PROSE STYLE IS IN THE EYE OF THE BEHOLDER.** What works for some may not work for all. This is an issue of being well-read within your genre, including the study of the masters of those niches. Some are more eloquent and fluent than others, so stop short of trying to imitate what you read. Rather, appreciate it. Notice how and why it works. A new author is as unlikely to duplicate the narrative eloquence of, say, John Updike as a new painter is of duplicating the brush stylings of Picasso or even Thomas Kinkade. The mission is to find your *own* voice and make it soar.

  When you read the work of authors you admire, you may find yourself leaning into their cadence and choices to some extent, which is usually a good thing. Every writer who keeps at it won't hesitate to say who has influenced them. And any writer who has been compared with a famous author will agree, it may be a compliment, but the voice they apply is their own.

- **WRITING VOICE CRITERIA #7: DON'T USE NAMES WITHIN DIALOGUE.** Here is a rule of thumb this is not quite, but almost, an absolute: When writing dialogue, at all costs avoid having the speaker state the name of the person he's speaking to. Usually this will be the first name. "Gee, Sandy, I just don't know." The only time using the name can work smoothly is when one character is greeting another, as in, "Hey, Steve, what's up?" But when your characters repeatedly use the name of the person right in front of them, you are announcing that you're new at this and that your dialogue ear is stuffed beneath a thick hat. People, as a reliable rule, just don't talk that way in real life. They only speak that way in poorly written dialogue created by new authors or nonwriters. You might encounter this once in a while in a published book, but rest assured, doing it in your own book will always put you at risk.

  Here's now *not* to write dialogue in this regard:

  "You know, Mark, I've thought the same thing on occasion."

"Really, Laura? I didn't think that would occur to you."

"Well, Mark, it does."

"Interesting. In any case, Laura, I appreciate you bringing it up."

"Thanks, Mark. By the way, who wrote this crap?"

You may think this excerpt has been overplayed to make a point, but too many manuscripts from newer writers are swamped with dialogue that sounds just like this. The best practice here is to *never* allow a name to appear within quotation marks when that name is a party to the conversation taking place (it's okay to use a name to reference a character outside of the scene). It always screams like a wrong note in a solo piano performance.

Make it your mission to avoid these dialogue mistakes.

ONE FINAL, CRITICAL CRITERION THAT COULD GO ANYWHERE.

I'm putting this one under the prose category due to several facets of this choice, one of them is the kind of prose you use in the execution of your story. This is about *narrative strategy*, which is the choice of person, tense, and point of view that always demands landing on a consistent preference. If you default to third-person omniscient narrative, you may be stepping over a dollar to pick up an easy dime.

- **NARRATIVE STRATEGY CRITERIA #1: EVERY AUTHOR MUST CHOOSE WHICH VOICE AND TENSE TO APPLY TO HER STORY.** The options are third-person omniscient narrative, third-person close narrative, first-person narrative, or some combination of these voices. Older writers will recall their creative writing teachers back in school telling them to never write in first person, but that advice is as dead and buried as the teacher who said it. First-person point of view is everywhere these days.

  Nelson DeMille has two first-person narrators in several of his books: one from the hero's point of view, one from the villain's. It's a great way to manage reader awareness and tension, because the reader may know things the hero does not.

In *The Help*, author Kathryn Stockett gave us three first-person narrative voices, each with a distinctive cadence and tonality.

In *The Hunger Games*, author Suzanne Collins writes in first-person *present* tense, which is another option. Because not only can writers choose between points of view, we can also choose between past and present tenses. Present tense is a high degree of difficulty, if for no other reason than you'll encounter the need to reflect to the past sooner or later, so make sure you can handle it before going there.

Many writers default to a favorite, comfortable choice, when in fact the story may benefit from a different way of telling the story. Narrative strategy is one of the six primary realms of story physics because it has the power to elevate a story above the crowd of stories it sits beside on the bookshelf.

Choose carefully, though. Narrative voice and tense become an all-or-nothing bet when you color outside the lines of traditional third-person past tense point of view. And even with that choice, there are options that may better serve you, so make sure you're considering the reader as much as you are your comfort level.

25 Caveats, Exceptions, Contradictions

....

And Other Realities of the Storyteller's Mantle

Perhaps—hopefully—we have come full circle in our discovery of the criteria-driven, mission-conscious perspective for developing and writing a story. But nothing in the writing business is an absolute. Exceptions abound, diverse views collide in every writing conference hallway, and authors become entrenched in their opinions and habits in ways that can blind them to—or at least bend them away from—truth and probability, or even best practices.

It serves us to revisit these truths and threats and opportunities following this survey of the principles and criteria that make fiction work. Think of this as simplicity on the other side of complexity.

Cultivate an awareness of the nature of conventional wisdom.

Much of the traditional conventional wisdom about writing fiction asks us to *just write* the story and then figure it out and fix it later. For me, this smacks of advising someone to *just get married and then work on the rough patches later,* which is the antithesis of conventional wisdom where relationships are concerned. Trust me, you and your story, as well as you and your reader, *are* having a relationship, so this becomes an apt analogy. To some extent we are by default engaging with this approach. We are always tinkering, listening to our gut, considering and reconsidering, and too often doing so without the context of a higher requisite.

In this way we are all pantsers *and* planners at some point along the way.

Organic story development works for many.

And many of those for whom it works are famous. And yet, it is less than an absolute, if nothing else, because there are just as many famous story planners out there. Every pantser is in search of a core story and its ending, just like every story planner. When a story emerges, the organic process becomes the same as that applied by planners and plotters, which is to envision the best available *option* at each waypoint along the story path, usually within the scenes we write. The idea isn't to grab the first notion that fills a space and move on to the next space. The higher skill is to land on the *best* option for any given story moment, something that is fresh and edgy and reflective of the emotional subtext of the narrative's unspooling.

Criteria exist to help us make better, more optimal choices in those moments. That's true for pantsers every bit as much as it is for planners and outliners.

The sheer star power of the advocates of an organic approach adds gravitas to the weight of their advice to write stories in the same way they write stories. Here's a quote from a famous author—George R.R. Martin, best known for his A Song of Fire and Ice (A Game of Thrones) series. Notice how he stops short of suggesting you proceed in his shadow and do things the same way. Yet he implies it, at least within the perception of a newer writer seeking to find her own path, by virtue of his name being attached to the quote.

> I think there are two types of writers, the architects and the gardeners. The architects plan everything ahead of time, like an architect building a house. They know how many rooms are going to be in the house, what kind of roof they're going to have, where the wires are going to run, what kind of plumbing there's going to be. They have the whole thing designed and blueprinted out before they even nail the first board up. The gardeners dig a hole, drop in a seed, and water it. They kind of know what seed it is, they know if they planted a fantasy seed or mystery seed or whatever. But as the plant comes up and they water it, they don't know how many branches it's going to have, they find out as it grows. And I'm much more a gardener than an architect.

George R.R. Martin is a rare breed of talent, indeed. But this argument doesn't lean into either method of writing as a preference to be emulated. In fact, notice how he leaves a crack of daylight for the inclusion of at least a little planning, which is probably the unavoidable tendency to write *toward* something, even if it isn't written down. Which is precisely why we should *not* attempt to write just like he writes, where process is concerned, until you are confident you can do what he does, as he does it. For the rest of us, grittier, principle-driven grist remains to be more fully understood.

At the end of the story there is always architecture, and there should always be flowers.

Know this: Both the architect and the gardener begin the process by staring at a blank plot of ground. Both depend on the emergence of a vision for a story in their head. The *only* difference is how and when that vision is imparted to the page. While both processes have their challenges, they are equal in their relationship to the criteria for excellence of the end product. Which, in this analogy, are not the same thing. But in writing from either of two preferences, they *are* the same thing at the end of the writing day, when THE END is typed on that last page.

The great caveat here, applied to all famously quoted authors like Martin, is this: *It'll work best when you know what he or she knows.* Until then, you may not know what you don't know, which leaves you exposed to the complexities and risks of the storytelling proposition.

While this *write-first-fix-it-later* strategy certainly works for many, it also absolutely sabotages the intentions of others. The criteria-driven approach flips that proposition on its ear, giving us the tools and criteria to figure it out—to whatever degree you can, as early as you can—even before you begin to write, and at each decision point along the arc of a story as well. In fact, an awareness of these criteria, at either the instinctual level or as something you espouse and apply along the path, serve the die-hard pantser every bit as much as they empower the story planner.

So while it's tempting to suggest that the criteria-driven, mission-focused, knowledge-based approach is a strategy for the rest of us, it is, in fact, a framework that applies to and serves all storytellers. Whatever their process, whatever their genre, whatever their ambition. I'm not arguing against pantsing any more than I'm arguing for plotting. What I am arguing for is that either choice is greatly empowered and enriched when you know what you're doing—too often poor choices are made precisely because one doesn't know better—and impart an understanding of the criteria shown here to your work as early in your process as possible.

Given the 96 percent failure rate of the traditional conventional wisdom—which is often explained by the degree to which they come up short of the criteria required—it makes immense sense to incorporate at least some of this knowledge into your process.

When you do, you will have become, at least to some degree, a criteria-driven author.

Consider formula vs. reality.

If you are writing commercial, genre-centric fiction, something that depends on plot and drama to render its requisite emotional resonance, then here's a newsflash you may not have considered: You actually *are* writing from a *formula*. Get over it if that doesn't suit your lofty vision for your craft. Genre fiction *is* a formulaic craft, and no less a form of art than the literary titles found elsewhere on their own rack. Hey, I don't like the word *formula*, either, but let's get real. Let's stop confusing the issue by avoiding nasty words like *rules* and *formula* and *reader manipulation*. All mystery novels basically take the same shape of narrative and archetypes, and then they're painted with unique characters, villains, and crimes. Same with romance. Same with the subgenres, mashups, and the vast library of adult contemporary fiction titles.

These stories almost always unfold in four contextual parts.

Each part with its own context, with major turning points that bear the weight of the story's pace and exposition. Sometimes these turning points are subtle, sometimes on the nose. I've been faulted for putting this out there as something that's new (which I've never claimed; rather, I've attempted to interpret and clarify it), and yet, a vast majority of new writers aren't in command of the nature and power of this truth. I know this after working with roughly a thousand stories over the past few years, almost all from newer and emerging authors. For many, these principles are indeed a new discovery, even a genuine epiphany, one that changes their writing experience, not to mention their upside. There are criteria for all of it, and when a book is successfully written within the genres, they end up honoring those criteria.

That's not a formula, that's just the truth.

A final note about literary fiction

What isn't by definition formulaic—though it certainly can be—are stories that present themselves, by intention or outcome, as *literary fiction*. That may include saga stories, multi-generational family or biographical fiction, and experimental fiction. When authors push back against this model (a much more palatable description compared to formula), they are juxtaposing the form and function of commercial stories with more literary forms.

And yet, those, too, are driven by emotional resonance, dramatic intention, and an arc driven by the presence of situational threat or antagonistic pressure, leading the hero through a journey of experiences and the navigation of her own limitations. All of which are intrinsic to the criteria you now understand.

Literary fiction lends itself to organic story development. And yet, when it works, it unfolds in pursuit of a vision for the resolution of questions posed within the story. And just as with genre fiction, the draft written after the entire story has been discovered works better than the draft written with the primary purpose of finding it.

Here's a simplistic guide to understanding the difference.

Genre fiction is driven by conflict leading to drama, which unfolds in the form of a plot that pits the goals of a protagonist against the intentions and agendas of an antagonist. The driving heart of the story is that evolving plot in the presence of stakes, thus illuminating character along the way. The plot, and the nature of the story as expressed by genre, is why readers come to it. When that ride becomes a thrilling vicarious experience for the reader, the writer has succeeded.

Literary fiction turns that inside out. The heart of the story *is* the character, with a focus on his inner landscape and journey. Sometimes the narrative voice itself can seem literary, though great eloquence is neither a criteria nor a deal-breaking expectation. The goal is emotional resonance and the internalization of the comprehension of themes that reflect the real world and inspire contemplation.

Notice this when someone pushes back on your criteria-driven context for storytelling and your valuing of criteria—if you interact at all within the writing community, they definitely will. Chances are, when this happens, they will compare the form and function and process, as a standard of excellence, to literary fiction, which is a different beast that lends itself to softer edges and more pliable expectations of its final form.

Own your craft, whatever your genre. When you do, the criteria will reside at the heart of what you understand to be true. Which is why *knowledge* is the gold standard in the avocation of storytelling, in any genre, with any process.

There are, of course, some famous exceptions that can and will be cited.

Get ready for them, they're out there, and they are the most available stones thrown by writers who reject anything that isn't the manifestation of their instincts. Every criteria shown here has been ignored or mangled in a story you've heard of. Even when, for every one of those, there are hundreds, if not thousands, of other successful titles that are clinics in what you now understand, from structure to the reliance on a premise that imparts its own compelling allure, executed in accordance with criteria at every beat of the story.

My favorite anecdote on this issue involves a blog post I wrote for a widely read website, wherein I waxed enthusiastic about the liberating nature of the core principles and modeling of four-part story structure. The owner of the site, who has never published a novel, cited Cervantes and his classic *Don Quixote* as an example of how everything I'd just written was nonsense. Thing is, *Don Quixote* is a 200-years-young classic considered by some to be the greatest novel ever written. Hardly the standard by which we should compare and model commercial genre fiction or even the literary works that are being written today. This is like comparing the gleaming Walt Disney Concert Hall in Los Angeles to Gaudi's still uncompleted Sagrada Familia in Barcelona. Apples and oranges, my friends, apples and oranges.

The guy didn't know what he didn't know.

Not everyone who falls off a building dies, though almost everyone who does so is gravely injured. For every incident in which the person ends up unscathed, there are thousands of others that become case studies in the principle that advises us not to jump off a building without a bungee cord or a massively thick landing pad.

For every experimental novel that hits it big, there are tens of thousands that never find a publisher, and tens of published thousands of others that aren't remotely experimental.

Why would you seek to be the one-out-of-a-thousand writer who beats the odds with an exception that defies genre tropes and expectations driven by principles and criteria, while for every one of those there are 999 opportunities to succeed simply by applying proven principles and criteria that define a rewarding reading experience? That's not noble. It's just naïve.

My goal here is to help you become part of the four percent who lives to see their writing dream fulfilled. In every avocation and profession that thrives in our modern times, there are principles and criteria in play that either reflect the instincts of its elite performers or become the form they have mastered to attain those heights.

It's an issue of proximity, timing, and perseverance.

Of course, nothing is certain in this business. And while there are no rules, there certainly are principles that frame and drive the probability of success. When you view the honoring of principles and criteria as the ante-in to the trade, when you cease trying to reach your goal by being an exception to the conclusions of decades of modern storytelling and readership, you're improving your odds accordingly. And likewise, when you accept nothing less than your best effort—and align it with the gravity-like physics of your trade—then you truly have a shot.

Add perseverance and a hunger for knowledge and growth, and then become a seeker and a student of craft, and continue your journey as a rabid consumer of fiction as well as a practitioner of it. Because now you can see inside the stories you read—like a doctor who has seen inside the bodies she is committed to heal, with a new clarity of order and function, of cause and effect—and you will find yourself engaging your writing dream from a new sense of bliss and hope.

It's always good to be in the right place at the right time. But half of that latter element is having the right project in hand, meaning that if you show it before it's time—before it's ready—you may be compromising your chances. A criteria-driven approach is a strategy that allows you to understand when that time has arrived, because you'll have a better sense of when the criteria have been met and hopefully optimized.

Seek to make your stories a gift to your readers.

There's another universal law in play here. It has to do with getting what you give, and reflecting the energy you hope to harness in return.

Before your writing dream can happen, *you* must become a gift to your stories the same way an enlightened parent is a gift unto their children and a loving soul mate becomes a blessing to her partner, even though it takes work to get there and remain viable. This happens not only through instinct, one informed by values and principles, but through the experienced application of knowledge as manifested in an elevated understanding of the inner workings and mysteries of storytelling. Of the principles that give it all a framework and the criteria that sets a qualitative bar for execution.

As an author who is no longer writing exclusively for yourself, this becomes the highest calling of all. One that will elevate you to the next realm of your experience as a writer. When all this gets into your head and begins to inform your gut instincts, then you can truly let your stories pour out of your enjoined heart and mind and onto the page with hope and a sense of bliss.

You can finally, in the most evolved sense and context, just write.

ABOUT THE AUTHOR

––––

Larry Brooks is the award-winning *USA Today* bestselling author of six novels and four writing craft books, including the bestselling *Story Engineering*, from Writers Digest Books. He is the creator of a widely respected craft-building website for fiction writers, and frequently teaches at workshops and conferences nationally and internationally. He lives in Chandler, Arizona with his wife, Laura, who is an artist. He can be reached through his website, www.storyfix.com.

ACKNOWLEDGMENTS

––––

No book, fiction or non-fiction, stands alone as the product of a singular effort. Just as no book stands apart from the experiences and intentions and mistakes that have brought the author to that first blank page. In this, my eleventh published book, I feel the presence of all that has brought me to this point.

The list of those who have, sometimes unknowingly, contributed to and colored my journey is long, and probably missing a few names that belong. It begins with my wife, Laura, who believes in me unconditionally and has the courage to risk telling me when something isn't there yet. She is a painter, which means she understands the iterative process of creating a story out of parts that embrace both context and other elements to become something that exists as part of a mysterious larger whole. She is the hero of our story. And while it has manifested the dramatic tension that all good stories require, the ending is clear. It is a Happily Ever After by any measure, and hopefully, a great many chapters remain.

I would like to thank my editor at Writers Digest Books, Amy Jones, for not only her keen insights and contributions, but for doing the intangible work of a professional who understands that support, empathy, and wisdom are just as critical to the process as the flagging of an editorial clunker, of which there were many before her deft touch imbued this book with coherence. Likewise, line-editor Kim Catanzarite's keen eye and sense of balance added much to the end product of this team effort.

I would like to thank Robert Dugoni for his contribution, his support, and his friendship. He is a role model and a selfless superstar in the universe we inhabit as authors, albeit at vastly different altitudes.

Others have contributed to this work in ways they may not understand: Art Holcomb, Jennifer Blanchard, Stephanie Raffelock, Mary Andonian, Jason Brick, Kerry Boytzen, James Scott Bell, James N. Frey, Phillip Margolin, Sue Colleta, Robert Jones, Mike Richardson, Melissa Haynes, Martha Miller, Scott Krager, and certainly others whose names this old brain has failed to summon forth in this moment, all of you have touched my work and my heart. And to my son, Nelson, who is living the phenomenon of the student becoming the teacher, in this case, for how to live with integrity and passion.

And to that sea of faces that over the years have stared back at me in the many workshops and conferences and online connections that explore this magnificent craft we pursue, this is for you. May this book take you one step closer, one day sooner, to the fulfillment of your writing dream.

Index

Great Stories Don't Write Themselves